SEVERUS OF ANTIOCH

Severus, patriarch of Antioch on the Orontes from 512 to 518, was an opponent of the decisions of the Council of Chalcedon (451), a council which has divided Christian churches ever since. He is venerated as one of the most important saints in the Old Oriental Christian tradition but has mostly been regarded as a heretic elsewhere.

Although Severus was an active lobbyist at the imperial court, a pastor, administrator and scholar, his works have come down to us only in fragments in the original Greek after they were condemned by imperial edict in AD 536. This volume translates a key selection of his writings and introduces readers to Severus's life and times, his thought, homiletic abilities, and his pastoral concern as expressed through his letters and hymns. Severus is a truly pivotal late-antique figure, who is here for the first time rehabilitated as such.

Pauline Allen is Director of the Centre for Early Christian Studies at Australian Catholic University. **C.T.R. Hayward** is Professor of Hebrew at the Department of Theology, University of Durham, UK.

THE EARLY CHURCH FATHERS
Edited by Carol Harrison
University of Durham

CYRIL OF JERUSALEM
Edward Yarnold, S.J.

EARLY CHRISTIAN LATIN POETS
Carolinne White

CYRIL OF ALEXANDRIA
Norman Russell

MAXIMUS THE CONFESSOR
Andrew Louth

IRENAEUS OF LYONS
Robert M. Grant

AMBROSE
Boniface Ramsey, O.P.

ORIGEN
Joseph W. Trigg

GREGORY OF NYSSA
Anthony Meredith, S.J.

JOHN CHRYSOSTOM
Wendy Mayer and Pauline Allen

JEROME
Stefan Rebenich

TERTULLIAN
Geoffrey Dunn

ATHANASIUS
Khaled Anatolios

SEVERUS OF ANTIOCH
Pauline Allen and C.T.R. Hayward

SEVERUS OF ANTIOCH

Pauline Allen and C.T.R. Hayward

Routledge
Taylor & Francis Group

LONDON AND NEW YORK

First published 2004
by Routledge
2 Park Square, Milton Park, Abingdon, Oxon OX14 4RN

Simultaneously published in the USA and Canada
by Routledge
711 Third Avenue, New York NY 10017

Routledge is an imprint of the Taylor & Francis Group

©2004 Pauline Allen and C.T.R. Hayward

Typeset in Garamond by Prepress Projects Ltd, Perth, Scotland.

British Library Cataloguing in Publication Data
A catalogue record for this book is available from the British Library

Library of Congress Cataloging in Publication Data
A catalog record for this book has been requested

ISBN 0–415–23401–8 (hbk)
ISBN 0–415–23402–6 (pbk)

CONTENTS

PREFACE

This volume has been a collaborative enterprise between many scholars, a testimony to the variety of talents which are needed to give Severus of Antioch his rightful place in the history of Christian thought. Robert Hayward (University of Durham) was responsible for translating from the Syriac Texts 1–15, 17 and 18–28. Youhanna Nessim Youssef (Australian Catholic University) provided specialist knowledge on the Coptic and Arabic traditions of the works of Severus. Witold Witakowski (University of Lund) put his specialist knowledge of the Ethiopic tradition at the disposal of the group, and translated Texts 29–34 from the Syriac. He wishes to acknowledge the assistance of Stephen Coombs in his 'battle with Severus's poetry'. Iain Torrance (University of Aberdeen) kindly made available his translation of Text 16, together with the notes to the homily which he compiled with Anna Wilson. Pauline Allen (Australian Catholic University) coordinated the project, and composed Chapters 1–3, the introductions to the text in Part 2 and the translation of Text 26. Youhanna Nessim Youssef procured a copy of the icon in the church of St George Hamamat al-Quabbah (Cairo) which appears on the cover of the book, and obtained the permission of the iconographers Youssef Nassif and Boudour Latif for its use here.

The next generation of Severan scholars, including Renato Roux, Frédéric Alpi and James George, have been generous in sharing information. John Cawte provided his usual theological insights, and Dinah Joesoef her technological competence. Richard Stoneman and Carol Harrison were their usual patient selves in the face of missed deadlines.

The entire project enjoyed the generous support of the Australian Research Council and Australian Catholic University.

ABBREVIATIONS

ACO   *Acta Conciliorum Oecumenicorum*, ed. E. Schwartz, Berlin: W. de Gruyter, 1914–40.

CCSG   *Corpus Christianorum. Series Graeca*, Turnhout-Leuven: Brepols, 1977–.

CPG   M. Geerard, *Clavis Patrum Graecorum*, vols 1–5, Turnhout: Brepols, 1974–87; M. Geerard and J. Noret, *Clavis Patrum Graecorum. Supplementum*, Turnhout: Brepols, 1998.

CPL   E. Dekkers, *Clavis Patrum Latinorum*, 3rd ed., Steenbrugge: Brepols, 1995.

CSCO   *Corpus Scriptorum Christianorum Orientalium*, Louvain: Secrétariat du CorpusSCO, 1903–.

HE   *Historia Ecclesiastica*.

JBA   John of Beith Aphthonia, biography of Severus.

PG   *Patrologia Graeca*, ed. J.P. Migne, vols 1–161, Paris: Apud J.-P. Migne Editorem, 1857–86.

PL   *Patrologia Latina*, ed. J.P. Migne, vols 1–221, Paris: Apud J.-P. Migne Editorem, 1844–64.

PLRE   *Prosopography of the Late Roman Empire*, vol. 2, AD 395–527, ed. A.H.M. Jones and J.R. Martindale, Cambridge: Cambridge University Press, 1980.

PO   *Patrologia Orientalis*, ed. R. Graffin and F. Nau, *et al.*, Paris: Firmin Didot, 1903–.

SC   *Sources Chrétiennes*, Paris: Editions du Cerf, 1941–.

SL   *The Sixth Book of the Select Letters of Severus Patriarch of Antioch in the Syriac Version of Athanasius of Nisibis*, ed. and trans. E.W. Brooks, vol. 1, London: Williams & Norgate, 1902; reprint Farnborough, Hants.: Gregg International Publishers Limited, 1969 (text); vol. 2, London: Williams & Norgate, 1903; reprint Farnborough, Hants: Gregg International Publishers Limited, 1969 (trans.).

Vie   *Vie de Sévère*, biography of Severus by Zachariah Scholasticus.

Part I

SEVERUS'S LIFE AND WORKS

1

SEVERUS'S LIFE

BACKGROUND

In 451 the Council of Chalcedon promulgated a definition of faith which outlawed the extremes of the theological traditions of Antioch and Alexandria, namely Nestorianism and Eutychianism, and attempted a balance between the christological terminology of each. Christ was proclaimed 'in two natures', as opposed to the expression 'from two natures' favoured by the Alexandrians. The Council also recognized the *Tome* of Pope Leo I of Rome as orthodox, and in harmony with the Fathers and with Cyril of Alexandria.

The definition was problematical from the start because in the East it was seen as only an interpretation of the symbol or creed of Nicaea, whereas for Pope Leo I it was an absolute definition which allowed no addition or subtraction. Also critical was the resolution of the Council, later known as Canon 28, which gave to Constantinople (New Rome) equal privileges with Old Rome in ecclesiastical matters, and decreed that the eastern city should hold second place after Rome. As a result of this canon, the traditional influence of Alexandria was short-circuited. To the bishop of Rome, the canon was also unfavourable, and he was reluctant to accept it explicitly. The issue of the formula 'in two natures' and Canon 28, as well as the ratification of the *Tome* (considered by many in the East to be Nestorian), were to cause unrest and resentment among Christians in both East and West in the century that followed, and a lasting division in the churches of the eastern Roman empire. Christians were polarized into 'dyophysites' and 'monophysites'. With good reason could this be called 'The Great Schism'.

The edict of 7 February 452, by which the emperors Marcian and Valentinian III enjoined their subjects to obey the decisions of the Council, was promulgated amid turbulence in Palestine, Egypt and

Antioch in the aftermath of the Council. That monks and lay people also defined and enforced orthodoxy at this time is clear from such cases as that of Bishop Juvenal of Jerusalem, who lost the support of the influential monks in his see, and on his return to Jerusalem after the Council was forced to flee in the face of their determined opposition. The amount of popular literature written in the century after Chalcedon both for and against the Council demonstrated that reaction to the perceived issues was not confined to emperors or patriarchs.

In the fifty years after Chalcedon, there were repeated efforts by the imperial government in the East to restore ecclesiastical and political unity. The most famous example of this was the *Henotikon* of Emperor Zeno in 482, which emphasized the faith of Nicaea. Although it was a masterpiece of imperial diplomacy, and nominally at least brought the eastern sees into communion, in the long run it was unsuccessful, because for those opposed to the Council only an outright condemnation of the *Tome* of Leo and of Chalcedon would suffice.

This is the background against which we must situate the life and thought of Severus of Antioch.

SOURCES FOR SEVERUS'S LIFE

The sources for the life of Severus, anti-Chalcedonian patriarch of Antioch from 512–18, are many and varied, with the result that we have a comprehensive and multidimensional picture of the man, his life and his times. In the first place, we have nearly 300 of his own letters, written prior to and during his patriarchate, as well as during his long exile. In addition, some of his 125 cathedral homilies, particularly Homilies XXVII and XXX, contain autobiographical information. In the Coptic version of Homily XXVII we find a section in which Severus narrates his conversion at Tripolis, showing that until he went to Beirut to study he was still a pagan (Garitte 1966: 335–90). To his friend and fellow-student Zachariah Scholasticus, later bishop of Mitylene on Lesbos, we owe the first biography of Severus. Composed in Greek around 515 and surviving in a Syriac translation, it was a response to a pamphlet defaming the patriarch (*Vie* 7–10, 75) on the grounds that he was guilty of pagan practices and of being baptized late. Although it is a contemporary document, it needs in part to be used with caution because some of its details are in conflict with those given by Severus himself (Darling 1982: 20). A second biography, similarly composed in Greek but surviving in a Syriac translation and some Coptic fragments, is that of John, abbot of the monastery of Beith Aphthonia on the Euphrates, who died *c.* 558. Another biography is ascribed to one of Severus's successors as anti-Chalcedonian patriarch of Antioch, Athanasius Gamala or the Camel-Driver (594–630/1), which has come down to us in Coptic fragments and in an Ethiopic version derived from an Arabic model, which in its turn was possibly a translation from Coptic. Dependent on John of Beith Aphthonia is the Syriac biography in metrical homiletic form of George, bishop of the Arabs, who was born around 640 (George, bishop of the Arabs 1993: XI–XIII). We have a fifth biography, written in Syriac by Qyriaqos, the Syrian Orthodox patriarch of Antioch from 793–817, which was discovered in 1975 and remains unpublished (Vööbus 1975–6: 117–24). A sixth biography, composed in Arabic by a certain bishop of Assiut, probably John, in the fifteenth century, was discovered by Youhanna Nessim Youssef in 2002 in the monastery of St Menas at Mariout. All of these hagiographical works need to be used with varying degrees of caution, and checked wherever possible against other historical sources.

Given his pivotal role in the ecclesiastical politics of his time, Severus features in most of the historical and theological works which were composed either in or about the period, from the Chalcedonian as well as the anti-Chalcedonian side. Because these are too numerous to list here, we mention only the anti-Chalcedonian *Church History* of Zachariah Scholasticus and his continuator, ps.Zachariah, which contains several of the patriarch's letters, and the Chalcedonian *Church History* of Evagrius Scholasticus (d. before 600), which preserves unique information about him.

BEFORE THE PATRIARCHATE

Severus was born around 456 in Sozopolis (Pisidia) to a well-to-do family. Despite the assertions of his friend and biographer, Zachariah, that his grandfather, also called Severus, was bishop of the city, had attended the Council of Ephesus in 439, and had been one of the bishops who condemned Nestorius, it is clear from Severus's own words that the family was pagan.[1] Thus his relatively late baptism should not be attributed – as it is by Zachariah – to an unduly long catechumenate as supposedly practised in Pisidia (*Vie* 11), but to a radical conversion from paganism to Christianity (Darling 1982: 24). After the death of his father, in 485 Severus and his two older brothers were sent by their mother to Alexandria to study grammar and rhetoric, both Latin and Greek (*Vie* 11), a prerequisite for legal studies. In Alexandria Severus met Zachariah, his future biographer, and for the next twelve or so

5

years the fortunes of the two young men were inexorably intertwined. Because Zachariah wrote his biography as a defence of Severus against claims that at the beginning of his career he had worshipped demons and idols and given himself over to magical practices (*Vie* 9, 75), much of the work deals with pagan and magical practices in Alexandria and Beirut, where the two fellow-students went on to study law. While the account is partisan, it discloses incidentally details of the students' timetables, programmes of courses, the names and provenance of students and the names of professors, the liveliness of paganism in the two cities at the end of the fifth century, and student life at the time (Poggi 1986: 59, 62; Blázquez 1998: 415–36). No doubt one of Zachariah's aims in dropping the names of young rich Christian men who went on to stellar careers in church and state was to add weight to his claims that Severus was not guilty of paganism or magic (*Vie* 10).

Severus is presented consistently as an unbaptized adviser to his fellow students, who as Christians were fighting paganism in both Egypt and Phoenicia (*Vie* 44, 65, 91). According to Zachariah, his Christian fellow students in Alexandria persuaded Severus to abandon the reading of the great Antiochene orator Libanius in favour of two illustrious Christian Cappadocians, Basil of Caesarea and Gregory Nazianzen (*Vie* 13). This study programme was to be continued by both Severus and Zachariah when they met up in Beirut in 488, a year after the future patriarch had arrived there (*Vie* 46). The Cappadocians in fact were to become models for Severus both personally and ecclesiologically, and he believed that they would be his judges at the Last Judgement.[2] Zachariah instructed his friend in the Scriptures and the Fathers: the two of them pursued their legal studies from Monday to Friday, rested on Saturday morning, then spent the remainder of the weekend studying theology (*Vie* 52–3). At the end of his five-year stay in Beirut, Severus had composed a legal work and graduated as master of law (Poggi 1986: 65). His legal training remains discernible in his writings, and accounts for his interest in canon law, as evidenced particularly in his letters.

Severus was given formal catechesis by a monk before being baptized in the church of the martyr Leontius at Tripolis (*Vie* 80–2). The choice of this venue was almost certainly not accidental, although Zachariah glosses over the motive. Leontius was credited with the power of converting pagans from demon-worship to Christianity, and in Homily XXVII (*PO* 36/4: 563), delivered in 513 in the church of Leontius in Daphne, Severus was to claim that before his baptism he was a pagan converted suddenly from his parents' religion (Darling

1982: 22–5). That both catechesis and baptism occurred outside the hierarchy of the church in Beirut may be explained by the fact that the local bishop was a Chalcedonian (Darling 1982: 20), and perhaps also by the close nexus in Syrian and Palestinian monasticism between baptism and asceticism (Escolan 1999: 41–2). For an ascetic is what Severus became, after his indisputably anti-Chalcedonian baptism. Despite the fact that after his graduation he went shopping for official legal robes before his planned return to Pisidia via Jerusalem, he was won over by meeting some disciples of the famous first-generation anti-Chalcedonian Peter the Iberian, and in *c.* 490 became a monk in Peter's monastery near Gaza (*Vie* 92–3). In so doing, he parted company with his friend and mentor Zachariah, who recounts sheepishly that he could not follow Severus into the monastic life because his father wanted him to become a lawyer in Constantinople (*Vie* 95).

Under Peter's charismatic leadership, the area around Gaza had produced an influential group of anti-Chalcedonian monastics and intellectuals (Steppa 2002: 163–4) that was to be involved in the course of both ecclesiastical and secular politics in the late fifth and early sixth centuries. In fact, with his entry into the monastic world of Palestine, Severus had 'joined the most volatile and influential subculture' of late antiquity (Darling 1982: 26), for it was a breeding-ground of theologians, bishops, and ecclesiastical administrators for the eastern empire. However, Chalcedonian monks in the area were even more influential under the leadership of Sabas, whose life was written by Cyril of Scythopolis in the mid-sixth century.

From the monastery of Peter, Severus graduated to the solitary life in the desert of Eleutheropolis, where, however, his health suffered so badly from the rigours of asceticism that he was taken by the abbot of the monastery of Romanus and nursed back to health.[3] This anti-Chalcedonian establishment was built *c.* 459 near Eleutheropolis, and soon after, according to John Rufus (Rufus 1912: 58), it housed 600 monks. According to John of Beith Aphthonia (JBA 229), at this stage Severus used his not inconsiderable family legacy to help the poor and to found his own monastery in Maiuma near Gaza.[4] Zachariah would have us believe that this establishment was necessary to accommodate the numbers of disciples who had gathered around Severus. By 500, Severus had received priestly ordination at the hands of Epiphanius, bishop of Magydon in Pamphilia (*Vie* 98–100).[5] Although in reading Zachariah's biography of Severus one is given the impression that the anti-Chalcedonian monks were in the ascendant in Palestine at this time, this was far from being the case, as Severus's encounter a little later with the theologian and Alexandrian monk Nephalius, a convert from anti-Chalcedonianism, illustrates.

A born agitator, Nephalius would have known that the safest region in which to launch an attack on the by-now outstanding anti-Chalcedonian monastic leader was Palestine. He attacked the future patriarch, who responded; then Nephalius delivered a speech 'in front of the church' in Jerusalem (*Vie* 103–4) and, with the aid of the clergy and monks there, succeeded in expelling Severus in 508. This is testimony to the decline of the anti-Chalcedonian cause in the region as a result of the vigorous propaganda of the great Abbot Sabas (Frend 1973: 265). Severus went to Constantinople with 200 monks (Moeller 1944–5: 105) to plead his case with Emperor Anastasius, and was followed by Nephalius and an entourage of Chalcedonian monks from Palestine (*Vie* 103–5). The two monks were to cross swords again publicly in the imperial capital, but in the meantime Severus had won the trust of the emperor and was soon acting as his theological adviser.

Shortly before this, the militant anti-Chalcedonian bishop of Mabbog, Xenaias (whose name was Hellenized as Philoxenus), had been invited to Constantinople by the emperor, perhaps in order to participate in an anti-Chalcedonian synod convoked by imperial order.[6] While Anastasius was sympathetic to the anti-Chalcedonian cause, the patriarch of the capital, Macedonius, was a strict Chalcedonian in a largely Chalcedonian city, and refused to communicate with Philoxenus in any sense of the word (de Halleux 1963: 61). Philoxenus had left the capital by the time Severus arrived in 508 (de Halleux 1963: 59), but, despite the differences in their age and backgrounds,[7] the two men developed a partnership which was a turning-point in the history of incarnational theology (Moeller 1951: 670).

Both Severus and Philoxenus would be content only with an outright condemnation of Chalcedon. Yet the eirenic Anastasius, whose aim was to minimize disruption in his realm, was committed to using the *Henotikon* as the main tool of his ecclesiastical policy, and indeed neither Severus nor Philoxenus would have rejected the document outright. The patriarchates of Constantinople, Antioch and Jerusalem were led by staunch Chalcedonians. Philoxenus campaigned relentlessly against Patriarch Flavian of Antioch, and perhaps also against Patriarch Elias of Jerusalem (de Halleux 1963: 69). Faced with the insistence of Severus and Philoxenus, and with the growing inefficacy of the *Henotikon* to achieve his aims, Emperor Anastasius apparently entrusted Severus with the task of drawing up a document known as the *Type*, which gave to the *Henotikon* an anti-Chalcedonian interpretation, without, however, anathematizing Leo and the council of 451 explicitly.[8] Judging from the embarrassed manner in which the

Byzantine chroniclers relate the event, it seems that Severus's formula was accepted at least temporarily or conditionally by the patriarchs of Constantinople, Antioch and Jerusalem (de Halleux 1963: 69).

It was about this time that the controversial doxology known as the Thrice-Holy or Trishagion came to play a decisive role in the career of Macedonius. Some forty years before, one of the first generation of anti-Chalcedonians, Peter the Fuller, patriarch of Antioch, had introduced into the doxology 'Holy God, holy mighty, holy immortal, have mercy on us', the words 'who was crucified for us', in order to reinforce the christological interpretation of the hymn such that the second person of the Trinity was said truly to have become incarnate and to have suffered. The addition was seen by anti-Chalcedonians in Syria as an antidote to Nestorianism,[9] but to those who understood the hymn to be addressed to the Trinity, it was deeply shocking because it implied theopaschite doctrine; that is, that the impassible Godhead had suffered. While the addition is described by Bacht as a liturgical extravagance (1951: 280) and by Moeller as baroque (1951: 652–3), it had become an anti-Chalcedonian catch-cry. It was this formula that was used by the monks who had accompanied Severus to the capital, and Anastasius acquiesced in the practice until Chalcedonian monks from Palestine objected. In this they were followed by Macedonius. This only served to sharpen the confrontation between Severus and the patriarch, who was eventually deposed by a synod on 7 August 511 and banished (Frend 1972: 168, 218). He was replaced by the more moderate Timothy (511–18). The extent to which the use of the addition 'who was crucified for us' could arouse religious zeal on both sides can be seen from the riots which the strict Chalcedonian Sleepless Monks (*Akoimetoi*) provoked in Constantinople the following year in objection to the formula. This turbulence ultimately led Anastasius to appear without his crown in the circus and offer to abdicate (7 November 512).[10] The Trishagion would also figure in the revolt of the Goth Vitalian, as we shall see.

Philoxenus's campaign against Flavian of Antioch had suffered a setback at the Syrian synod of Antioch in 509, when the bishop of Mabbog and his monastic supporters constituted a small minority (de Halleux 1963: 65). The anti-Chalcedonian militant was also not impressed at being summoned to an Oriental synod in Sidon in 511, the imperial aim of which was the re-establishment of relations between Flavian and John of Nikiu, patriarch of Alexandria, with whom Flavian had broken communion in 505/6 when John had repudiated Chalcedon. Despite the fact that, according to his biographers, Severus had left Constantinople (September 511) to return to his monastery in Maiuma out of a preference for the monastic life, he was present at Sidon, a synod which was to be a decisive point in his elevation to the patriarchate of Antioch. In Sidon, the anti-Chalcedonians were no match for their opponents, and, when the impossibility of restoring unity between the patriarchates of Antioch and Alexandria became apparent, the assembly was disbanded by the imperial legate, Eutropius.[11] Notwithstanding, a synod in Laodicea, probably comprising a small number of Philoxenus's supporters who were soon to appear at the consecration of Severus (de Halleux 1963: 74), declared Flavian deposed, on trumped-up charges. The church historian Evagrius, reporting eyewitness accounts, describes the ensuing violence between anti-Chalcedonian monks who arrived in Antioch from Syria Prima, and the largely Chalcedonian populace of the city, who slaughtered their opponents and threw their bodies into the river Orontes (*HE* III.32). Such violence flew in the face of Anastasius's eirenic policies. Flavian was forced to leave his patriarchal throne, and was banished to Petra, in present-day Jordan (Honigmann 1951: 15). The way was clear for Philoxenus's party to put forward the patriarchal candidate of their choice – the monk Severus (November 512).

Meanwhile, the agitation of Severus in the imperial city and Philoxenus in Syria between 508 and 511 had contributed to the crystallization of a new christology known as neo-Chalcedonianism, of which Severus's former harasser, Nephalius, was one of the earliest exponents. In *c.* 508 (Lebon 1909: 120–1), Nephalius had written an *Apology for the Synod of Chalcedon* (*CPG* 6825) in which the debate over Christ's natures had taken a decidedly linguistic and terminological turn (Grillmeier 1995: 49). From Severus's two addresses to Nephalius, which unfortunately do not survive in their entirety but which we know from Severus himself were written in Palestine,[12] we can reconstruct to a large extent the neo-Chalcedonian position which Nephalius had come to embrace.[13] In the face of the determination of the two champions of the one-nature christology – champions who had no equivalent on the Chalcedonian side – dyophysites were almost forced into some rapprochement (Moeller 1951: 645). Thus characteristic of the neo-Chalcedonian movement were the attempts to reconcile the two contentious formulae 'from two natures' and 'in two natures', and to show that Cyril of Alexandria, who for Severus and his party was the touchstone of orthodoxy, was in accord with Chalcedon. It was precisely at this time that *florilegia* were circulating which were intended to prove that Cyril, the great enemy of Nestorius, did not therefore have to be considered the enemy of two-nature christology as well, but could be claimed as a witness in favour of Chalcedon (Grillmeier 1995: 22). When one of these *florilegia* came into Severus's hands while he was in Constantinople, he felt obliged to refute it in a work entitled the *Philalethes*, or 'Friend of Truth', by which Cyril was meant. The *Philalethes* is a classic christological work from the anti-Chalcedonian side (Grillmeier 1995: 23). Since a *florilegium* is of its very nature selective, it was Severus's aim in this work to prove that, by selectively citing Cyril, the Chalcedonians had made the great Alexandrian out to be a proponent of the two-nature christology. 'The historical development of Cyril was in fact so ambivalent that his works could be an common arsenal for contrary christologies depending upon what one sought in them' (Grillmeier 1995: 23), and it was precisely this ambivalence that was to cause Severus from this point on to take up his pen repeatedly to defend Cyril's understanding of Christ.

From the time before his episcopacy comes also a variety of letters which demonstrate that Severus was already building up the networks which were to stand him in good stead for the next thirty years. He was clearly on good terms with Constantine, bishop of Seleucia in Isauria, an ally of Philoxenus (*SL* I.1), and with Solon, the metropolitan of the same city (*SL* I.2, 3). He had the ear of a group of patricians (*SL* II.1), and of secular officials: John the tribune (*SL* V.1), Theodore the tribune and notary (*SL* X.3), Conon the silentiary (*SL* X.4), Oecumenius the count (Letter I), and Eupraxius and Phocas the imperial chamberlains (Letters LXVII, LXVIII). In addition we find from this period letters to laypeople (*SL* X.1, 2), giving evidence of a keen pastoral sense which we are to encounter again in the letters written during his episcopate and exile.[14]

THE PATRIARCHATE (512–18)

For a long time we have wanted to partake of the Holy Mysteries.
Set our city free from the Council of Chalcedon!
Anathematize now this (council) which has turned the world (upside down)!
Anathematize now the council of the distorters (of the faith)!
The cursed Council of Chalcedon!
The cursed *Tome* of Leo!
Let all the bishops anathematize (it) now!
Who will not do so is a wolf and not a shepherd.[15]

According to the Syrian anti-Chalcedonian tradition, these were the acclamations which greeted Severus when he ascended the patriarchal throne of Ignatius of Antioch, after having been summoned, as Zachariah tells us, from his monastery in Maiuma by Emperor Anastasius (*Vie* 111). Severus's election possibly took place on 6 November 512 (Malalas 1986: *Chron*. 16), and it was followed by the ceremony of consecration in the Great Church on 16 November, at which twelve bishops, including Philoxenus, assisted.[16] During the ceremony, Severus delivered the first of his 125 Cathedral Homilies, so-called because they were delivered from the *cathedra* or episcopal throne in his role as bishop. This homily survives in Syriac fragments and in a complete Coptic version (*PO* 38/2: 254–69), from which we learn that the address was repeated two days afterwards in the sanctuary of the martyr Romanus in Daphne outside Antioch, because on 16 November many people were prevented by the tumult and the shouting from hearing its delivery.[17] This may indicate that not all residents of Antioch were as happy with Severus's accession as the acclamations in the Syriac tradition would have us believe. The title of the homily as preserved in the Syriac version reveals that the main topic was the necessity of confessing 'Christ out of two natures, a single Lord, a single Son, and not two natures after the ineffable union' (*PO* 38/2: 255). In expressions which would become familiar to his new congregations, to his readers and to opponents, the new patriarch denounced the madness of the new Jews; that is, those who joined the Council of Chalcedon, and who divided the indivisible into two natures – for the word 'two' dissolves unity and destroys the economy of salvation (*PO* 38/2: 261–2). At the conclusion of the ceremony of consecration, Severus signed a declaration of faith, which was witnessed by thirteen bishops.[18]

While the depositions of Macedonius and Flavian spelled the end of the efficacy of the *Henotikon* and were followed by the exile of Chalcedonian bishops, clergy and monks (Theophanes, *Chron*. AM 6004), in his new role Severus was far from being uncontested. Thanks to the influence of Philoxenus and the support of the latter's monks, the frontier area between Roman and Persian territory was staunchly anti-Chalcedonian. The situation in and around Constantinople was, however, problematical, as the proffered abdication of Emperor Anastasius, just one day after Severus's accession to the patriarchate, illustrates. In Palestine and Jerusalem, there was vociferous opposition among Chalcedonian monks and clergy to Severus's consecration, portrayed later by Cyril of Scythopolis, who claims that 'on seizing the patriarchate Severus exhibited great cruelty towards those not in communion with him', that he was arrogant and relied on imperial power, and that he was a 'destructive corrupter of souls'.[19] In Syria Secunda, in such cities as Apamea and Epiphaneia, where Greek influence was strong, there was also opposition, as the oral tradition reported by Evagrius testifies (*HE* III.34).[20] But there was trouble for Severus and his followers from a perhaps less likely quarter – the moderate Chalcedonian or neo-Chalcedonian party, from whose conciliatory ranks Severus's next theological opponent, John the Grammarian, had just emerged (Lebon 1909: 61–2). In Cilicia, the problem which faced Severus was of quite a different kind: there the Antiochene theological tradition of Diodore of Tarsus, Theodore of Mopsuestia, and Nestorius was still strong, and in the city of Tarsus the name of Nestorius was still retained in the diptychs and he was venerated as a martyr.[21]

The Hellenized city whose patriarchal throne Severus ascended in 512 would have been largely recognizable to Libanius and John Chrysostom.[22] It was a well-to-do city whose status rivalled Rome, Alexandria and Constantinople, a fact which was a source of some pride for Libanius, but a cause of concern for John and Severus. Situated on trade routes to the north, south, east, and west, it was a prosperous centre through which many non-Antiochenes passed, including pilgrims on their way to and from the Holy Land. As well as being the capital of Syria, it was the administrative hub for the secular diocese of Oriens, and in the recurring wars between the Roman and Persian empires, the latest of which had taken place between 502–5, it had been a base for military operations. The imperial family had at least one palace there, on the island in the Orontes, and perhaps another in Daphne (Downey 1961: 641–6). The increasing imperial centralization in the late Roman empire and the stationing in Antioch of the *magister militum per Orientem*, the commander-in-chief of the army on the eastern frontier, and the *comes Orientis*, who was responsible to the emperor for the eastern diocese, meant that its citizens could experience perceived imperial oppression first-hand. The fiscal and financial reforms of Emperor Anastasius entailed further centralization to execute them, such that imperial officials were given extensive powers, and the city council was left in the hands of a few rich families (Liebeschuetz 1972: 241). This perception was translated into numerous public disturbances during the fourth, fifth and sixth centuries, the best known of which was that of 387, when an angry mob destroyed the imperial images and statues in the city. As in other cities in the late Roman empire, in Antioch public events connected with sport or entertainment often gave rise to violence. After the Council of Chalcedon in 451, these acts of public disorder acquired an additional dimension, with manifestations of violence between proponents and opponents of the council. Serious riots had broken out between circus factions in 494–5 and at the celebration of the local Olympic games in the hippodrome in July and August 507, during which churches and public buildings were destroyed (Downey 1961: 504–7). During his patriarchate, Severus was to rail repeatedly in his homilies against the Olympic games, indeed against the circus and the hippodrome as well. To some extent, physically isolated from the *polis* but nonetheless engaged with it were numbers of monastics who lived in the hills around Antioch, various manifestations of whose lifestyles were already well attested to in the homilies of John Chrysostom (Mayer 1998: 275–88).

If Antioch was affluent, it was also certainly home to many poor.[23] Although the archaeological evidence from the reigns of Emperors Zeno and Anastasius (474–518) shows a major growth in the production of olive oil in the Belus region, east of Antioch (Downey 1961: 501–2), an industry that was presumably in the hands of wealthy Antiochenes, there is little hard evidence for increased affluence in Antioch itself. From the Syriac *Chronicle* of Josua the Stylite (Ch. 44) we know that there was a widespread famine in 500/1 in the area between Antioch and Nisibis, and in his first year as patriarch Severus speaks in his preaching of a severe drought around Antioch (Hom. XIX; *PO* 37/1). The Persian War (502–5) would also have had a significant impact on the city's finances. Leaving aside the numerous passages in Severus's homilies where he exhorts his congregations generally to almsgiving – these are commonplace in the homiletic repertoire – we still find specific mention of the poor and the sick. There was harassment of tenant farmers and their families in the hinterland of Antioch by owners (Hom. XIX; *PO* 37/1: 39, 41); similarly there were cases of richer people dragging the poorer into court and having them put in irons (Hom. CIII; *PO* 22/2); there were beggars in the streets and market-place of Antioch[24] and specifically around the church of St Babylas (Hom. XXXIII; *PO* 36/3). Severus's congregations are urged to give money, jewellery and superfluous items of clothing to the poor.[25] It was the custom in Antioch during Lent to give to the church clothing or pieces of linen which were distributed by the protodeacon to the sick and needy. However, the patriarch's congregations were not keen to part with their possessions, as three different homilies testify.[26]

The church of Antioch may not have been well-off at the time of Severus's accession: there are numerous passages in his homilies and letters where he complains of financial burdens. The affairs of the church bring more worry than profit, he says (Hom. XXXVII; *PO* 36/3), and material worries make him incapable of teaching (Hom. LIV: *PO* 4/1). At one point, during a homily on the local martyr Drosis (Hom. CXIV; *PO* 26/3: 301. 6–11), he reports that his congregation have expressed their displeasure at always hearing the same homily on this feast-day, and at the same time an appeal for them to give money. The effects of the flourishing olive industry east of Antioch are not detectable in episcopal social welfare programmes in the late fifth and early sixth centuries: it may be that the ecclesiastical turmoil in the area following the Council of Chalcedon had taken a financial toll.[27] Apart from one reference to the construction of a well which Severus financed by a loan (*SL* I.42: 120), and the mention of a small gift which he presented to a new monastery (*SL* I.35: 102–3) – in both places he points to the financial embarrassment of his see – there is no evidence of largesse during his patriarchate. The deposed Flavian, whom Severus accuses of corruption and simony (*SL* I.48: 131), may have had to resort to such measures to ensure some degree of solvency for his see.

At the beginning of the sixth century, as there had been since Hellenistic times, there would have been an affluent and influential Jewish community in Antioch. Indeed, in the days of John Chrysostom a little over a century beforehand, it had made its presence felt in the everyday life of the Antiochenes, including the Christians. The cult of the Maccabees, for instance, was attractive to Christians, as were the various Jewish festivals. John rails against those of his congregation who 'Judaize' or behave like Jews in certain circumstances or at certain times of the year (Allen and Mayer 2000: 148–9). However, we have little direct evidence for the activities of the Jewish community during Severus's patriarchate. We do know that the Jews, as associates of the Blue circus party, were involved in the riots at the time of the Olympic games in 507, and that their opponents, the Greens, attacked and plundered the synagogue in the course of the violence and killed many people. Adding insult to injury, the Greens placed a cross on the burnt-out site, which later became the martyrial shrine of St Leontius (Downey 1961: 505–6), where Severus was to deliver Homily XXXVI. There are few factual references to Jews in Severus's works: Jews are synonymous with unbelief and with the followers of Chalcedon. One rare example of the concrete threat which they posed to the self-identification of Antiochene Christians was their introduction of good-luck amulets, which was greeted with displeasure by Severus (Hom. LXXIX; *PO* 20/2: 321).

Possibly because of his own pagan background and his familiarity with paganism and its adherents in Alexandria and Beirut, we find more concrete references to pagan practices in Severus's works, particularly in his homilies. However, as in the case of the 'Jews', the question of the self-identification of Antiochene Christians against their pagan fellow citizens is pertinent to our interpretation of the data. The theatre, the circus and the hippodrome are regarded by the patriarch on numerous occasions as 'pagan', but this is commonplace in homiletic literature, and the appropriation by Christians of aspects of paganism which had been traditionally associated with life in the *polis* can come as no surprise. We know from the chronicler John Malalas, who would have been in Antioch during Severus's patriarchate, that several old Roman pagan festivals – the Brumalia, the Consilia and the Februalia – were still celebrated there.[28] Then, when in Homily LXXII (Text 17 below) the patriarch berates as pagans those who accord angels such a degree of devotion that they come close to worshipping them, as pagans worship many gods (*PO* 12/1: 72, 73, 83), this is not a denunciation of paganism per se (*pace* Darling 1982: 111).

In November 512, Severus assumed responsibility for a see which included Isauria, Cilicia, Syria, Phoenicia, Arabia and Mesopotamia. Since the aftermath of the Council of Nicaea in 325, it had been no stranger to religious discord and, even at times, to religious anarchy. From AD 330, Antioch had been led by a series of Arian or Arianizing bishops, some of whom were violent, and during the subsequent schism caused by the resistance of the Nicene bishop Meletius, who ordained John Chrysostom to the diaconate, there were no fewer than four rival bishops (Downey 1961: 412–4). In the fifty years after the Council of Chalcedon, we find similar unrest, beginning with the visit to the city of the future emperor, Zeno, an anti-Chalcedonian and at that stage (AD 469) *magister militum per Orientem*, in the company of a priest, Peter the Fuller, whom we have already met as the instigator of the addition to the Trishagion hymn. With Zeno's support, Peter ousted the Chalcedonian patriarch Martyrius, and with the aid of imported and local monks, and especially his addition to the Trishagion, set about building up anti-Chalcedonianism in the city and its environs. So troubled were the ecclesiastical affairs of the city from this point to around 488 that Peter was banished on four separate occasions (AD 469–70, 470–1, 475–6 and 484–8). One of his Chalcedonian successors, Stephen, was murdered by anti-Chalcedonians in the church of the local martyr Barlaam, or Barlaha, being stabbed with sharp reeds, and his body was thrown into the river Orontes.[29] Both Peter's successor, Palladius, who died in 498, and Severus's predecessor, Flavian

(498–512), were moderate Chalcedonians who tried to make the *Henotikon* work, and for a time there was peace in the see of Antioch. This, however, was cut short by the agitations of Philoxenus.

Because the religious situation in Antioch was characterized by its pluralism, it would be odd to think that other Christian groupings, in particular Nestorians or Nestorian-sympathizers, were not to be found there on the accession of Severus, even if their numbers were small. Yet in the case of Nestorians, the picture is complicated by the fact that most of Severus's references to 'Nestorians' are rhetorically coded to mean 'anti-Chalcedonians'. Thus, in the letter to Bishop Nicias, translated below (Text 19), the two would-be clerics who sailed west from Cilicia to be ordained by 'Nestorians' were probably transferring to the Chalcedonian side (*pace* Frend 1972: 226). Severus's complaint that the monk Pelagius had introduced a 'Nestorian' into the monastery of the apostle Thomas at Seleucia has to be read similarly (*SL* VII.4; 420–6). The case of Homily LXIV, delivered on 29 December 514, which is a denunciation of Theodoret of Cyrrhus, that luminary of the Antiochene School and disciple of Nestorius, may be different: it was pronounced in a church in the new quarter of Antioch, where, in the words of the title of the homily, 'these foxes of the Nestorian heresy were sneaking in' (*PO* 8/2: 313. 6–9). More significant among other Christian groupings, at least among monastics in and around Antioch, seems to have been the quietist movement of Messalianism, whose adherents believed in the inborn sinfulness of humanity, which could be eradicated by ascetical practices and prayer under the guidance of the holy Spirit, rather than by the administration of baptism. A synod had been held in 390 in Antioch itself to condemn this movement definitively (Downey 1961: 417), but it lived on, even experiencing a reformation at the beginning of the sixth century (Escolan 1999: 113–14). Severus addresses one of his letters to an archimandrite, Simeon, who had decided to outsource his monastic responsibilities and devote himself to continual prayer (*SL* VII.3: 371–3). The patriarch also writes to Abbot Mark near Tarsus, asking him to renounce both Chalcedonianism and Messalianism (*SL* V.4: 286–90). That Manichaeism was an additional force to be reckoned with is demonstrated from the serious attempt which Severus makes in Homily CXXIII to refute its tenets point by point (Wallace-Hadrill 1982: 22–5).

Such was the city whose spiritual and temporal concerns were to occupy the outsider Severus for the following six years. While the new patriarch was adept at politicking and lobbying, which his years as court theological adviser had put beyond doubt, and while he had

had some brief administrative experience running his own monastery in Maiuma, he was first and foremost a monk-theologian, probably unfamiliar with directly catechizing laity, and he was a stranger to the city of Antioch (Darling 1982: 46). Even according to his close colleague Philoxenus, it was only gradually that Severus rallied people to himself (*Letter to Abbot Simeon of Teleda* 193: 3–6).

Among Severus's first official duties would have been the dispatch of *synodika* or a letter to other bishops containing the new patriarch's profession of faith and a list of anathemas. The addressees of this letter then replied with their own professions of faith and lists of anathemas, if they agreed to enter into communion with him. Severus sent his letters to John of Alexandria (Letter XLVI; *PO* 12/1: 321) with the aim of re-establishing communion with Egypt, and to Timothy of Constantinople (*SL* I.27: 88), who, although a moderate Chalcedonian adhering to the *Henotikon*, apparently subscribed to Severus's list of anathemas (de Halleux 1963: 81 n. 38). Epiphanius of Tyre, brother of the deposed Flavian, refused to accept the *synodika* (Letter LI; *PO* 12/1: 325–6), as presumably did other Chalcedonians. Extracts of these letters survive only in an Arabic translation. We have a good example of this practice in the *synodika* which Patriarch Theodosius of Alexandria sent on his consecration in 535, and Severus's reply to it (Text 28 below).[30]

The monk-patriarch began his reforms.

> He sent away the scullions and cooks from the bishop's palace, with all the edibles they had prepared. He overturned the baths which were there, like the God-loving kings Hezechiah and Josiah when they tipped over the statues of Baal. He continued the hard life he had taken as a monk, in sleeping on the earth, in no baths, in the long service of song, and in a diet of vegetables like the youths of Babylon, and buying rough and common bread from the marketplace, such as bakers customarily make for the poor.[31]

Severus also took the usual step of ordering the removal of the names of heretical bishops from the diptychs in Antioch and its environs (*SL* I.19: 68), although, like Philoxenus, he was measured enough not to insist on the removal of the names of all Chalcedonians (de Halleux 1963: 87).

In April or October 513, together with Philoxenus, the new patriarch convoked a synod at Antioch to ratify his election, to ensure anti-Chalcedonian orthodoxy and safeguard the anathemas on Chalcedon and Leo's *Tome*, and to maintain ecclesiastical harmony.[32] [Until the work of de Halleux (1963: 80–5) this synod was thought to have been held in Tyre in 514.][33] All the aims of this meeting were realised, thus making good the setback which the anti-Chalcedonians had suffered at the synod of Sidon two years previously. The fortunes of the opponents of Chalcedon began to turn, particularly after the deposition of Elias of Jerusalem (1 September 516), the last of the patriarchal triumvirate on which Philoxenus and Severus had set their sights. The names of the first-generation Alexandrian anti-Chalcedonians, Dioscorus and Timothy the Cat (Aelurus), were restored to the diptychs (Frend 1972: 228).

There was, however, trouble on another front, which was eventually to contribute to the demise of the anti-Chalcedonian party in 518. A substantial number of clergy in the eastern empire, led by Alcison, bishop of Nicopolis in Epirus, were in communion with Rome, and this arch-Chalcedonian party looked to Vitalian, the Thracian count, as its champion. Vitalian had substantial numbers of barbarian troops and close ties with Rome, and was a supporter of Macedonius and the godson of Flavian. A letter sent to Alcison by the monks of Palestine towards the end of Anastasius's reign in fact documents the events leading up to the depositions of the patriarchs of Constantinople and Antioch.[34] At first, Vitalian's demands were confined to the eastern empire: the restoration of the Trishagion doxology without the anti-Chalcedonian addition, and the reinstatement of Macedonius and Flavian. He marched unsuccessfully on Constantinople three times, in 513, 514 and 515.[35] His first repulse was commemorated by Severus in Homily XXXIV, delivered at the end of 513, where the insurgent's 'impious' name is associated with Jeroboam, who 'plotted rebellion against his master' (*PO* 36/3: 430–4). Vitalian's final defeat was seen as an anti-Chalcedonian triumph, celebrated by Severus in a hymn *On Vitalian the Tyrant and on the Victory of the Christ-loving Anastasius* (*PO* 7/5: 710). Unsuccessful though the Goth's initiatives, both ecclesiastical and military, had been, they nonetheless polarized the debate about Chalcedon, on the one hand between East and West, and on the other within the eastern empire itself.

In reading the letters which survive from Severus's patriarchate, one has the impression of an 'immensely busy administrator attempting to right in a few years disorders resulting from generations of neglect' (Frend 1972: 225). The patriarch complains that his workload is overwhelming (*SL* I.23: 92), but it is also clear that in dealing with his administrative load he relied on a large number of people (*SL* VII.5: 379–80). One of these was his own brother Peter, a priest, who was one of his *apocrisarii* or representatives in Constantinople, having followed Severus there in 508 (*SL* I.1: 11). Peter died, however, during his brother's patriarchate (*SL* XI: 461; I.49: 134–50). Relying on such infrastructure had its pitfalls, as Severus himself wryly comments:

> nothing is likely to impair the whole administration of those who preside over a people (not only spiritual administration but also political or any other kind whatever) so much as intercourse with those who are constantly with them and serve them and are entrusted by them with things that cannot be entrusted to those without.[36]

Severus's concerns, as expressed in his letters, range widely, from the conduct of episcopal elections (e.g. *SL* I.29: 101) to matters as trivial as declaring illicit the dismissal of a steward of church property and the removal of keys by others while the local bishop lay dying (*SL* I.30: 106–7). In matters of process, such as episcopal ordinations and the administration of ecclesiastical justice, we encounter a tidy and business-like mind, formed by legal training (Poggi 1986: 65, 70).

Although Severus states in one of his letters to the noblewoman Caesaria, translated below (Text 23), that 'one should not even offer an ordinary greeting to those who bring another doctrine and do not teach the orthodox faith', his position regarding Chalcedonians was somewhat more nuanced. In the same letter, he acknowledges that those who occupy official positions, like Caesaria herself, may at times be required to be present at ceremonies in a Chalcedonian church: it is legitimate for them on those occasions to listen to the readings and prayers, as long as they do not communicate.

Severus felt responsible for the inclusion or striking of names from the diptychs,[37] not only in his own see but also in the churches of his suffragan bishops (*SL* I.13: 62). In regulating the ordination of a bishop, he was involved in a personal way, having the casting vote in an election process (*SL* I.29: 101). If problems arose concerning the choice of an episcopal candidate, it was Severus who referred the matter to the emperor, a procedure perhaps facilitated by his *apocrisarii* in the capital. Severus could prohibit a bishop from performing ordinations outside his own district, unless the bishop's presence was necessitated by the 'heresy' of the local bishop (*SL* I.1: 10). There are various references in the letters to the regular presence in Antioch of a number of bishops who probably assisted Severus in the administration of the ecclesiastical courts.[38] On this point, however, the evidence in the letters refers only to ecclesiastical cases, rather than to secular suits being brought before an episcopal court (the *audientia episcopalis*); in fact, the presbyter Julian of Tarsus, when accused of profiteering from church property, shunned the ecclesiastical court and dragged his case to the secular courts, a fact which Severus reported to the *magister militum per Orientem* (*SL* I.40). At least in some cases brought before the ecclesiastical courts Severus was personally involved.[39]

The venality of Julian seems not to have been an isolated case. The letters are riddled with comments on the corruption of the clergy in Severus's patriarchate. To be sure, as we have seen, the finances of the see were not robust when he came into office, and he complained that Flavian, 'the trafficker in all divine things', had been prepared to admit men to ordination for payment (*SL* I.48: 131). As we read in the letter to the prefect Timostratus, translated below (Text 19), Severus was also troubled by requests for ordination from men who were interested only in priestly vestments and being supported by the church. The problem of clerical corruption seems indeed to have been endemic (Frend 1972: 224–5).

A large amount of Severus's time and energy was directed towards ensuring that those for whom he was responsible maintained a correct attitude to Chalcedonians, in particular those Chalcedonian clergy who wished to join the anti-Chalcedonian party. This 'correctness' (Greek *akribeia*) in canonical matters is typical of Severus and is paralleled, as we shall see, by a 'correctness' in doctrinal matters. Like Timothy Aelurus (the Cat), Peter the Iberian and Philoxenus before him, Severus believed that those who renounced Chalcedon should not be subjected to the humiliation of re-ordination or re-baptism, but should rather make a written profession of faith and do penance.[40] Even the former followers of the deposed Flavian were treated in this manner, a fact for which some blamed Severus at a later date (*SL* V.15: 353). Severus could defend himself by citing the actions of the first-generation anti-Chalcedonian, Timothy the Cat, who had practised the same policies in order to avoid excessive zeal. In commending Timothy Severus writes:

> Though these things seem contradictory to many, yet nevertheless their one purpose was the salvation of those who had perished, and that those who stood upright might not under the influence of immoderate zeal leave the royal road, and turn away to that which is rather on the right side.[41]

Like the letters written before his patriarchate, those dating from 512–18 show the range of networks which Severus had at his disposal, among them a number of archimandrites[42] and groups of monks.[43] Perhaps because of his own monastic background and his experience of administering his own monastery in Maiuma, Severus seems to have taken a great interest in the administration of those monasteries under his jurisdiction. His letters reveal something of the protocol which had developed in anti-Chalcedonian monastic establishments in Syria, partly evidenced by his exchange with the abbot of the monastery of Simeon Stylites, translated below (Text 20). The archimandrite was in the first instance responsible for the monks; on all matters he was approached by the bishop; and the monks were contacted only through the archimandrite. The bishop, however, laid down the law in matters of ordination, although even here the formal consent of the archimandrite for the ordination of the monk was required. The reception of heretics into monasteries, the dismissal of monks and the supervision of the archimandrite also fell within patriarchal jurisdiction.[44] While there is little or no direct evidence of the administration of monasteries in Antioch itself or in its immediate vicinity, we have a charming story, related by John Rufus soon after Severus's accession, concerning public asceticism in the city at the time. John saw with his own eyes how an ageing man had set up a tent outside the main door of a disused palace in Antioch, and lived there for many years. The man was an anti-Chalcedonian, and his manner of life was open testimony to the spirit of asceticism fostered by Severus (*Pler.* LXXXVIII–LXXXIX: 140–8).

Both during and after his patriarchate, Severus was involved in an epistolary exchange with a certain Sergius, an anti-Chalcedonian of exaggerated views, who seems to have been influenced by Apollinarian ideas. This correspondence contains three letters from Sergius, followed by Severus's three replies, and finally an *apologia* by Sergius. The beginning of this exchange, namely Sergius's first letter, can perhaps be dated to after the synod of Antioch in 513,[45] and it lasted until after Severus's exile in 518 (Torrance 1988: 7). Since the debate between the patriarch and his opponent arose out of Sergius's misconceptions and concerns technical christological terms, Severus's letters are more like doctrinal treatises than most of the letters in the other two collections.

On the basis of his 125 surviving homilies, Severus has been called one of the greatest orators of the early church (Olivar 1980: 403). In many cases the place and date of delivery of these homilies have come down to us (Brière 1960: 50–62). As well as in the Great Church in

Antioch,[46] the patriarch preached in the martyrial shrines and other churches in the city: the New Church (Hom. LXIV), the church of the Angel Michael (Hom. LXXII), the martyria of Babylas (Hom. XI), the Forty Martyrs (Hom. XVIII), Leontius (Hom. XXVII), Ignatius (Hom. XXXVII), Barlaha (Hom. LXXIII) and Julian (Hom. LXXV).[47] He also preached outside the city, in a monastery (Hom. XXX), in Seleucia (Hom. XXVIII), Chalcis (Hom. LVI and LVII) and Cyrrhus (Hom. LVIII, LIX, LX), and in Aigiai (Hom. CX and CXI). From these homilies, we see a developed cult of the saints, which could act as an antidote to the pagan attractions which the city and even the countryside still had to offer. The increasing importance attached to the Mother of God is reflected in the dedication of Homilies XIV (Text 15 below) and LXVII to her under this title. Apart from the major feasts in the liturgical cycle, Severus also preached on the feasts of the apostle Peter, Thecla, Antony of Egypt, Athanasius, and his heroes Basil of Caesarea and Gregory Nazianzen. Although the number of catechumens in Antioch in the sixth century could not have been significant, each year of his patriarchate, Severus delivered a homily to them on the Wednesday of Holy Week (Hom. XXI, XLII, LXX, XC and CIX). The absence of any reference, in other homilies preached in Holy Week and Easter Day, to his further personal involvement with them, however, seems to suggest that systematic catechesis was carried out by other members of his clergy. It is worth noting that many of Severus's homilies contain passages that are uncompromisingly technical in their christological development, and that there is a harsher anti-Chalcedonian tone present than that found in his letters.

An energetic administrator and a gifted orator, Severus also put his poetic talents at the service of the patriarchate of Antioch. John of Beith Aphthonia, who for the rest has only scant information in his biography for the years 512–18, relates that, on seeing how the people of Antioch loved both secular and ecclesiastical songs, Severus set about composing hymns. In this way he wooed them away from the theatre and back to the church. These hymns, John informs us, also taught about theology, contemplation, correct dogma, the depths of Scripture, good works and suffering (JBA 244–5). Of the 365 hymns surviving from the ancient church of Antioch, 295 are attributed to Severus (Honigmann 1951: 20). The patriarch was also a great liturgist: from him we have a eucharistic liturgy surviving in Syriac and a Coptic fragment; a rite for baptism transmitted in Greek, Syriac and Coptic; and liturgical hymns, such as *O Monogenes*, which is still sung in Greek and Coptic churches.

As Severus's patriarchate continued, it became obvious that he was unable to influence the largely pro-Chalcedonian areas of Palestine and Jerusalem, and that his former champion, Emperor Anastasius, was too concerned about Vitalian and his barbarian troops to support the patriarch in Antioch (Bacht 1951: 287). Patriarch Timothy of Constantinople died on 5 April 518 and was replaced by John, a Cappadocian, who formally condemned Chalcedon.[48] For his part, Severus believed that John was rather 'more desirous of adopting a deceitful middle course' (*SL* VI.1: 361). Soon after John's installation, rumour circulated to the effect that the new patriarch had anathematized him (*SL* VI.1: 362) – a sign of impending trouble. When the aged Emperor Anastasius died on 9 July 518 and was succeeded by the Latin-speaking Justin, a comrade of Vitalian, the acclamations of the crowds to their patriarch in Constantinople did not bode well either for the patriarch of Antioch.

> For many years we have wanted to take communion.
> You are orthodox; of whom are you afraid?
> You are worthy of the Trinity.
> The holy Mary is the Theotokos.
> You are worthy of the [patriarchal] throne.
> The holy Mary is the Theotokos.
> Long live the emperor; long live the empress.
> Throw out Severus the Manichaean.
> Whoever does not say so is a Manichaean.
> Dig up the bones of the Manichaeans.
> Proclaim the holy synod [of Chalcedon] now.[49]

The crowd continued, demanding the restoration of the relics of the late Macedonius to the church, and the despatch of the decrees of Chalcedon to Rome. Severus's days were numbered, but it was above all Vitalian, intent on avenging the disgrace of his godfather Flavian, who sought to undo him. The patriarch was summoned to Constantinople to be tried or to have his tongue cut out – the sources do not agree (Honigmann 1951: 142–3) – but eventually Irenaeus, the *comes Orientis* or count of the East, was charged with preventing Severus's escape from Antioch. Nonetheless, Severus managed to get to the port of Seleucia Pieria, where he took ship for Alexandria on 29 September (Maspero 1923: 70–1). After 518, no fewer than fifty-five bishops were expelled from the patriarchate of Antioch (Honigmann 1951: 87).

EXILE

On his arrival in Egypt, Severus was welcomed by Patriarch Timothy IV[50] and went to the monastery of Enaton outside Alexandria (Liberatus, *Brev.* 19), where the deposed bishop of Halicarnassus, Julian, also sought refuge. After his flight, Severus was accused by the clergy of Antioch of the stock crimes of embezzlement, conspiring with Jews and sorcery; a further, more original, allegation was that he had removed gold and silver statues of doves, representing the holy Spirit, which hung above the baptismal fonts and altars in his patriarchate.[51] Both Severus and Philoxenus fell foul of accusations of iconoclasm regarding doves, but in Syria these birds were sacred to the goddess Aphrodite, and their removal should rather be seen in the context of stamping out pagan practices.[52]

In the capital, Emperor Justin, who was sympathetic to western interests, was keen to restore unity between Pope Hormisdas and the East. On Easter Day, 31 March 519, the emperor solemnly restored the communion between Old and New Rome which had lapsed at the beginning of the Acacian schism. Justin's reign was to be characterized by the restoration of Chalcedon, close ties with the West,[53] and persecution of anti-Chalcedonians (Michael the Syrian, *Chron.* IX.13). The exception to the persecution was Egypt, which remained immune (Zach. Rh., *HE* VIII.5), although Severus describes it as united against Leo's *Tome* and Chalcedon (*SL* V.11: 328). The forced exodus of anti-Chalcedonian bishops from their sees occurred on a large scale: the Syriac chronicles record the names of fifty-two banished bishops – and this is an incomplete catalogue because it does not include, for example, the name of Severus (Honigmann 1951: 146–8). Many of the exiles looked for a safe haven in Egypt, although danger followed them wherever they went, as Severus's letters testify, and a safe passage always had to be guaranteed if they were summoned to Constantinople. For his part, Philoxenus was exiled to Thrace, to be kept under surveillance by a Chalcedonian bishop until his death in 523 (de Halleux 1963: 93–8).

Severus was to spend the next twenty years in exile. It was a difficult and dangerous period for him. Nobody knew where he was living except those who brought him the necessities of life (*SL* V.12: 339); he was forever on the move, sometimes changing his abode when some news reached him (*SL* V.12: 341); and even for those who did know where he was, access appears to have been possible only through certain officials (*SL* VIII.5: 415). Despite the isolation, however, the sophisticated networks which he had established even before his patriarchate ensured that he was kept informed of events and that he could be reached by letter. The volume of post could in fact be overwhelming:

> During the whole time of summer, and that though I have been hiding in corners, I have never ceased being worried by constant letters from men who in various ways ask different questions at different times, and beg to have now scriptural expressions, now doctrinal theories explained to them. Also the loneliness of solitude, and the fact that I have not men at hand to serve as scribes when I want it in addition to the other things hinder me from writing.[54]

The lack of books was also a serious concern for Severus (Letter XXXIV; *PO* 12/2: 276). Yet his years in exile were to be extremely productive ones in terms of sustained theological writing, both against the Council of Chalcedon and its proponents and against erring members of his own party.

Despite the fact that he was in exile in Egypt, there was no suggestion that Severus had abandoned either the duties of his patriarchate or the anti-Chalcedonian cause. He continued to administer his diocese from exile, while his successor, Paul, nicknamed 'the Jew', made life difficult for anti-Chalcedonians (519–21). In 521, there were widespread expulsions of monastics from monasteries in Syria. Most of these seem to have survived in desert areas, and it was incumbent on Severus to continue to give such groups advice and solace from his distant exile. This appears to have been done through the offices of two priest-archimandrites, both called John, to whom a number of letters is addressed from Severus's exile.[55] These men, whose whereabouts are uncertain, seem to have assumed Severus's responsibilities for the anti-Chalcedonian churches in Syria:

> nor can you on your part avoid doing everything in the capacity of my representatives. For, what you do, that men will justly reckon to me; for all, both brothers and strangers, both friends and enemies, know clearly that I and you are one, as in fact we are.[56]

With regard to Palestine, it seems that Severus was represented by a certain Theodore, who may have been the archimandrite of Severus's former monastery of Romanus near Gaza (Honigmann 1961: 152 n. 2). One of Severus's letters is addressed jointly to the two Johns and

Theodore [Letter XXVII (CXVI); *PO* 12/2: 248–59]. During his patriarchate, Severus had had to struggle with low numbers of committed anti-Chalcedonian clergy; in his exile, his concern must have been that there was little opportunity among the anti-Chalcedonians of the diaspora to have canonically ordained priests or bishops. The persecution waged against anti-Chalcedonians by the successors of Paul the Jew, Euphrasius (521–6), who perished in the great earthquake in Antioch in 526, and more especially Ephrem (527–45), would have exacerbated the problem. Only the ordaining of a rival clergy and hierarchy after *c.* 530 was to resolve this situation.

About the time that Severus was returning to Maiuma from Constantinople in 511, a presbyter and grammarian, John of Caesarea,[57] composed an *Apology for the Synod of Chalcedon* (*CPG* 6855), demonstrating a more structured approach to the topic than that found in Nephalius's work of the same name. Like Nephalius, John was motivated by the neo-Chalcedonian movement; in particular his aim was to reconcile Severus and his party to the Council of Chalcedon, using Cyril as the basis for argument. John's work is mostly lost to us, but its argument can largely be reconstructed from Severus's rebuttal of it, provocatively entitled *Against the Impious Grammarian*, which does not survive complete.[58] Perhaps because of his patriarchal workload, Severus's treatise was published only in 519, after his deposition. In one of his letters, he explains that the composition of his refutation was hindered by his having to cast the introduction to the work in such a way that it looked as if it had been written while he was still patriarch of Antioch (Letter XXXIV; *PO* 12/2: 276), and thus still a legally recognized citizen of the empire. The enterprise was also made difficult because of the lack of resources:

> It was a very difficult task and needed a great store of books, and it was so to speak difficult for me to correct, because I am moving from place to place, and I have not everywhere at hand fitting testimonies and demonstrations from the Scriptures. For I thought it right to meet not only the lamentable babblings of the grammarian, but also the whole web of impiety contained in what was defined and done by way of innovation at Chalcedon by the synod which met there, and the impious Tome of Leo . . . .[59]

As previously mentioned, Severus's exchange of letters with the exaggerated anti-Chalcedonian Sergius was not completed until he was in exile. From the anti-Chalcedonian side, too, there now emerged another irritating menace for Severus in the shape of his former ally Julian, the deposed bishop of Halicarnassus. The two had met in Constantinople during Severus's stay there and had acted in concert against Patriarch Macedonius (Theod. Lect., *HE*, fr. 484). They found themselves together again at the monastery of Enaton in Egypt after Julian's flight from his see in 518. Julian's thesis was that, even before the resurrection the body of Christ was incorrupted (*aphthartos*) and incorruptible, a position that to anti-Chalcedonians and pro-Chalcedonians alike was alarmingly close to that of Eutyches and the docetists. The movement was therefore known by its opponents as aphthartodocetism. From about 520 to 527, there was a protracted, vehement and voluminous debate between the two exiled bishops, during and after which Severus did not succeed in quashing the embarrassing influence of the Julianists. Their influence did indeed live on, particularly in Egypt and Armenia.

In 527, after acting for several months as co-regent with his uncle, Justinian became emperor. His aim was to ensure orthodoxy, and unity between Chalcedonians and anti-Chalcedonians, and he realized that the support of Severus was essential for the latter. His consort, Theodora, was openly sympathetic towards anti-Chalcedonians and engineered the appointment of anti-Chalcedonians to key positions. By *c.* 530, after more than a decade of persecution, the anti-Chalcedonian church, particularly in Syria, was suffering from a dearth of clergy that even the energetic Severus and other exiled bishops were incapable or unwilling to make good. When John of Tella in the district of Osrohoëne in east Syria began to ordain anti-Chalcedonian clergy, the response was overwhelming.[60] A separatist and independent church was born. Justinian subsequently relaxed the persecution, and in 531 recalled exiled monks (ps.Zach. Rh., *HE* X.1). The following year, he granted safe passage to six anti-Chalcedonian bishops living in the desert, to enable them to go to Constantinople to negotiate ecclesiastical unity with six Chalcedonian bishops. Severus was also invited, but excused himself because of his advanced age. In declining the imperial invitation, he wrote a long letter to Justinian, translated below (Text 27), in which he defended himself against accusations of stirring up sedition by distributing large amounts of money in Alexandria, and attacked Julian and his teaching. We have detailed minutes of parts of these 'conversations' of 532 (Grillmeier 1995: 232–40), which were inconclusive. It was in the course of the discussions that the anti-Chalcedonians appealed in support of their christological position to the authority of Dionysius the Areopagite (*ACO* IV/2: 172–3), behind whose name lurked a contemporary Syrian monk whom Severus was the first to cite (Text 26). Justinian, who had presided over a session of the talks, responded by publishing an edict in the following year (*Codex Justinianus* I.1.6), in which he set out a statement of correct faith, without, however, mentioning either Chalcedon or the *Tome*. In winter 534/5,[61] in response to repeated invitations from Justinian which may have been prompted by Theodora, Severus finally went to Constantinople, accompanied by a large group of anti-Chalcedonians, and took up residence in one of the imperial palaces (ps.Zach. Rh., *HE* IX.15, 19). He probably did not hold out much hope of a successful outcome, for he supposedly remarked before leaving Egypt:

> Don't be deceived. In the lifetime of these emperors no means of peace will be found, but so that I do not appear to hinder or oppose it, I will go, though with heartsearchings. I will return without anything accomplished.[62]

Soon after Severus's arrival in the capital, Timothy of Alexandria died, and Theodora successfully replaced him with the deacon Theodosius, a member of Severus's party, who was almost immediately challenged by Gaianas, a follower of Julian.[63] Severus received and replied to Theodosius's *synodika* in the capital. Patriarch Epiphanius of Constantinople died soon after Timothy of Alexandria, and was replaced by the ascetic Chalcedonian, Anthimus, who had been part of the 'conversations' of 532. Here too Theodora intervened, bringing the influence of Severus to bear on the new patriarch, who was not long in embracing the anti-Chalcedonian position and entering into communion with Severus and Theodosius (ps.Zach. Rh., *HE* IX.21). This anti-Chalcedonian ascendency was not, however, to last long. Theodosius was driven out of Alexandria by the Julianist faction on 24 May 535 (Liberatus, *Brev.* 20) and went to Constantinople, where he lived in exile until his death in 566; Anthimus was denounced to Rome by Palestinian and Syrian monks and was forced to withdraw. Severus was left. Not even the patronage of Theodora could withstand the alliance between Justinian and Pope Agapetus, an alliance which had as its basis the orthodoxy of Chalcedon. At a Home Synod in Constantinople in May–June 536, Anthimus and Severus were condemned. Severus was accused of being an 'acephalist', a Eutychian and a Manichaean, of performing uncanonical baptism, of holding unlawful assemblies, and of having been a pagan (Torrance 1988: 23 n. 33). The decision of the synod was ratified in August of the same year by imperial edict. The persons of Anthimus and Severus and their followers were declared exiled, and the works of Severus condemned.

With the help of Theodora, Severus fled once more to Egypt (John Eph., *PO* 2/3: 302), where he lived in various places in the desert, including Kellia, south of Alexandria (John Eph., *PO* 2/3: 300), Scetis, and the mountain of Assiut, where a monastery was named after him. He died in the town of Xoïs (Sakha), east of Alexandria, on Monday, 8 February 538, just two days after John of Tella. His body was transferred at a later date to the Monastery of Glass at Enaton (Honigmann 1951: 154 n. 3). The cult of Severus became widespread in Egyptian monasteries and intellectual centres, where he was venerated not as a miracle-worker but as the greatest theologian of the one-nature christology.[64] In Syria too, he was an object of special devotion, as the religious hymns composed on him by his biographer, John of Beith Aphthonia, and others testify.[65]

After Severus's death, Theodosius became the acknowledged leader of the anti-Chalcdeonian party, directing it from Constantinople for the next thirty years. It was a church with a depleted episcopate and clergy, but Theodosius, like Severus, was reluctant to jeopardize possible ecclesiastical unity by establishing a rival hierarchy. In 542, however, when the Arab leader al-Hareth approached Theodora asking for two anti-Chalcedonian bishops to be consecrated for the critical border areas with Persia, events took a significant turn. Jacob Baradaeus was consecrated for Mesopotamia and Syria, and Theodore for Arabia and Palestine. Both bishops began ordaining men to the priesthood and to minor orders; it was only *c.* 557 that they progressed to the consecration of bishops and metropolitans (Grillmeier 2002: 197–200). Jacob's long career (542–78) left its mark on the post-Severan church, which came to be called Jacobite.

2

SEVERUS'S THOUGHT

TRANSMISSION

The condemnation of Severus's person and works by the imperial edict of 536 effectively put an end to the transmission of his works in Greek, with the exception of numerous fragments preserved in *catenae* (chains of quotations), in Homily LXXVII, which was transmitted under the name of Gregory of Nyssa or Hesychius of Jerusalem, or in the works of his opponents after his death, such as that of the monk Eustathius.[1] A number of the fragments found in the *catenae* have been published, most recently by Dorival (1984) and Petit (1999), both of whom can be consulted for previous literature. Also transmitted fragmentarily in Greek is the work *Contra Felicissimum* (*CPG* 7032), which survives as well in Syriac fragments.

The chief medium through which we know Severus's works is the Syriac tradition. The indefatigable Paul, bishop of Callinicum on the Euphrates, who, like Severus, was exiled in 518, spent his years in banishment in Edessa translating many of the works of Severus into Syriac. Before 528, he had translated Severus's voluminous works against Julian of Halicarnassus (Brière 1960: 17); he was also responsible for the Syriac rendition of the Cathedral Homilies, which received a revision by Jacob of Edessa in AD 701. It is possible too that he undertook the translations of Severus's correspondence with Sergius (Torrance 1988: 19) and the tractate against John the Grammarian. The *Select Letters* were translated into Syriac by the priest Athanasius of Nisibis in 669 (Brooks 1903: x), who also translated the *Ad Nephalium*, while the hymns and liturgical works were rendered into Syriac by Paul of Edessa (later revised by Jacob of Edessa). The translator of the *Philalethes* remains unknown to us.

The Coptic tradition preserves many fragments in exegetical *catenae* [see *CPG* 7080 (18)]: Severus's first Cathedral Homily,[2] Homilies XIV, XXVII, L, LX, LXXVII and CIII. However, the Coptic version of the Cathedral Homilies reflects another tradition from the Syriac. Four letters [*CPG* 7071 (9, 12–14)], and prayers (*CPG* 7078) also survive in Coptic. Two letters have come down to us in Arabic [*CPG* 7071 (15–16)], and recently Youhanna Nessim Youssef discovered two manuscripts containing the Arabic translation of the *Philalethes* (Youssef 2001a).

In some cases the same work is preserved in more than one tradition. A good example of this is Severus's letter to the deacon Anastasia (*CPG* 7071 (12)), which is preserved in Syriac, Coptic (Youssef 2001b: 126–36), and Arabic, and partially in Greek. In the Syriac version, we find more biblical and Patristic quotations than in the Coptic and Arabic. The Arabic is in fact a literal translation from Coptic. Both the Coptic and Arabic versions have come down to us through a liturgical book dedicated to the feast of Zachariah the priest, the father of John the Baptist, while the Syriac is preserved in the corpus of Severus's letters. Youssef notes that the Copto-Arabic tradition caters for a general public who attended church, while the Syriac is aimed more at a scholarly audience.

From the Copto-Arabic tradition is derived an Ethiopic, which is relatively unknown and is being investigated by Witold Witakowski. While it does not seem that all of Severus's writings were translated into Ethiopic, those that were apparently became quite popular, because there is a substantial number of manuscripts containing them. We do not have Ethiopic translations of Severus's major polemical works: before Youhanna Nessim Youssef's discovery of Arabic versions of the *Philalethes*, this situation was not surprising because it was assumed that there were no Arabic versions either, and Ethiopic literature was simply repeating the pattern of its parent. By searching manuscript catalogues, Witakowski found six works or groups of works attributed to Severus: two homilies, one of which is not authentic, two prayers, extracts supposedly from various works, and a homily or treatise by or on Severus. The extracts that so far have been matched against the Syriac tradition betray a non-literal translation technique, and point to a model different from that used by the Syriac translators.

REHABILITATION

While Severus continued to be revered in the traditions of the Syrian, Coptic, Arabic and Ethiopic churches, the sentence of condemnation passed on him in 536 was a far-reaching and enduring *damnatio memoriae* in the Byzantine and Byzantine-influenced churches as well as in the West. The Chalcedonian monk Eustathius, writing in the middle of the sixth century, called him 'the double-tongued snake' and 'the double-headed fox'. Edward Gibbon gave him the title 'the tyrant of Syria'. The French church historian Monseigneur Louis Duchesne (1925: 99–100) accused him of having a cold and fanatical soul and of continuing a regrettable schism, which it would have been easy for him to mitigate if he had wanted. Branded as 'monophysites', Severus and his followers were thus connected with the infamous Eutyches, who supposedly taught that the union of the two natures, divinity and humanity, in Christ results in a *tertium quid*, consubstantial neither with God nor with human beings.

Although several of Severus's works were printed on the basis of Syriac manuscripts in the Vatican by the orientalist Joseph Assemani in the eighteenth century, it was not until the twentieth century that most of the patriarch's known works surviving in Syriac were published. Perhaps the greatest catalyst for this was the Belgian scholar, Joseph Lebon. It was suggested to Lebon by Jean-Baptiste Chabot, the editor and translator of the massive Syriac chronicle compiled by the Jacobite patriarch Michael the Syrian in the twelfth century, that he should edit and translate the theological works of the eleventh-century Syrian 'monophysite', Nonnus of Nisibis. Once he had embarked on this project, however, Lebon realized that Nonnus's christology was far from heretical, and he felt obliged to return to the christological developments in the period 451–543, where the figure of Severus of Antioch cannot be sidestepped. The result was his 1909 monograph of some 600 pages – a historical, literary and theological study of one-nature christology according to Severus of Antioch. Lebon's conclusions were decisive for the rehabilitation of Severus: he found unmistakeable similarities between 'monophysite' christology and the christology of Cyril of Alexandria. *'The monophysite doctrine of the incarnation', he wrote adamantly, 'even and particularly in the scientific form which was given to it by Severus, is nothing other than Cyrillian christology. Severus in combat with the grammarians is Cyril explaining and defending himself after the union of 433'* (Lebon 1909: XXI; italics in original).[3] Lebon pointed out (1909: XXI–XXII) that Cyril could not be called a monophysite because he died before the Council of Chalcedon, and that this was the only reason that he escaped the label which was subsequently attached to Severus and his followers. The christology of the anti-Chalcedonians is thus a verbal monophysitism, where the hypostatic union in Christ receives an orthodox expression in formulae which stress the unity of the natures, rather than in the two-nature formula of the definition of Chalcedon.

The publication of editions and translations of Severus's works throughout the twentieth century followed. The availability of his dogmatic, homiletic, epistolary and liturgical compositions helped to round out the existing portrait from historical sources and show him as a significant figure in his various roles – monastic, political, theological, episcopal, pastoral and liturgical – during four decades. It is to a consideration of the works and their contents that we now turn.

SEVERUS'S THOUGHT

For Severus, as for the anti-Chalcedonians in general, when speaking christologically there exists a synonymity between nature (*physis*), hypostasis, and person (*prosopon*). He even points out that because of their derivations the terms *ousia* (substance), *physis*, *hypostasis* and *hyparxis* (existence) do not differ.[4] In other words, *physis*, when used christologically, is not an abstraction, but refers to the one concrete individual, the incarnate Word. Thus Severus considers it an impossibility for Chalcedonians to confess two natures if they do not confess two hypostases and persons as well.[5]

There are three aspects to the process of incarnation as understood by anti-Chalcedonians: before the incarnation, the act of incarnation, and the result of the incarnation. Before the incarnation, there are two elements from which is Christ, namely the Word and a certain human being. Whereas the former existed from eternity, the human being never existed separately – if it had, we would have to speak of two separate natures, hypostases, or persons in Christ (Lebon 1951: 463–4 n. 28) The humanity is, however, intellectually (*en theoria*) considered as existing, in order for the incarnation to be thought of as a union (*henosis* or *synthesis*) of divinity and humanity. As such, the humanity is, as it were, a mental construction, and the duality of the natures disappears with the union.

In the second aspect of the process, the act of incarnation, the emphasis in Severus is on the union effected, and the terms used for this act of union (*henosis*) are a union of natures or a hypostatic union. This union is a new state of the Logos, who, as Severus says, 'is believed immutably and without change to have become a child, while he remained that which he was and did not change or convert that which he took up'.[6] The union of the two natures, i.e. of the two hypostases, is seen as a mystery, but a mystery which reaches its fulfillment by a process (Lebon 1951: 437 with n. 41), since, like human beings, the body of the Logos is first conceived, then formed and endowed with a soul. The peculiarity of this union, as Severus stipulates by recapitulating Cyril, is that:

the hypostases are in composition and are perfect without diminution, but refuse to continue an individual existence so as to be numbered as two, and to have its own person impressed upon each of them, which a conjunction of honour cannot possibly do.[7]

Furthermore, the two hypostases united in Christ have an iconic relationship, each reflecting the other on a different level of reality (Chesnut 1976: 15). While, however, the divinity and humanity are united inseparably, Severus strenuously and repeatedly denies that the force of this union demands a confusion or mixture (*mixis*) (Chesnut 1976: 18): indeed, a mixture of the two natures is impossible, because they represent two different levels, the suprasensual and the perceptible.[8] In order to guard against mixture and confusion, Severus took over from Cyril the term *synthesis* (composition) and its cognates *kata synthesin* and *synthetos*, and used them systematically to exclude a mixture of natures, as can be seen in his second letter to Sergius.

The most common formula used by the anti-Chalcedonians to express the result of the incarnation is 'one incarnate nature of God the Word' (*mia physis tou Theou Logou sesarkomene*), considered by them to have a Patristic pedigree, whereas in fact it derived from the (ps.)Apollinarian writings through the intermediary of Cyril of Alexandria. Severus, who seems first to have exploited *synthesis* systematically as a synonym for *henosis*, employs as well the expressions 'a single composite nature' (*mia physis synthetos*) and 'composite Word' (*Logos synthetos*) (Grillmeier 1995: 126–8). 'One nature of God the Word' relates to the Logos; the word 'incarnate' introduces the incarnation. Since for Severus the humanity in Christ has no independent status (Torrance 1988: 89), the 'one nature' of Christ is that of the Word. Because the formula was originally directed against Nestorianism, its insistence on the unity of the individual is natural, as are the concerted attempts to dismiss any suggestion of duality. The anti-Chalcedonians assert that in Christ there is one nature, one hypostasis and one person; there is also said to be one will (*thelesis/thelema*) and one activity (*energeia*) (Chesnut 1976: 17). Severus characterizes the union with respect to activity as 'a single activity of the God-human' (*mia physis theandrike*), a term adapted from ps.Dionysius the Areopagite that was to play a significant part in the monenergist and monothelite controversies in the following century (see Text 26 below).[9] The union of the two natures in Christ is understood strictly in the sense of numerical unity. Thus the formula 'a single double nature' (*mia physis diple*), which is attested in the works of Fathers before Chalcedon and could have provided a useful modification to the strict interpretation of 'one nature of God the word incarnate', is rejected out of hand by Severus, on the grounds that, after the Nestorian controversy, 'double' was suspect (*Ad Nephalium* I.2: 3–5). While their insistence on the strict union in Christ led the anti-Chalcedonians to reject expressions such as 'two natures' or 'in two natures' of the Chalcedonian definition as being Nestorian, it was equally the case that the Fathers, including Cyril, had also used dyophysite expressions. Both Philoxenus and Severus admit this, but Philoxenus defends them on the grounds that they used the expression 'two natures' to convey a truth about the incarnation (de Halleux 1963: 379–80), and Severus points out that the Fathers used the term correctly, not in the sense that the Chalcedonians use it. Severus adds, however, that after the advent of Nestorius the term is better avoided (*Ad Nephalium* I.2: 1–9). Although in his first Cathedral Homily he claims that the word 'two' destroys the economy (*PO* 38/2: 261.33–263: 1), in the face of increasing accusations from Chalcedonians that emphasis on the one nature involves mixture and confusion of divinity and humanity in Christ, he followed the example of Cyril and admitted two natures 'in thought' or 'in contemplation' (*theoria/kat'epinoian*).[10]

For his part, Philoxenus admits the expression 'from two natures' as a concession to the dyophysites, but on the understanding that the two natures had no time to exist (de Halleux 1963: 380 n. 7). Once again, Severus's handling of this expression is characteristic in that he follows Cyril's interpretation of it as being tantamount to 'two natures in contemplation' (*dyo physeis en theoria*) (Lebon 1951: 525–7), and sets the tone for his successors. He points out that Nestorius shunned the formula 'from two', which confirms the composition and establishes one hypostasis and nature of the Word incarnate (*Ep. 2 ad Sergium*; Torrance 1988: 179). Unlike Timothy Aelurus and Philoxenus, Severus, returning once again to the arsenal of the Cyrillian vocabulary, uses the expressions like 'property' or 'propriety' (*idiotes*), 'physical quality' (*poiotes physike*), and 'difference in physical quality' (*diaphora os en poioteti physike*) to convey the preservation of the qualities of the two natures in the union. These terms were for him useful correctives to extreme monophysitism, that is, to Synousiast or Eutychian positions, such as that adopted by Sergius the grammarian. Against Sergius, Severus asserts that the divinity and the humanity in the Emmanuel are not only completely different, but are distant from each other and separate as well. But when union is professed from the two of them, the difference, again in the quality of the natures from which there is the one Christ, is not suppressed, but by the hypostatic union division is driven out (*Ep. 1 ad Sergium*; Torrance 1988: 149). Unlike Leo in his *Tome*, Severus does not assign these physical qualities to a particular nature – this would lead to dissolving the economy. Julian of Halicarnassus, however, for whom the unity of Christ always remained in the foreground, did not accept as legitimate the terminology of 'property/propriety' or 'physical quality' (Draguet 1924: n. 61, 62) because their use was tantamount to dividing Christ himself into two natures (Grillmeier 1995: 94–5). For the relation between human and divine properties, he preferred to use the expression 'undifferentiated difference' (*diaphora adiaphoros*). The Severan terminology was, however, not adopted by all anti-Chalcedonians.

Among the anti-Chalcedonians in general, the emphasis on synthesis and henosis over against *synapheia* (conjunction) leads to an insistence on the fact Christ's body is his own by birth from the virgin. It is only if the Theotokos is truly the mother of the one she gave birth to that he can be substantial with her, and then consubstantial with all humankind. In Severus's words:

> If anyone says that the flesh of the Lord descended from heaven or passed through the Virgin as through a channel, and describes it not rather as from her in accordance with the law of conception, even if formed without man, he is condemned. Neither the conception nor the birth from Mary, nor the dealings with human beings, nor cross, tomb, resurrection from the dead, ascension into heaven happen according to appearance, but all according to truth: for we needed real healing, because we had really sinned.[11]

Hence Mary's true maternity is soteriologically of great significance. However, we shall see that for Severus's opponent Julian of Halicarnassus the fact that Mary gave birth to God necessitates some qualification of this true maternity: the virginal conception and birth guarantee the superiority of Christ's body from the moment of its conception (Grillmeier 1995: 109).

For Severus, as for the anti-Chalcedonians in general, the union of the two natures in Christ is intrinsically redemptive, and thus the preservation of the human nature in the union is a soteriological necessity. In this sense, the incarnation is, according to Severus, a 'second divine creation' (Hom. LIV; *PO* 4/1: 56). Despite the orthodox language in which such soteriological principles are enunciated by Severus and other monophysites, it is difficult to escape the impression that it was not only Julian of Halicarnassus who believed that, while Christ was a true human being, he was not an ordinary one. The interpenetration of the two natures results in a dominance of the divine nature in the union, and the exchange of properties (*communicatio idiomatum*) seems one-sided. Time and again Severus, like Cyril, stresses the voluntary nature of the submission of the Logos to the human condition.

> If he sometimes permitted his flesh by dispensation to undergo the passions proper to it, he did not preserve its property undiminished: for in many instances it is seen not to have undergone the things which manifestly belong to its nature; for it was united to the Word, the Maker of nature.[12]

This 'possession' by the Logos leads to an ambiguity not only in the sphere of the passions, as evidenced in Severus's debate with Julian, but also in that of activity (*energeia*), will (*thelema/thelesis*) and knowledge (*gnosis*) in Christ. For all that, however, Severus conceived of the union of natures as continually dynamic and adaptative (Torrance 2000: 185).

3

SEVERUS'S WORKS

AD NEPHALIUM

We have already encountered the ex-anti-Chalcedonian Alexandrian zealot Nephalius and his harassment of Severus in Palestine before 508, when Severus went to Constantinople to seek the protection of Emperor Anastasius. Nephalius, we have seen, followed his opponent there. While in the capital, he wrote a work called *Defence of Chalcedon* (*CPG* 6825), which is lost to us except for quotations in Severus's rebuttal of it. Compared with his tone in the letters to Sergius and his writing against John and Julian, in *Ad Nephalium* Severus is polite and generally non-personal: it is even significant that his refutation of Nephalius is entitled not 'against (Greek *kata*) Nephalius' but 'to (Greek *pros*) Nephalius' (Grillmeier 1995: 48). As the title of his work suggests, Nephalius set out to corroborate the definition of Chalcedon, first by composing a florilegium, which apparently included Gregory Nazianzen, John Chrysostom, Proclus and Cyril (Grillmeier 1995: 48), and second by an attempt to reconcile the expression 'out of two natures' and 'in two natures' by speaking of 'united natures'.

Severus's reply to Nephalius was divided into two parts, the first of which is almost completely lost except for fragments in the writings of the patriarch's next opponent, John the grammarian, and the ending of Severus's work itself. From these fragments we can reconstruct that Nephalius had argued in favour of the definition of Chalcedon that some of the Fathers had used the expression 'two natures'. Even if we concede this, runs Severus's argument, they did not use it in the sense that Nephalius intended: in the face of the threat of the 'gabbling' Nestorius, the expression was rejected by Cyril as a remedy against christological sickness, and even if, conjecturally, the term were to be found in the earlier works of Cyril, this would not be convincing either (*Ad Nephalium* I.1). After the demise of Nestorius, it was also reprehensible to say that Christ was 'double' (*diplous*), even if Gregory Nazianzen used the term, as he used the expression 'God the Word assumed the human being' against Apollinaris, which likewise became suspicious after Nestorius. While Nephalius and his supporters apparently gave Severus some leeway by conceding that, in the fight against Eutyches, Chalcedon had employed 'blunt' words, the anti-Chalcedonian was not prepared to give ground.

The second part of the *Ad Nephalium* is addressed to Nephalius and 'to the same people who assert that Christ is to be recognized in two natures after the union, and add the phrase "which are united and not divided"' (*Ad Nephalium* II.8: 26–8). Here, Severus repeatedly uses Cyril's dictum 'Leave off dividing the natures after the union', taken from the five books against Nestorius, and adduces citations from the 'heretical' Theodoret, Andrew of Samosata, and other Antiochenes to demonstrate how close they are to the two-nature christology. If one is serious about not separating the natures, Severus maintains, then there should be talk not of two united or undivided natures after the union, but of one nature (*Ad Nephalium* II.19: 4–6). Similarly, to say 'two natures' after we have confessed the union removes the hypostatic union and attacks Cyril's Twelve Chapters and all his writings (*Ad Nephalium* II.20: 23–6). He highlights what he perceives as the dyophysite absurdity of confessing 'two natures', which separates them; and then confessing the union and being constrained to say 'one nature of the Word incarnate' (*Ad Nephalium* II.21: 22–4). Nephalius and his followers are reported as having said: 'If the two natures are gathered into themselves and are united, it is therefore necessary for us to say that this one Christ is acknowledged to be two natures' (*Ad Nephalium* II.35: 25–7), which is contrary to the teaching of Cyril. Towards the end of the second part of his work, Severus defends himself against the charge of theopaschitism which his opponent brought against him, calling on the witness of the Fathers: Ignatius, Irenaeus, Alexander of Alexandria, Julius of Rome, Athanasius, the Cappadocians, John Chrysostom, Atticus of Constantinople, Amphilochius, Proclus, Theophilus of Alexandria and Cyril himself. He anathematizes those who speak of a union, only to say that those things which are once and for all united are 'two united into a union' (*Ad Nephalium* II.44: 27–9). Without mentioning Nephalius by name, Severus claims that the one who says there is one hypostasis, but two natures, in Christ after the union is similar to the one who calls that same object 'one' and 'two', and 'falls into a contradiction more stupid than all stupidities'. Confessing one hypostasis of necessity entails also confessing 'one incarnate nature of the Word' (*Ad Nephalium* II.50: 13–20).

PHILALETHES

We have already seen that during his stay in Constantinople between 508 and 511 Severus came into contact with an Alexandrian neo-Chalcedonian or neo-Cyrillian compilation, known as the *Florilegium Cyrillianum* (*FlorCyr*), which he felt compelled to refute.[1] John of Beith Aphthonia alleges that the *FlorCyr* was passed on to Patriarch Macedonius by its authors; Macedonius then presented it to Emperor Anastasius, who alerted Severus to its existence (JBA 235–6): this supposed chain of events is, however, to be treated with caution (Lebon 1909: 125). The *FlorCyr* comprised 250 chapters of quotations from Cyril, and was intended as a reading of the Chalcedonian definition in a Cyrillian sense. For his refutation of it, Severus chose the name *Philalethes* ('Lover of Truth') because of his aim of establishing the authentic ideas of Cyril by completing or correcting the way in which the compiler(s) had quoted him. On the basis of Syriac fragments of a work entitled *Apology for the Philalethes*, Lebon (1909: 131–7) assumed that Severus had written a follow-up work, but the publication of the complete Syriac text subsequently demonstrated that the *Apology* was part of Severus's campaign against Julian (see further below). As previously mentioned, Youhanna Nessim Youssef recently discovered Arabic manuscripts of the *Philalethes*, a work formerly thought not to have survived in that linguistic tradition.

The 250 chapters of the *FlorCyr* are more like excerpts. Numbers 1–10 work through the Cyrillian definition, which is broken up into parts for the purpose of commentary. To each part is then attached a citation from Cyril, with the intention of showing that the Council had not departed from the christological tradition of the great Alexandrine. The two natures and one hypostasis in Christ are central here. Numbers 11–250, the bulk of the *florilegium*, focus on the two contentious issues in the Chalcedonian definition: the distinguishing of two natures in Christ, and the correct interpretation of the theopaschite formula ('one of the Trinity suffered in the flesh'); the citations from Cyril are meant to show that the council was in agreement with him.

In his rebuttal, Severus sought to bring down the argument that Cyril was close to two-nature christology and to show that he was a pure representative of one-nature christology. The problem for both the compiler(s) and Severus was that Cyril's works were written at different stages in his long career, and against quite different christological opponents – Arians, radical Apollinarians or Synousiasts, and Nestorius, against whom it was necessary to stress either the one-ness or the two-ness in Christ. Thus, for example, the compiler(s) did not attempt to scrutinize the distinction which Chalcedon made between *hypostasis* and *physis* and to demonstrate that it was in line with Cyrillian terminology. Nor did the extracts in the *FlorCyr* make it clear that Cyril had taught a two-ness only in abstract consideration (*theoria*) of the natures after the union. For his part, Severus cannot afford to deal with some extracts from Cyril's earlier works which, in the face of the Arian denial of the divinity of Christ and the Synousiasts' dismissal of the body of Christ, stress the difference between the divinity and humanity in the union of the two natures. In the *Philalethes*, Severus consequently pleads for a purification of language with regard to the use of expressions, particularly those to do with 'mixing', in earlier Patristic writings, so to exclude any idea of a duality in Christ.

AD SERGIUM GRAMMATICUM

While Severus's exchange with Sergius the grammarian is in epistolary form, the letters are more like christological tractates, and will consequently be dealt with here as dogmatic/polemical works. Because the entire correspondence between Severus and Sergius has been given a fine English translation and commentary by Torrance (1988), it was decided not to include translations from *Ad Sergium Grammaticum* in the present volume.

As we have seen, the beginning of this correspondence dates from the patriarchate of Severus, and its end from after his banishment from Antioch in 518. Seven texts are involved: three letters from Sergius, three replies from Severus, and an *Apology* by the grammarian. The first of Sergius's letters was in fact addressed to Antoninus, bishop of Aleppo, a correspondent of Severus (Honigmann 1951: 25–6), who was apparently asked by his fellow-bishop to reply. It was an unequal exchange, for Sergius was an amateur theologian lacking the terminological or conceptual tools necessary for a clear expression of the one-nature christology. He was also an extreme anti-Chalcedonian, who exaggerated the unity of the two natures in Christ to a point where he believed in the unification of propriety (*idiotes*) as well as of nature (*physis*) in the union (Torrance 1988: 16): he was 'the zealot of the unity in Christ' (Grillmeier 1995: 113). In this respect, namely the emphasis on the complete unity in Christ, there is a similarity between the grammarian and the patriarch's later opponent, Julian of Halicarnassus. Severus's replies to Sergius concentrate on the nature of the unity and its constituent parts, with a strong emphasis on the soteriological implications of the union as he conceives it. In the face of Sergius's somewhat confused and obscure thought, he was obliged to clarify his own concept of 'propriety', basing himself, as always, on the thought of Cyril.

Severus understood Sergius's declaration of 'one propriety' in Christ as 'one particularity', to the extent that the flesh had become consubstantial with the Logos by losing its intrinsic difference (Torrance 1988: 34). The grammarian believed that this close union was based on a 'mixing without mingling', and that not to conceive of the union in this way was to embrace Nestorianism. Severus rejected the idea of 'mixing without mingling', and, having recourse to Cyril once again, substituted the word *synthesis*, which removed from Christ any division, duality or mingling (Grillmeier 1995: 126–8). Particularly in his first letter to Sergius, Severus is at pains to confess the particularity of the two natures from which there is the one Christ: difference is in fact intrinsic to the union, for the Godhead remains the Godhead and the humanity remains the humanity, but the two are one. However, in this union the humanity becomes as it were possessed by the divinity, such that, while it is integral, it is no longer independent.

> But he made the human soul his own that he might show it superior to sin, and he imparted to it the firmness and unchangeableness of his own nature, as dye in a fleece.[2]

This understanding of the union is crucial to Severus's soteriology: it is an active process, with the Word as the subject of this activity (Torrance 1988: 86).

> For there is one who acts, that is the Word of God incarnate; and there is one active movement which is activity, but the things which are done are diverse, that is (the things) accomplished by activity.[3]

Consequently, only sometimes does the human nature undergo the passions proper to it, because the properties of the constituent natures are not distributed each to its own nature, as Leo argued in his *Tome*.[4] This would result not in a union but in a kind of partnership. Thus, although there is a *communicatio idiomatum*, it is in a way one-sided (Torrance 1988: 87). Following Cyril, Severus argues that the union of the two natures in Christ is continually adaptative and voluntary, and that the adaptation of the Word incarnate occurs for the redemption of humankind. In other words, the possession of the human nature by the Logos is something which is 'active, intentional, and soteriological'

(Torrance 1988: 104). Although in this process the differences in the natures are preserved for soteriological reasons, division is removed for soteriological reasons, but not through mixture or confusion. For Sergius, such argumentation could only imply a two-nature christology, and he calls Severus a Nestorian unless he agrees to a mixture of natures in Christ.[5] However, in his *Apology* the grammarian changes his tune, avoiding words implying mixture, and making Severus an adversary of Nestorius.

CONTRA IMPIUM GRAMMATICUM

Shortly before 518, John, presbyter and grammarian of Caesarea, composed his *Apology for the Council of Chalcedon*. Severus did not have a chance to refute it until he was in exile in Egypt, and we have seen the difficulties which he encountered in accessing the necessary books there. John's *Apology* seems to have played an important role in the synod of neo-Chalcedonians held at Alexandretta in Syria between 514 and 518 (Richard 1977: VI-VIII). It survives in Syriac fragments found in Severus's rebuttal, *Contra impium Grammaticum* (*CPG* 7024), and in Greek fragments cited in other works. John also composed *Seventeen Chapters against the Acephaloi*, a work against the aphthartodocetists or followers of Julian of Halicarnassus, and two homilies against the Manichees, and he made a collection of syllogisms of the Fathers against the Manichees (*CPG* 6855–61). He was perhaps also responsible for the *Dispute between John the orthodox and a Manichaean* (*CPG* 6862).

Severus's reply to John contained three parts, the first two of which do not survive in their entirety, and in it his opponent is cited often, indeed at length, and vituperatively. The exiled patriarch had an able dialectical opponent in the grammarian, even though the latter does not seem to have been a professional theologian, and Severus had to deal with the fact that in his *Apology* for the council John had said nothing about Leo's *Tome*, had not cited explicitly from the conciliar definition of faith, and only once had cited the Acts of the council (Richard 1977: XII). This posed a problem for Severus. But because John's christology was not quite the same as that of Chalcedon, Severus seized the opportunity to point out that some of John's propositions were, in fact, a direct critique of the council's definition of faith (Richard 1977: XII). Like Nephalius, but more adeptly, the grammarian attempted to mediate between the 'one incarnate nature' christology of Cyril and the two-nature christology of Chalcedon. He did this in two ways – he worked on the definition of terms or concepts, and he attempted to reconcile the formulae of Cyril (the dominant figure in the controversy) with the terminology of Chalcedon.

Both ways riled and embarrassed Severus, and this fact was reflected in the opprobrium of his response. He addressed John as the 'inheritor of foreign humbug, lacking knowledge and having no sense',[6] 'the thickest of all thick grammarians',[7] as 'concussed with a huge case of pride and giving oracles out to us to fit his own judgement, just like from a Delphic tripod'.[8] In his first approach, the grammarian, while not denying the suitability or appropriateness of the term *physis* (nature), had recourse to the terminology of Basil of Caesarea used in discussion of the Trinity, and applied Basil's terminology of essence (*ousia*) and hypostasis to christology. Like the neo-Nicenes or followers of Basil of Caesarea, John distinguished between *ousia* and *physis*, whereas Severus and the anti-Chalcedonians, representing the old-Nicene, Alexandrian or Athanasian tradition, understood *physis* as what had existed from birth, which in the case of Christ could only refer to the divinity. *Ousia*, on the other hand, as used by Basil, refers to 'essence' as universal. With Severus directly and deliberately in his sights, John gave preference to *ousia* over *physis*, because then, on the basis of Basil's use of the term in Trinitarian theology, he could still maintain a duality in Christ. While there was a duality in *theoria* or abstract contemplation with regard to the abstract *ousia*, there was unity with regard to the concrete hypostasis. Two essences (*ousiai*) exist. Severus was forced back into his own defence lines by this clever and adept attack. He must have recognized that his able contestant could not only return to the terminology of Basil and call upon the homoousios of Nicaea, but could also utilize Cyril's formulae by providing new interpretations. He also had to admit that the grammarian was able to use the same weapons as his, and at times to better effect (Grillmeier 1995: 56 n. 99).

In his second mode of defence of Chalcedon, John used and combined the two formulae 'in two natures' (Chalcedon) and 'out of two natures' (Cyril, and subsequently Severus). Because of his definition of terms, as we have seen, John was able to use Cyril's and Severus's phraseology of the one-nature christology while still maintaining a duality or doubleness (*diplous/diple*) in Christ. Expressions of 'doubleness' had a respectable Patristic pedigree, even in Cyril and Athanasius, much to the displeasure of Severus. It was in this contest that John introduced the term 'enhypostaton', which means that the two abstract essences (*ousiai*), viewed abstractly (*en theoria*), had been united 'hypostatically' in the concrete.

As Cyril had done before him, Severus rejected these propositions out of hand, on the grounds that they smacked of Nestorius, and called John 'a Moabite and an Ammonite, and a foreigner to the laws of Israel' (see Text 10 below). The former patriarch was impervious to his opponent's reasonable suggestion that compromise about Chalcedon was possible on the basis of Cyril's position at the time of the union with the Antiochenes in 433, namely not to reject 'two natures', but to demand the confession of 'the one incarnate nature of the Logos', preferring to base himself on Cyril's anti-Nestorian letters after 429 (Grillmeier 1995: 70–1). This abhorrence of Nestorius was continually the motivation for Severus to reject any talk of duality in Christ, to the point in which the two natures are so united that the Logos is, as it were, in charge, particularly with regard to free decision or will in the matter of human activity (*energeia*).[9] The development of this idea was to continue throughout the sixth century and to culminate in the monenergist/monothelite controversy.

While in his rebuttal of John the grammarian Severus resorted to and maintained the literal usage of Cyril, his opponent attempted in a clever way, and with orthodox Patristic support, to be a reconciler and mediator of opposite words. What he aimed at was a functional balance of formulae to ward off both Apollinarianism and Nestorianism.

WORKS AGAINST JULIAN

We have already encountered Julian, the exiled anti-Chalcedonian bishop of Halicarnassus, during the sojourn which he shared with Severus in the monastery of Henaton in Egypt. Shortly after their arrival there in 518, Julian wrote a speech *About the Confession of Faith*[10] in which he claimed that his doctrines were corroborated by Severus himself in the *Philalethes*. The former patriarch of Antioch found this claim particularly galling, and a protracted and voluminous exchange between the two men ensued. We have Syriac translations of three letters which Julian wrote to Severus, and the replies he received (*CPG* 7026). The rest of Julian's works survive only in Syriac and Greek fragments.[11] Julian composed a *Tome*, received retorts in Severus's *Censura tomi Iuliani* (*CPG* 7027) and *Confutatio propositionum Iuliani* (*CPG* 7028), and published a second edition of the work, *Additiones Iuliani*, to which Severus replied in *Contra additiones Iuliani* (*CPG* 7029). An *Apologia tomi* followed, in response to which Severus wrote *Adversus apologiam Iuliani* (*CPG* 7030). Subsequently, Julian attacked his opponent's critique of his *Tome* in a work entitled *Contra blasphemias Severi*. Finally, Severus was so nettled that he defended his masterpiece, the *Philalethes*, in the *Apologia Philalethes* (*CPG* 7031). The entire exchange, to judge from the works of Severus, which survive practically in their entirety, was characterized by invective. It needs to be asked why the doctrines of Julian irritated and alarmed Severus so much.

In the *Philalethes*, Severus had found himself constrained to stress, against the Chalcedonian compiler(s) of the *FlorCyr*, the unity in Christ, and to do this he had emphasized the predominance of the divinity in Christ and the importance of the divine activity or power (*energeia*) in the union. Christ's human nature was depicted as 'vibrating with divine powers' (Grillmeier 1995: 83–4). From this it was but a small step for Julian to transfer divine power to the flesh of the earthly Christ, and to posit that, even before the resurrection, Christ's body was distinguished from that of human beings by its immunity from corruption, suffering and death (*aphtharsia, apatheia, athanasia*). The former bishop of Halicarnassus could even point to Severus's Homily LXVII on the Theotokos and virgin Mary, delivered on 2 February 515, where the patrarich stated that 'the whole pure body of Christ had no share in sin and the corruptedness resulting from it' (*PO* 8/2: 358. 7–9).[12] Hence, it could be argued that Christ's body was safeguarded from corruption by virtue of both the virginal conception and its union with the Logos, who was without original sin and corruption. For Severus this position was tantamount to that of Mani, Eutyches, and the docetists and had far-reaching soteriological implications: if Christ is not truly human, then there can be no salvation for human beings. For his part, Julian argued that to accept human suffering and death in Christ would mean that Christ was a mere human being, and would be tantamount to the doctrine of Nestorius, and of Paul of Samosata and Photinus before him.

While Julian's doctrine is somewhat obscured by the harshness of Severus's rebuttals of it and by the position eventually taken by extremists in Julian's own party, it is clear that the fundamental point of contention between the two exiled hierarchs was a terminological one.[13] As he had done previously in the *Philalethes* and in his work against John the grammarian, in his altercation with Julian Severus attempted a purification of language: thus when Christ is said to be 'incorruptible' it means 'without sin'; he is 'corruptible' when suffering so-called 'blameless passions' (*pathe adiableta*), such as hunger, cold and death; and only after the resurrection is he absolutely incorruptible.[14] On the one hand Severus had to safeguard the reality of Christ's body in order not to be regarded as Nestorian, while on the other hand he wanted to emphasize the one activity (*energeia*) in the union, the activity of the Logos which permeated the humanity. At the same time, he had also to show that the divine properties in Christ had, as it were, limits into which the human properties had to fit. Julian's focus was on the union from divinity and humanity, to the extent that the difference between the two faded into the background. Much to Severus's derision,[15] he coined the contrived and overly subtle term 'undifferentiated difference' or 'non-different difference' (*diaphora adiaphoros*) in the properties in Christ, such that he did not differentiate even in abstract contemplation (*theoria*) between the divinity and the humanity. Although Severus presents him as maintaining that the two essences (*ousiai*) in Christ are the same, it is doubtful whether this was in fact the case (Grillmeier 1995: 98). Using the distinction between 'essence' and 'nature' which, ironically, he had taken over from John the grammarian, Severus hammers home the point that, although there is one nature in Christ, two abstract essences have to be distinguished in *theoria*. As Grillmeier (1995: 162) has shown, the debate between Severus and Julian demonstrated that the former saw the union in Christ established both in the exchange of properties and in the unity of the energeia or activity in Christ, such that the human activity in Christ in the areas of willing and knowing was 'owned' by the divinity. Again, as we have seen in Severus's altercation with John the grammarian, this concept was to be crucial in the development of anti-Chalcedonian christology for the remainder of the sixth century and well into the seventh century, culminating in the monenergist/ monothelite debate.

It is clear that Julian's influence on the anti-Chalcedonian community was felt before Severus's banishment, for as patriarch he preached between 6 January 518 and Lent of the same year Homily CXIX, on the doctrines of one of Julian's extreme followers, Bishop Romanus of Rhosus in Cilicia, an exaggerated encratic or ascetic.[16] The fact that in this homily the patriarch embarked on a detailed denunciation of Romanus and his work *The Ladder* demonstrates that the attraction of Julian's doctrine extended beyond the circle of academic theologians. Letter XCVII (*PO* 14/1: 194–9) from banishment, to the noblewoman Caesaria, corroborates this: Severus had to deal with her question concerning the Julianists' claim that an incorruptible Christ could not have been circumcised. Severus's work against the shadowy Felicissimus (see below) also testifies to the virulence of the debate against Julianism.

Despite Severus's misrepresentations of Julian's doctrine of *aphtharsia*, it seems that the former bishop of Halicarnassus did not intend to abolish the reality of the body of Christ, but rather to portray Christ as a new Adam, with special prerogatives. This new Adam is not subjected to the limitations of humankind, but voluntarily undergoes 'passions' such as suffering and death. Julian's followers were not so careful in their formulations, and Severus's alarm at the rise of so-called aphthartodocetism was proven to be well grounded. Julianism acquired a firm footing in Egypt, particularly in monastic circles (Maspero 1923: 95) and spread elsewhere in the Roman empire, notably to Armenia (Grillmeier 1996: 45), causing a serious schism among anti-Chalcedonians and, like Julian himself, encountering strong opposition from adherents of both the one-nature and the two-nature christology.

CONTRA FELICISSIMUM

Against Felicissimus, Severus directed a work which survives only in some Greek and Syriac fragments.[17] It was obviously a substantial composition, encompassing at least fifteen books (*Doctrina Patrum* 21: 14). Felicissimus himself was a follower of Julian, disseminating his master's ideas in Armenia (Honigmann 1951: 127 n. 5), and indeed he suffered as Julian (and John the grammarian) did from Severus's invective.

> The stupid fellow (sc. Felicissimus) having been unable to prove this, those who devised the last murky volume with him go the rounds to collect proof-texts for him, as it were in a begging bowl, and have even collected indeed some texts which are quite irrelevant to the point proposed i.e. which say that in the beginning man was made not mortal but immortal. The lunatic forgot that nobody quarrels with him on that point.[18]

Elsewhere Felicissimus is mentioned by Severus in the same breath as Julian,[19] and the former patriarch says of him: 'for it is good to reply to you, because you are close'.[20] He is also named in the biography of Severus ascribed to Athanasius, but without further details.

HOMILIES

The 125 so-called Cathedral Homilies that Severus delivered during the six years of his patriarchate (512–18) circulated as a collection during his lifetime (Brière 1960: 63) and were quickly translated in two separate enterprises, first by Paul of Callincum in 528, and subsequently by Jacob of Edessa in the second half of the seventh century

(Graffin 1978a: 243–55). Of Paul's version we have only three of the original four tomes, and there are other lacunae; this means that Homilies I–XXX and LX–LXXII are missing. The meticulous revision by the polymath Jacob, which was completed in 701, is more or less complete. The numbering of the homilies is ancient.

The schema of Severus's surviving preaching activity, the annual inventory beginning on the anniversary of his consecration as patriarch in November 512, looks like this:

- November 512–November 513: thirty-three homilies;
- November 513–November 514: twenty-six homilies;
- November 514–November 515: nineteen homilies;
- November 515–November 516: nineteen homilies;
- November 516–November 517: fourteen homilies;
- November 517–some time after April 518: thirteen homilies (cut short by his banishment).

This collection was influential during his lifetime, and today constitutes a valuable resource for the study of early Christian homiletics, because many of these texts can be dated and topographically located (Cumming 1990). Unfortunately, the negative opinion of Anton Baumstark (1897: 36–7) regarding Severus's efforts as a homilist ('tiring', 'inconclusive', with 'no synthesis' and 'no clear objective', 'always going off on new tangents') was not conducive to a study of this corpus, particularly since subsequently it took most of the twentieth century to edit the homilies and furnish them with French translations. However, more recently Dom Alexandre Olivar (1980: 403), as we have already noted, was able to claim that Severus was one of the greatest orators of the early church.[21] The homilies, like the letters and the liturgical works of the patriarch of Antioch, provide a useful foil to the dogmatic/polemical works, and a complement to the portrait of Severus as pastor.

Despite his low opinion of Severus's homiletical abilities, Baumstark (1897: 36) provided a useful division of the corpus into four parts: principal feast-days in the liturgical cycle; saints' days; exegetical homilies on Sundays; and occasional or annual events or ceremonies. As we shall see, Severus's hymns can also be grouped in much the same way. The first group of homilies is devoted to such feasts as the Nativity, Epiphany, the beginning of Lent, Easter, Ascension and Pentecost. Incorporated here are six homilies (one delivered each year) to the catechumens of Antioch.[22] In the second group are homilies on saints, martyrs, Fathers of the church and the Theotokos (see Text 15 below), and there is a close similarity to the subject-matter of the hymns. Martyrs local to Antioch, such as Thecla, Ignatius, Barlaha, Drosis and Babylas, as well as those beloved of his congregations, such as Severus's own patron Leontius of Tripolis, Basil and Gregory, Antony or the Forty Martyrs of Sebaste in Armenia (Text 16 below), are commemorated. In his visitation to outlying areas, the patriarch also preached on Sts Sergius and Bacchus in Chalcis, and Thalleiaios in Aigiai in Cilicia. The third group comprises mostly exegetical works, extracts from which also found their way into many catenae and hence survive in Greek, Syriac and Coptic fragments (cf. Brière 1960: 66–7). As is the case with the hymns of Severus, the most intriguing homilies are those in the fourth group, which form a miscellany dealing with such diverse subjects as the theatre, horse-racing and the actions of the emperor (see for example Text 14 below).

The homilies were delivered in various locations, not only in Antioch and its suburb Daphne but also in outlying towns. In Antioch itself, Severus preached for example in the Great Church,[23] the Church of the Angel Michael (Hom. LXXII), and the shrines of Babylas (Hom. XI), Ignatius (Hom. XXXVII), Barlaha (Hom. LXXIII), and Julian (LXXV). Homily XXX was delivered in a monastery, Homily XXVIII in Seleucia Pieria, Homilies LVI and LVII in Chalcis, Homilies LVIII, LIX and LX in Cyrrhus, and Homilies CX and CXI in Aigiai in Cilicia. Many of the homilies, Severus tell us, he took the trouble to prepare beforehand,[24] but Homily CXI, for example, was delivered in Aigiai in response to a question put to him by one of the congregation (PO 25/4: 789. 2). On another occasion, a congregation in Antioch requested that he preach a homily, which, they had heard, he had delivered in Cyrrhus two months earlier. Severus obliged, but had to adapt his material to the feast being celebrated, namely the Massacre of the Innocents, and to add a section at the end to make the homily fit into its new milieu in Antioch.[25]

Although as a preacher, too, Severus loses no opportunity to hammer home uncompromisingly the one-nature christology (Grillmeier 1995: 131 n. 341), his homilies are a rich source for details of everyday life in a late antique city, and for the development of liturgy and 'popular' theology. Demons, angels and heretics (real or imagined) abound, and there is increasing importance attached to the Theotokos (see Text 15 below).[26] We have vivid pictures of liturgical practice at the time, for example, in Homily XXVII, delivered on Tuesday, 18 June 513 on the martyr Leontius, whom Severus credited with his conversion from paganism to Christianity (PO 36/4: 558–73). Leontius's relics resided in his martyrium in Daphne outside Antioch in a building which had formerly been a synagogue and which stood at the top of the road from Antioch to Daphne. The programme for the faithful on this occasion is set out by their patriarch as follows: they are to go to the shrine, remember the martyr's achievements and sufferings, anoint themselves with the holy oil from the urn there, go and eat and drink in moderation, avoiding the carnal pleasures of Daphne, and return home. Almsgiving is also prescribed in favour of the many beggars who line the streets around the martyrium and bar the way for those who refuse to give them money. On the eve of Leontius's feast some of his remains had processed on a cart, and were fêted by the people, who threw objects of clothing, loaves of bread, and jewellery onto the vehicle, and held up small children to touch the reliquary (Allen 2002: 714).

In the course of his preaching, Severus uses ethical imperatives and literal and figurative exegesis. Although, as we have seen, most of his homilies were prepared beforehand, they still contain evidence of audience reaction, of the dynamic which existed between the patriarch and his various congregations, and of a preacher who had a keen sense of his teaching role.

LETTERS

Like his homilies, Severus's letters (CPG 7070–71) have for the most part come down to us in early Syriac translations and in several groups.[27] Originally they were divided into three classes: those before episcopacy (before 512); those during his patriarchate (512–18); and those during his banishment (518–38). These contained respectively four, ten and nine books, but there were additional letters outside these groups. How prolific Severus was as a letter-writer can be seen from Brooks's calculation that the total number of his letters must have exceeded 3759 (Brooks 1903: ix–x). Of this total fewer than 300 have survived.

There are two main groups of letters, in the first of which we have 123 translated by the priest Athanasius of Nisibis in 669, the so-called *Select Letters*. These deal solely with ecclesiastical affairs and are not in chronological order. However, at the beginning of each letter its place in the original collection is stated. In the second main group we have 117 letters, edited by Brooks on the basis of twenty-eight Syriac manuscripts (*PO* 12/2 and 14/1). In only twenty-six of these do we find any indication of where the letter originally belonged, and once again the rationale behind the ordering of the collection is not clear.

In addition there is a Letter to John the Soldier (Brock 1978), and another six letters survive in the *Church History* of Zachariah Scholasticus, one of which, Severus's *Defence* to Emperor Justinian, is translated below (Text 28). The Synodical Letter which Severus composed on 26 July 535 on the accession of Theodosius to the patriarchate of Alexandria is preserved in an anti-Chalcedonian dossier (see Text 28 below), and at least four letters are preserved in a Coptic translation, and two in Arabic. Numerous fragments survive, mostly in Greek, Syriac and Coptic, and we know of the existence of other letters which are so far unedited (Brock 1975: 17–24).

In following the biography of Severus (see Chapters 1 and 2 above), the importance of his letters has already been noted. Despite the somewhat haphazard manner in which about only one-fifteenth of them has come down to us, the surviving letters show the wide range of his addressees and the topics he discussed with them, and they highlight their author as a pastor and administrator, rather than as a polemicist or dogmatician. To be sure, in the letters too we find polemic on the topic of the one-nature christology, but it is balanced by the other concerns manifested by Severus. We know that his epistolary networks were already in place before his patriarchate, and that during that time he used his letters to lobby for the anti-Chalcedonian cause as a complement to his lobbying in person in the imperial capital. The letters dating from his patriarchate reveal his concerns with endemic corruption amongst his clergy, and with canonical matters like the administration of monasteries, the re-admisission of lapsed anti-Chalcedonians, or the admission of Chalcedonians to communion, matters of dispute in which his legal training served him well. His epistolary interaction with high officials like the *magister officium* (*SL* I.21), the chamberlain Misael (*SL* I.17; XI.1), and the general (*stratelates*) Hypatius (I.40) are testimony to the civic responsibilities which the bishops of late antiquity had increasingly to assume. But pastoral care is in evidence as well. The same Misael, who wrote to the patriarch about becoming an ascetic, is advised by Severus rather to retain his place in the imperial administration (*SL* XI.1); the reader Stephen, who lived among Chalcedonians, is given advice about recycling one of Severus's homilies for liturgical use (*SL* VIII.1: Text 21); while Andrew, a reader and notary, is counselled about visiting the grave of a relative in a Chalcedonian shrine (*SL* IV.9). After his exile in 518, Severus's letters became both a lifeline to the outside world and an essential means of continuing the administration and pastoral care of the anti-Chalcedonian church in Syria and elsewhere. They reveal the personal dangers and difficulties which he encountered during banishment in Egypt, and at the same time the sophisticated

networks which he had with exiled bishops such as Proclus, bishop of
Coloneia in Cappadocia II (*SL* I.56), Sergius, bishop of Cyrrhus, and
Marion, bishop of Sura in Syria (*SL* V.15).

HYMNS AND LITURGICAL COMPOSITIONS

According to the biography of Severus by John of Beith Aphthonia
(244–5), the people of Antioch loved songs, either those of the theatre
or those of the church. Their patriarch consequently set about composing hymns for them, in order to save them from the perdition of
the theatre and to encourage them to attend church. Some of these
hymns, explains John, taught theology, contemplation and doctrine;
others expounded on Scripture, good works and natural disasters. In
fact, in the *Octoechus* of Syria, a hymn-book in which the works are
arranged according to the eight tones to which they were sung, 295 of
the 365 hymns are attributed to Severus. The collection was made for
liturgical purposes, and was translated into Syriac by Paul of Edessa
between 619 and 629. In 675 it was revised by Jacob of Edessa.

Like Severus's homilies, his hymns can be roughly divided into four
categories: those sung on major feasts in the liturgical cycle; those
sung on saints' days; those devoted to Scripture; and those com-
memorating special occasions or recurring celebrations. In the first
group we find hymns on the Nativity, Epiphany, Lent, Palm Sunday,
the Passion, the Resurrection, mid-Pentecost, the Ascension and
Pentecost. The second group is dominated by hymns on the martyrs,
including Severus's patron Leontius, Romanus, Babylas, Sergius and
Bacchus, the Maccabees, the Forty of Sebaste, Drosis, Thecla and
Ignatius. However, Basil of Caesarea and Gregory Nazianzen also
feature, as does the Theotokos. Although scriptural quotations and
allusions permeate the entire collection, hymns on scriptural themes
are not numerous, and are mostly confined to Old Testament figures
such as Job or to miracles in the New Testament. The fourth group is
a fascinating miscellany, dealing with emperors, the rebel Vitalian, the
theatre, the Persian wars, the Huns, drought, earthquakes and rain.
In addition, various individuals are commemorated, such as Peter,
Severus's deceased *syncellus* or associate administrator, and there are
series of everyday, morning, evening and funeral hymns.

Some of the hymns are dated, 256 being sung on 7 September
513 after earthquakes and 255 on 15 January 515 after drought-
breaking rain. On 22 November 517, Hymn 181 was sung at a syn-
axis in the church of the Theotokos. In two cases there are links to
Severus's homilies. We have seen how, in 514, the patriarch carried

out a prolonged visitation to towns and monasteries in the hinterland of Antioch, returning to preach on the feast of John the Baptist on Tuesday 14 October (Hom. LXI). His return is commemorated in Hymn 271, which recalls the monks he visited during his absence and contrasts their devotion to the religious life with his own 'vain profitless labours' as patriarch (*PO* 6/2: 719–20). The second case concerns Hymn 198, which was sung in 517 as Severus entered the town of Aigiai in Cilicia to meet the general Hypatius, who was on his way to Persia (*PO* 6/2: 661–2). It was at this same time that the visiting patriarch delivered two homilies in Aigiai, Homilies CX (20 May) and CXI.

Severus's talents and output as a hymnographer were complemented by his liturgical works. In Syriac there survives an anaphora or eucharistic prayer (*CPG* 7073), as well as liturgical orders or rites (*CPG* 7074–7), mostly concerning baptism. In addition, at least four liturgical prayers attributed to him survive in Coptic, three of which have already received an English translation (*CPG* 7078).[28]

Part II

TEXTS

4

DOGMATIC AND POLEMICAL WORKS

In the following text, which is the opening of the second part of *Ad Nephalium*, Severus argues that the Council of Chalcedon, by confessing the 'in two natures' formula, then adding either 'one hypostasis' or 'which are united and not divided', introduced an absurdity. Cyril's dictum 'Leave off dividing the natures after the union' is cited repeatedly to support Severus's argument. To be noted is that apparently the future patriarch of Antioch had the *acta* of the Council at his disposal.

Text 1 *Ad Nephalium, Or.* II

Translated from *CSCO* 64: 10–21

Of the same man again, a second discourse to Nephalius: to the same people who assert that Christ is to be recognized in two natures after the union, and add the phrase 'which are united and not divided'.

Now we ourselves, according to the saving and truly divine statement of the three hundred and eighteen,[1] believe (p. 11) and confess that the only-begotten Son of God, who is equal in essence to the Father through whose power all things existed, came down at the end of days and became incarnate and was made man – that is, he was united to flesh which had a soul possessed of reason and intelligence by means of a free and hypostatic union from the holy Spirit and from the ever-virgin Mary, Mother of God; and that his nature was one, even when the Word had become incarnate, just as the God-inspired men and mystagogues of the church have instructed us; and we know him as simple, and not compound, in that which he is understood to be God, and composite in that which he is understood to be man. For since we believe him to be Emmanuel, even the same God the Word incarnate out of two natures which possess integrity (I mean out of

59

divinity and out of humanity), we know one Son, one Christ, one Lord. We do not affirm that he is known in two natures, as the Synod of Chalcedon declared as dogma, putting the expression 'indivisibly' onto its declaration as a kind of apology.

For that very synod bears witness that it is not the same thing to say that after the union he is 'out of two natures' as it is to say that he is 'in two natures', even if the word 'united' be added. For the *acta* state as follows:

The excellent and illustrious leaders have declared: Dioscorus was alleging: 'I accept the phrase *out of two natures;* the phrase *in two natures* I do not accept'. Moreover, the holy archbishop Leo declared that the two natures which are in Christ, himself the one only-begotten Son and our Saviour, are united without confusion and without change. To whom, now, are you attached? To the holy Leo, or to Dioscorus? The devout bishops shouted: 'Like Leo thus we believe! Those who are at variance (p. 12) are Eutychians! Leo has made affirmation in orthodox manner!'[2]

See how they dubbed the phrase 'out of two natures' a heretical expression, whereas they determined the phrase 'two natures united' to be of orthodox character, by this means making provision for him to be described after the union as being 'of two natures'. But if they had thought that the former and latter phrases had meant the same thing, it would have been proper for them to state plainly that Dioscorus was disputatious, and was being contentious for no reason about words which had possessed the same force and meaning. But they had known correctly that the phrase 'out of two natures' was the cause of (the formula) 'he is one through composition', and they were duly careful lest it should be stated 'one nature of the Word incarnate'; rather, they accepted the phrase 'in two (natures)' and alongside it the expression 'united' (that is to say, without division) subtly and according to their own understanding, without regard for what would follow.

For the phrase 'out of two natures' in fact denies that they are two, and demonstrates that he himself is one through composition, and that those things out of which he was compounded as the same Lord did not cease to exist because they were joined together without confusion; and that same one continues firm and unshaken after the sublime union. That formula, however, which is expressed as 'two (natures) after the union' is one of those things which have no substance: for if two persisted, they would not be united, since union is that which erases duality. And I shall try to make this plain from what will be brought to bear later on, namely this: I maintain that the hypostatic union does not admit of division into two.

Pay attention, then, to what that loathsome Theodoret says by way of contradiction against the second anathema,[3] when he indeed affirms two natures and confesses them as united, but (p. 13) denies the hypostatic union, about which the Synod of Chalcedon was also silent. For he states as follows: THEODORET: 'Now it is fitting to believe the Lord as manifesting two natures when he says to the Jews, "*Destroy this temple, and in three days I raise it up*" (Jn 2: 19)". Now if a mixing had taken place, then God would not have remained as God, and the temple would not have been known as the temple (for the principle of mixture requires such a thing), and our Lord would have said to the Jews, "*Destroy this temple, and in three days I raise it up*" superfluously. For it would have been appropriate for him to say: "Destroy me, and in three days I rise up", if indeed there had been some mixing and confusion. But now he manifests the temple as destroyed, and God as the one raising it up. Therefore the hypostatic union which they propound to us instead of mixture is, as I suppose, superfluous; but it is enough that one should speak of a union which both demonstrates the properties of the natures and teaches (us) to worship one Christ.'[4] And again, by way of contradiction in respect of the tenth anathema, he states as follows: THEODORET: 'But what was from the seed of David, what was mortal, what was liable to suffering, what was afraid of death was assumed by him, even though this nature afterwards destroyed the power of death because of its union with God who assumed it; and what walked in perfect uprightness and said to John, "*Allow it now, for so it befits us to fulfill all uprightness*" (Matt 3:15), this (is what) received the title of the high priesthood *according to the order of Melchizedek*'. (Ps 110: 4 etc.)[5]

While this man, therefore, acknowledges two natures and also speaks of union, let us consider that the holy Cyril says by way of defence of his own tenth anathema: CYRIL: 'How, then, do you assert that that Word who is from God was united (p. 14) to what was from the seed of David, if you have ascribed priesthood only to the one who is from the seed of David? For if the union is truly a union, there are not two entities at all, but Christ is known as one and sole, out of the two (natures). Therefore it is clear that they hypocritically declare that they acknowledge the union, since they are willing to delude the minds of those who are more simple, but themselves regard the conjunction (of the two natures) as external and in appearance, a conjunction which we ourselves copy when we are shown as being partakers of his divine nature through the Spirit'.[6]

But perhaps you will say: 'Theodoret, because he said "Who is of the seed of David", rightly bore the blame, since it was as if he were speaking of a unity of persons (*prosopa*).' Yet in fact he spoke rather of 'what is of the seed of David'; and afterwards the holy Cyril himself (in those discourses which were composed before the latter) also finds fault with him because of the term 'nature', when he states as follows: CYRIL: 'Now this careful Theodoret, being an accurate imitator of that man's[7] abomination, was not ashamed to say that he assumed human nature, and showed this nature as greater than that of ordinary high priests.'[8]

But this moaning Theodoret also states in his complaint about the same anathema: THEODORET: 'Now for the experiencing of these sufferings of ours our nature was assumed on our behalf; and it was not the case that he assumed this nature for the sake of our salvation.'[9] How this man is reproved by his own words, in that both above and below he describes without fear 'what was of the seed of David' as both person (*prosopon*) and nature in what he says himself: 'Who is the one who is perfect in labours of virtue?'[10] And again: 'Who is the one who has lived in virtue?'[11] And again: 'The nature which was from us was assumed on our behalf.[12] Thus Leo, too, in his *Tôme* now says in fact: 'Let him examine which nature (p. 15) was pierced with the nails and hung on the wood',[13] and now: 'For nevertheless in our Lord Jesus Christ there is, rather, one person of God and man'.[14] For what man of those who reason, when he hears that there is one person of God and man in our Lord Jesus Christ, would not at once think concerning that expression that it conveys to us the sense of a union of persons, and not an hypostatic union out of two realities, I mean out of divinity and out of humanity? For if he had thought that he would show to us one and the same reality, then he would have needed to say: 'For because our Lord Jesus Christ is one out of perfect divinity and perfect humanity, the same is God and man at the same time'. For what he has stated: 'In our Lord Jesus Christ there is one person of God and man', shows first that there is one entity, God who is set apart, and then another entity, man; and that thence that title of 'Christ' binds the two of them together – as Nestorius also asserted: 'For this reason also God the Word is named Christ, because he possesses perpetual conjunction to the Christ'.[15] For in another place the same man also states that the title 'Christ' is indicative of two natures, as also are 'Lord' and 'Son', and of the latter and of the former individually, such that there are two Christs, and two Lords, and two Sons, and again whichever of the two you wish together by means of the conjunction. And he states as follows: NESTORIUS: 'Therefore when the divine

Scripture is about to speak either of the birth of Christ from the blessed virgin, or of his death, it nowhere seems to put "God", but "Christ", or "Son", or "Lord", since those three expressions are indicative of the two (p. 16) natures, now of this, now of that; now of the one, now of the other.'[16]

But you can say that the Synod of Chalcedon understood the union as hypostatic, for it says in its definition that there is to be acknowledged 'one and the same Christ and Son and Lord and only-begotten in two natures without confusion, without change, without separation, and without division; the difference of the natures being in no way taken away on account of the union, but rather the distinctive characteristic of each being preserved from two natures concurring together into one person (*prosopon*) and one hypostasis'.[17] But it is plain to all those who are even moderately educated and learned in the dogmas of orthodoxy that it is in the nature of a contradiction to say concerning the one Christ that on the one hand there are two natures, but on the other one hypostasis. For the person who speaks of 'one hypostasis' necessarily affirms one nature as well. [There follow two citations, allegedly from Athanasius, but in fact from the ps.Apollinarian writings.]

(p. 17) See how he (sc. Athanasius) has affirmed him as being one Christ, one person (*prosopon*) and one nature and one hypostasis. Furthermore, with the same words that holy Cyril comes forward. For he says, in the second treatise against the blasphemies of Nestorius: CYRIL: 'Leave off from dividing the natures after the union.'[18] But immediately a malicious hearer disputes this and says: 'Look, he forbids us to divide the natures after the union, and I declare that they are united!' But that person shall hear from us: 'We do not pay attention to your disputations; but we shall enquire of the source of the statement what he defines as the meaning of (the instruction) that we should "not divide the natures"'. Now in the same discourse he had stated earlier: 'Thus everything shall be spoken of as if referring to one person: for one nature is perceived as existing after the union, that of the Word himself incarnate.'[19] Now according to you, he ought to have said: 'For the two natures are perceived as united after the union.' But he himself knows that the union demonstrated to me one nature incarnate, that of the Word himself; and the fact that he also calls that same Christ 'hypostasis' we can observe without any trouble. For he wrote as follows in the third chapter of his anathemas: CYRIL: 'If anyone divides the hypostases in Christ after the union, joining them together merely by a conjunction in dignity (p. 18) or authority or might and not rather by a conjunction of a union according to nature, let him be anathema.'[20]

But yet again those who attack these things which have been stated are calumniators, and assert that that union according to hypostasis allows us to speak of two hypostases, that is, two natures, after the union. But I do not need many words to deal with this, since I shall give testimony from the enemies themselves to the effect that this conjunction of hypostases, which is effected through a natural union, brings about one incarnate hypostasis in the composition of the Son himself. For Andrew[21] says, in his complaint against this anathema: ANDREW: 'Again, let us remind him of these words of his, since they show him speaking of two hypostases (in those matters which he discusses in the first volume[22]): "So then, that Word which is from the Father was not sanctified with us according to his own nature, even if one were to suppose that he alone was also born of the holy virgin, was anointed, and sanctified; and because of this also assumed the title Christ".[23] How, then, as if disregarding these words of his, does he gather (the natures) into one hypostasis by confusing the natures, when he calls the divine union "natural"?'[24]

Look: he evidently complains of the anathema as something which introduces one hypostasis. How, then, do you presume to call the gathering together of the hypostases according to a natural union 'two natures', that is, two hypostases united, when you do not perceive as a result of the union one entity in composition? Now that this is indeed the case, hear along with the testimony of the enemies the voice of Cyril himself as well. For he states in that letter to Nestorius, in which he also cites the anathema: CYRIL: 'Therefore let us ascribe to one person all the Gospel expressions, to one hypostasis of the Word (p. 19) incarnate. For the Lord Jesus Christ is one according to the Scriptures.'[25]

Thus it is clear that those who were at Chalcedon, when they promoted the dogma that Christ is in two natures, threw in for us the term 'one hypostasis' to lead to deception. For if there is one hypostasis, there is, in short, also one nature, as has been demonstrated before. For the God-inspired voice of the Fathers clearly affirmed neither two natures nor two hypostases for the one Son, regardless of whether anyone should say that the natures were either united or separated. For the lack of definition of both terms is understandable and challenging because it is generic, according to external authorities as well as general opinions. Furthermore, on account of irreverent mouths especially is added also that phrase 'but one nature of God the Word incarnate'. Nor may they assert that by saying 'incarnate' he established that other nature separately: for that God-inspired man who had Christ speaking within him did not utter an expression so base and perverse, but had stated clearly that there were not two natures divided, but two united. [A citation from Gregory the Wonder-worker follows.]

(p. 20) Why, then, do you frighten those who are more simple when you say: 'See! the holy Cyril in sending letters to Nestorius states that the natures which were gathered together into the true union were different from one another';[26] and thence you bring forth those matters which come out of your own heart when you assert: 'So, then, if the natures are gathered together into a union, is it necessary for us to speak of them as two natures united'?[27] For that man deserves to be believed rather than your opinion or your soothsaying, as though he were explaining himself, and saying: 'Now one Christ and Son and Lord is understood from the two (natures), not as if the difference, but rather the separation of the natures were taken away on account of the union.'[28] With understanding indeed let us add this: for the natures from which comes the one Christ are in fact different, inasmuch as divinity and humanity are not the same. But we do not make their difference a cause of duality, in that they are gathered together into the union; for from them Emmanuel is composed. For the teacher cries aloud: 'Cease from dividing the natures after the union!'[29] However, this command that we should not divide the natures does not mean that we should affirm (as you yourselves affirm) that the two natures are united; but it means this – that we should affirm one incarnate nature, as he himself (Cyril) says. For he declares as follows (just as he also asserts above when he says): 'So just as everything is spoken of the one person – for one nature is recognized as existing after the union, namely that of the Word (p. 21) incarnate.'[30] Thus these words 'after the union' were said not with reference to distinction. It is not the case, as certain people supposed as a result of this, that before the union there were two natures of Christ; for these words are the words of a drunken mind, and mere twaddle.

For indeed before the union and the incarnation, the Word was simple and incorporeal; but when, according to the Scripture, it pleased him to become flesh, that is, to be united to flesh which possessed a rational soul; then, from that conception, God the Word was incarnate and yielded himself for our sake to our composition in a manner inconceivable and inexpressible and as he himself alone knew. For we do not set up the human nature separately, in the manner of the foolish Nestorians, and then make God the Word dwell in it afterwards. For this would constitute an indwelling, and not incarnation; with the consequence that God would not be incarnate and made man, but rather there would be found a man inspired by God, a Christ. For indeed when we examine things altogether, we know that the divinity is one thing and the humanity another, and that they are greatly distant from one another. But when we consider the divine union, that is to say, the incarnation as conceivable for us, we see that out of two, divinity and humanity which are perfect, is composed Emmanuel in a union which is indivisible. And this is what was meant by the holy Cyril: 'Leave off from dividing the natures after the union', that is, after we have affirmed the union.

TEXTS 2 AND 3

The following two texts set the scene for Severus's argument against the selective use which the compiler(s) of the *Florilegium Cyrillianum* made of the writings of Cyril of Alexandria in order to prove that Cyril was close to a two-nature christology and that the definition of Chalcedon could be read in a Cyrillian sense.

Text 2 *Philalethes*, from prologue and ch. 1

Translated from *CSCO* 68:158–63

(p. 158) So then, since investigation of these people has been undertaken earlier, and all the treachery of their evil cunning has been disclosed, I now proceed to the refutation of this accusation, persuading my hearers of this one thing: that they have in mind those things which we have just now rehearsed before, inasmuch as they openly state (p. 159) of what kind of opinion is the compiler of this book or, rather, of this network of perdition. He has made a compilation out of some treatises of the holy Cyril, entirely changing them in the process to fit his own doctrine, imagining that they support his iniquitous teaching; while others of them he has wilfully mutilated – all those which perfectly demonstrate the meaning of what has been said, and which were able to reprove his cunning.

Now we must at present begin the account by finding fault, and rightly so, with the definition of those who were assembled at Chalcedon, and who defined and affirmed that our one Lord Jesus Christ is recognized in two natures as follows: FROM THE DEFINITION CHAPTER 1: 'One and the same Jesus Christ our Lord, the only-begotten, is recognized in two natures, without confusion, without change, without separation, without division.'[31] After quoting this chapter, the wicked defender of evil doctrines (as a support for his own, as he supposes) cites a statement of St Cyril from the first letter to Succensus, which goes as follows: 'Now when we contemplate the manner of the incarnation, as I have said, we see that the two natures are gathered together with one another in a union which is indivisible, without confusion, without change. For the flesh is flesh and not divinity, even though it has become the flesh of God. And in the same way also the Word is God and not flesh, even though he has made the flesh his own according to divine dispensation.'[32] After he has quoted these words and has removed those which occur in the middle, he cites the text as follows, while cutting out other parts from the same (p. 160) discourse: 'We say that there are two natures, but one Christ and Son and Lord, of the Word of God who was incarnate and was made man.'[33] Now the things in the middle which have been left out are those very things which perfectly demonstrate Cyril's teaching. He states that out of the union of the two natures there is but one nature of the Word who is incarnate, such that he is 'out of two natures' and not 'in two natures', as those who were at Chalcedon defined Emmanuel to be. CYRIL: 'When, therefore, we contemplate this, we do not in any way detract from the concurrence of one nature with the other, when we affirm that the union has come about "out of two natures". And after the union we do not separate the natures one from another; neither do we divide into two sons him who is one and indivisible; but we affirm one Son in the same way as the Fathers asserted: one nature of the Word incarnate. So then, in so far as it is proper to see with the mind and the eyes of the soul alone the manner in which the only-begotten was made flesh, we affirm two natures which were united; or, in accordance with what is known from certain writings, we declare that the two natures have been united but there is one Christ and Son and Lord, that Word of God who was incarnate and was made man. And if it seems good, let us take as example our own composition through which we are constituted as human beings. For we are composed of soul and body, and we discern two natures – the one that (p. 161) of the body, the other that of the soul – but one human being from the two of them in union. And the fact that we are composed out of two natures does not make us consider that single individual as two human beings, but as one man by the composition of soul and body, as I have described. But if we take away (the doctrine) that the one unique Christ is out of two natures, and different natures to boot, although he is without division after the union, those who fight against orthodoxy would say: "If he is entirely one nature, how did he become man, and make the flesh his own?" '[34]

Behold, it is plainly shown that St Cyril was affirming that from the union of the two natures there came about one nature of the Word not, however, of the discarnate Word, but of the Word incarnate. And he added that we see only with the eyes of the soul the manner in which the only-begotten was made man. We see two natures which have been united; but, after we have accepted the union with our mind, we affirm not two, but one nature incarnate. For the fact that we confess 'out of two natures' elicits the notion of 'one composition'. Therefore we find fault with those who are joined to Chalcedon, because they have rejected the formula 'out of two natures', and have not acknowledged that Christ is one nature of God the Word incarnate; and because their amazing defenders, in adducing the arguments of St Cyril, everywhere mutilate both this formula 'out of two natures' and the one nature affirmed of the incarnate Word as has been stated in what has just now been quoted. For in like fashion they also mutilate something they adduce as not stated by the Council of Chalcedon, namely this – the statement that God the Word was hypostatically united to flesh which was possessed of reason.

(p. 162) Now let none of those who are simple be deluded because those who were gathered at Chalcedon acknowledged one and the same Christ and Son; nor let him suppose for this reason that they did not divide him. For it was the custom of those who were infected by these opinions of Nestorius on the one hand to affirm hypocritically the Son as one and the same by reason of the equality of the title of sonship or of fellowship, and on the other to confess two natures after the union. Now observe what Andrew says in what he wrote by way of complaint against the tenth anathema of St Cyril: 'For the sonship after the union exists in their two natures, since they are not separated one from another. For there was no separation after the union: for the union is enduring, for ever. But in fact even in the sufferings of the flesh the Godhead was not distant, while it itself continued without suffering; and those things which were proper to the Godhead were accomplished through the agency of the flesh. For that reason we confess one and the same Son, the natures remaining without confusion; and we do not affirm that he is one thing and another (God forbid!), but one and the same.'[35]

While up to this juncture he has spoken deceitfully, he has also said at the start that the sonship is one 'in two natures', and has demonstrated his point of view: he supposes that the common property of sonship is the union of the two natures; then, from that point on without danger, he has introduced its sequel as he supposed it to be – once the two natures are set in place, he acknowledges one and the same Christ, like one who fears that perhaps when he spoke these things obscurely, it would have been supposed by people that he was in truth affirming one Son! But he reveals the falsehood in what comes after it, for immediately (p. 163) after what has been quoted he adduces (the following): ANDREW: 'There is none who does not confess our Lord Jesus as our *high priest and apostle* (Heb 3: 1) according to the Scriptures, without the man who was born of woman being separated from the Word who is from the Father in such a way that he who was of the seed of David was united, without confusion and incomprehensibly and inseparably, to the Word who is from the Father.'[36] Thus he who is of the seed of David is other, apart from, the Word who is from God the Father, and not the same. And how has he all of a sudden changed for us the natures into persons, namely the Word who is from the Father, and the one who is of the seed of David? The reason is near at hand, namely, that they are united, for 'in two natures the sonship is one'. Therefore it is because of the single title of sonship that the union exists; and not because God the Word was united hypostatically to the flesh which possessed a rational soul. But if you had recognized as one and the same the one who was generated from the Father in respect of the Godhead, and the one in the flesh as from the seed of David, you would have recognized him as Christ, the Word who was incarnate for our sake, and you would not have said that he was united to himself. For that is madness! Likewise, no-one thinks it sensible to say that every individual human being is united to himself! Indeed there are things out of which a man exists which are united together, and the union of these things perfectly forms a single individual. But after he has once been completely formed as a single being, it is no longer sensible to say that he is united to himself. So it is evident that those who were gathered at Chalcedon declared vainly, and as it were with trickery, and in appearance only, that they were affirming that the Christ and Son is unique and the same, since they affirm two natures after the union, in view of the fact that they define one Christ in two natures.

Text 3 *Philalethes*, prologue to florilegium

Translated from *CSCO* 68: 183–5

(p. 183) Thus far the chapters of the inspired utterances of Cyril which this robber of the sanctuary has quoted at the beginning of his book, as a defence of those who are joined to Chalcedon. Now we move on from this, to those remaining items which he has also quoted in order, first writing a preceding title for each item which makes known the wicked intention of his doctrine. His treatise is set out in the preceding title in this fashion: TITLE WHICH PRECEDES: *Different arguments of Cyril, archbishop of Alexandria, in which it is possible to find the difference of the two natures, and in which God the Word is preached by him as being impassible and immortal, the temple, however, as being passible and mortal.*

THE REFUTATION OF THIS. If you had the aim of making a defence of the Synod of Chalcedon, (p. 184) the title which precedes ought to have been an indicator of this kind: that St Cyril affirmed two natures after the union when he defined one Lord Jesus Christ in two natures. For it is not because he acknowledged differences in the natures from which Emmanuel exists that from then on (according to your opinion) he divides into two natures that which is one, so that the temple (as you allege) is separately acknowledged as mortal while God the Word is apart from it and separately immortal, the one being mortal and the other immortal, and the one being passible and the other impassible. But the divinely inspired Doctors of the church did not think like this. Rather, they recognized the same as impassible and the same as passible. For even though the Word according to his nature was impassible, nonetheless he experienced suffering, because he had as his own a passible body to which he was hypostatically united. So then, do not take the difference of the natures out of which Christ is one as a division. For it is one thing to say two in this sense, as referring to division; but it is another to recognize the difference of those things out of which he as one is assembled.

Of St Cyril, from the defence of the third anathema against the objections of Theodoret: 'Far indeed from all blame is the one who acknowledges perhaps that the flesh according to its own nature apart from the Word who shone forth from the Father is one thing; and on the other hand that the only-begotten, by reason of his own particular nature, is another thing. But that he should recognize these things does not mean that he divides the natures (p. 185) after the union.'[37]

TEXTS 4 AND 5

In the following two extracts we see Severus's method in the *Philalethes*: he cites each chapter of the *FlorCyr* before proceeding to a defence of Cyril's words, in order to stress the one incarnate nature of Christ. Severus's proof-texts from Cyril come in the main from the Alexandrian's later writings, rather than from his earlier works, where two-nature terminology was used against the Arians and Synousiasts.

Text 4 *Philalethes,* florilegium ch. 8

Translated from *CSCO* 68: 197–202

(p. 197) The opponent's eighth chapter. Of the same Cyril, from the letter to John, archbishop of Antioch, of which this is the beginning: *Let the heavens rejoice and let the earth exult* (Ps 95: 11). 'So then we confess our Lord Jesus Christ, Son of God, only-begotten, perfect God and perfect man, of rational soul and body, who was begotten of the Father before the ages as touching his divinity, and at the end of days the same for our sake and for our salvation begotten of the virgin Mary as touching his humanity, consubstantial with the Father in respect of divinity: for there was a union of the two natures. Therefore we confess one Christ, one Son, one Lord. According to this doctrine of union without confusion, we confess the holy virgin to be Mother of God, because God the Word was incarnate and made man; and from that conception he was united to the temple which was assumed from her. Now as concerns the evangelical and apostolic expressions about the Lord: we know that the theologians make some of them of general purport as referring to one person (*prosopon*), but make distinction among others as referring to the two natures; and those which are proper to God they assign to Christ's divinity, while those proper to low estate they assign to the humanity. When we encountered holy expressions like these and thus found as well that we were of the same mind – *for there is one Lord, one faith, and one baptism* (Eph 4: 5) – we gave thanks to God the Saviour of us all, rejoicing one with another, that the churches among us and among you rightly understand the faith which is according to the inspired Scriptures and the tradition of the holy Fathers.'[38]

DEFENCE OF THIS: When (p. 198) the holy synod was assembled in Ephesus the metropolis, and demanded of Nestorius recantation of his unclean doctrines, and he was summoned three times and did not obey; he persisted in his presumption, and poured out blasphemous utterances against those who were sent to him, and at the same time, moreover, he did not restrain his unbridled tongue. At that point the blessed meeting of all these bishops – when they set out his poisonous doctrines in public, and demonstrated to everyone their Jewish character, and tested as it were in a crucible his discourses which he had delivered in the church to those under his authority, and had shown up their abomination through the rational fire of investigation – passed a just sentence against his atheistic language, and dismissed the rogue from the honour of pastoral superintendence. But the bishops of the East, since they had voluntarily abstained from this holy synod (because they were contending on behalf of Nestorius's unclean doctrine and shared communion with all) were not in any way willing to consent to the degradation of this evil demon. And as to the expression 'Mother of God', many of them either did not at all desire to say it of the holy virgin or, when they were compelled to say it, added that she must also be called 'mother of man' in accordance with this vacuous terminology of Nestorius and, by way of these vicious doctrines, proceed towards a duality of sons and Christs. And when Theodosius (whose end was that of a God-fearing man) at that time advised and wrote to them to come back into communion and unity with the other bishops, they said: 'On the contrary! we accept that we should consent to the degradation of Nestorius, and that we should cherish communion with the bishops, only if all the writings of holy Cyril be destroyed along with the doctrine (p. 199) common to them all, because along with these treatises there would be destroyed as well the refutation of Nestorius's unclean teachings.'[39] Now when the holy Cyril did not even admit his ears to this demand, and they stepped down from their unequal and irrational conflict, sending to Alexandria Paul bishop of Emesa (this city which belongs to Lebanon of Phoenicia) bearing a document of reconciliation in which all the bishops of the East, after they had put far away the empty terminology of Nestorius, they confessed with mighty voice the holy virgin to be Mother of God, and one Son and Christ, the same who was begotten of the Father in respect of divinity, and the same begotten of Mary the virgin in respect of the flesh. So when the holy Cyril came upon these statements as it were in a net, he readily made peace with them and wisely took charge of the net for himself. For he also demanded of them that they consent to the degradation of Nestorius, and that they declare anathema the vanity of the unclean terminology. In the writings of St Cyril himself, I declare, there is confirmation of this. Now when they had thus acknowledged these things, he accepted from then on as being without danger these phrases which featured in bungling fashion in the document of reconciliation, as if they were words of children who prattle, so that by way of prattling along with them he might elevate them to purer modes of expression.

So that we do not devise these things out of our own mind, we demonstrate them from the writings of St Cyril themselves. [Two citations from Cyril's letter to Acacius of Melitene follow.]

(p. 201) So then, after the holy Cyril's report that the union has taken away the separation into two, and has perfected one nature of God the Word incarnate which shows only those things from which there exists the one and sole Christ without confusion and without dividing into a duality those things which have been united into one, how do you, dissolving that which is one, affirm two natures after the union? But again, perhaps, you declare: 'Why then do you mention the statements which are quoted in the document of reconciliation of the Easterners?' These are the things which (I mean): 'Regarding the evangelical and apostolic statements which relate to the Lord, we know that God-inspired men treat some of them as common relating to one person, but distinguish others of them as relating to the two natures: those which are proper for God they ascribe to the divinity of Christ, but those which refer to lowliness they refer to the humanity.'[40] You have uttered gross statements, which are typical of people who are sick. Do not hide from concern for (your) healing. For as regards the distinguishing of the evangelical and apostolic statements, it is not acceptable that these should be divided in this way between the two natures, as one might allot some of them to the divine nature alone, others of them only to the human nature. But since there is one nature of the Word incarnate, we recognize a variety of statements, of which some are proper (p. 202) for God, others are spoken in terms of the humanity, and others at the same time indicate the divinity together with the humanity. Because he was God by nature, and because he, truly the same, became man for us, it was necessary that we should have recourse to the two (kinds of) statements, as St Cyril himself somewhere declares.[41] But do not let him for this reason be divided into two natures. For all the statements, of whatever sort they be, refer to a single individual, God the Word who was incarnate for us: for the nature, that of the Word himself who was incarnate, is affirmed as one after the union. So then, let no-one understand the distinguishing of the (evangelical and apostolic) statements as a division, but as an enquiry which merely distinguishes the difference of the expressions, as also the blessed Basil has stated in the discourse *On Faith* or *On the Trinity*, as follows: 'For the abasement (of Christ) to your weakness did not involve any deficiency in the glory of the mighty one. But first perceive how it befits God; then accept according to the economy the words referring to (his) low estate.'[42] [Another citation from Cyril's letter to Acacius of Melitene follows.]

Text 5 *Philalethes*, florilegium ch. 12

Translated from *CSCO* 68: 221–3

The twelfth chapter of the opponent. Of the same Cyril from the letter to Eulogius, *apocrisarius* of Constantinople. This is the beginning of it:

'Some people complain of the statement which the Easterners have made'. 'Now because all the Easterners suppose that we orthodox agree with the evil doctrines of Apollinaris, and are of the opinion that there was no mixture or confusion – for expressions like these are the ones they use, as if God the Word had changed into the nature of flesh, and the flesh had been converted into the nature of the divinity – we had not allowed them to divide into two the one Son (God forbid it!), but only to confess that it was without confusion and without mixture; rather, that the flesh was from the flesh, (p. 222) as that which was assumed from the woman; and that the Word as that which was begotten from the Father was the Word: but there is *one Christ and Son and Lord* (Jn 1: 14), according to John's statement.'[43]

DEFENCE IN RESPECT OF THIS: What are you doing, you fellow in all things rash and unclean? Why in the manner of an impudent dog are you attacking the words of the saint, and in vain tearing at things which have been fittingly expressed? For it is enough for us here again by way of refutation of your abomination to quote the statements which precede the chapter, statements which you have wilfully mutilated. For it is plainly demonstrated from there that, although the flesh which was assumed from the woman is not mixed with the Word, nonetheless he exists as one out of two, and his nature is one, as he who is the Word was incarnate.

OF ST CYRIL, FROM THE LETTER TO EULOGIUS – the matters which are cited before the chapter which the opponent has left out: 'Some people complain of the statement which the Easterners have made and say: "Why, when they have designated two natures, does the Alexandrian agree with it and praise it? Those who hold the opinions of Nestorius say that he, too, is of the same view, and do violence to things of which they have no accurate knowledge". Now to these complainers we must say this: it is not necessary to take flight and abstain from everything which the heretics say, for they acknowledge many things, some of which we also acknowledge. For example, when the Arians affirm that the Father is the creator of all things and Lord, why should it follow from this that we should take flight from confessions of this kind? And so in the case of Nestorius, even when he asserts two natures in (p. 223) acknowledging the difference between the flesh and God the Word. For the nature of the Word is one thing, and that of the flesh another. However, he does not confess along with us the union as well. For uniting these things to one another we confess one Christ, one Son the same one Lord, and therefore a single nature of the Son incarnate, as is also the case in respect of human beings in general. For they exist out of different natures – I mean from the body and the soul. Now both reason and intuition acknowledge this difference; but after we have united them, from that point onwards we produce a single nature, that of "human being". Therefore, the fact that we acknowledge the difference of the natures does not mean that we separate into two the one Christ.'[44]

See, with these statements he plainly tells that the fact that we acknowledge the difference of the natures from which the one Christ is made does not mean that dissolves the union; and that Nestorius does not acknowledge the union like us, inasmuch as he does not acknowledge a single nature, that of God the Word incarnate. How, then, when you have taken away all these things, do you imagine to bring to the discussion the rest of these materials which you have torn away by force? And because of what St Cyril said, (namely) that the natures out of which the one Christ exists were without confusion, are you leading the simple astray so that we confess two natures after the union and acknowledge no longer that from the union a single nature was formed, that of God the Word incarnate?

TEXTS 6–11

The following extracts from *Contra impium Grammaticum* illustrate the theological intent of John the grammarian and the anger and embarrassment which his deft opponent roused in Severus. Text 6 shows John arguing in favour of reconciling Chalcedon and Cyril and of adding the one-nature formula to Chalcedonian language. In Text 7 we see the grammarian cleverly giving preference to the term *ousia* over *physis*, following Basil of Caesarea's Trinitarian language in order to be able to maintain a duality in Christ. Severus is at pains in Text 8 to stress the hypostatic union of the two natures, following Cyril in distinguishing the two natures in Christ after the union only 'in contemplation' (*theoria*) or intellectually. In Text 9 the former patriarch defends the one-nature christology from the charge of introducing mixture and confusion in the union of Christ's two natures, and refuses to admit any talk of 'two' after the union, which, he argues, equates to the Nestorian position. Texts 10 and 11 are a reply to the grammarian's attempt to use Cyril's phraseology of the one-nature christology while still maintaining a duality or doubleness (*diplous/ diple*) in Christ.

Text 6 *Contra impium Grammaticum, Or.* III.12

Translated from *CSCO* 45: 218–28

(p. 218) *Concerning the fact that the wicked one seems to contradict himself when he says that he will not, along with the Easterners, describe the abasement (of Christ) as a conjunction (of natures), and when he declares that they have been in darkness, not agreeing to confess the one nature of the Word incarnate. And concerning the fact that by means of his unclear terminology he displays St Cyril as wavering, blaming us as if we had brought this about; and concerning the fact that, as he wrongly and impudently expounds the text which is in the letter to Eulogius, he makes up a case for understanding the difference of the substance of the natures from which exists the one Christ as referring to a division into two.*

For behold! You are being dislocated in all directions, like those who are cast into the deep sea. And when you decided that St Cyril had not condescended to the Easterners, you wrote that the same Easterners had not submitted so as to affirm the one nature of God the Word incarnate, and therefore 'they had been in darkness' when the wise Cyril said he had written to Eulogius. Now it is right that we should quote your drunken stupidities; for it is right for me to gather together things cited here and there and which stumble over and contend with one another and represent the same things many times turned over and over, and which are never able to stand. (p. 219) GRAMMARIAN: 'But perhaps some will say: see, as regards the definition, he said that "they were in darkness". But if it had been right to affirm Christ in two natures, he would not have said that they were in darkness. Now it is more necessary to guard against people of this kind than to receive them. And it is to be observed from the things which they cite how they constantly cut to pieces the meaning of the things said, and hunt out little tit-bits which are far removed from the intention of the people who said them. For he does not say that they had been in darkness with regard to the fact that they acknowledge two natures: for it would have been folly, and folly in no small measure, for him to praise and then disparage the same thing. But because the Easterners, while noisily stating that there are two natures in Christ, would not agree to speak of one nature incarnate, but were for a long time contradicting and denying the formula, since for them it was under suspicion to such an extent that the blessed Cyril, who was defending and explaining the formula, was suffering immense weariness because of this, as he points out in the second letter to Successus – because of this, when he saw their contention, he said that they were in darkness: not because of their confession as it was stated, but because of their ignorance of the fact that they should affirm one nature of the Word incarnate. Now he makes it known that this formula was straightforwardly proclaimed by him, and indicates that it was of the same force, in the very same sentences which he utters, as follows (for I shall repeat them): "But from that time onwards there was one Son, and one nature of him as of the Word incarnate. The Easterners acknowledged these things, although they were briefly in darkness as regards the formula".[45] Those men, he declares, acknowledged our views and came to the same mind, even though through the use of other terminology they were in darkness and did not recognize that our formula (p. 220) was in agreement with them in the same particulars. Therefore he was not refusing to speak of two natures, but sought that he should acknowledge one nature incarnate in flesh which was animated with a rational soul. So you yourselves are in darkness even now, while the Easterners are enlightened and confess with equity and integrity both formulae.'[46]

So then, in these matters you acknowledge along with us that the Easterners were then in darkness, since they were not agreeing to admit that there is one nature of God the Word incarnate. For that reason, since they had composed a statement which was deprived of this definition, the wise Cyril accepted it. How, then, did he not humble himself when he did this, so as to show the way to those who were in darkness, or rather, in accordance with your expression, to heal those who were blind? How did he not appear like a huckster, and a pliant one to boot, when he accepted their statement which was bereft of this principal formula? For you have also written in this wicked pamphlet these things: GRAMMARIAN: 'For in this letter the blessed Cyril wrestles only against those who do not accept the affirmation "one nature of God the Word incarnate", but who accept only the formula "in two natures", which is a token of a bad confession of faith if it is absent from the other confessional formula, as has been shown.'[47] AND AGAIN: 'Oh! the impudence of the opponents! For if we were affirming two natures and were never acknowledging the other confessional formula that there is one nature of the Word incarnate, there would be a reason for their accusations.'[48] AND FURTHER: 'For this reason blessed Cyril was accepting also those who affirm two natures for Emmanuel, since he was shunning the heresy of Apollinaris, and was furthermore acknowledging that he should affirm one nature of God (p. 221) the Word incarnate on account of the excommunication of Nestorius. For when the two of them are acknowledged, it is a sign of orthodox doctrine; but when the one confessional formula is thrust aside, the evil supposition of heresy enters in.'[49]

So then, as you have said, there is an indication of madness (see above) in the Easterners' letter, which was distant from that confession which acknowledges that there is one nature of God the Word incarnate, and which was defiled by 'the supposition of an evil heresy', as you have said. Why, then, did he accept this insane letter? And if it was insane, how will you not be caught out again as contradicting yourself – you who write and declare: 'the wise Cyril recognized their formulae as his own'? For call to mind these fair words: GRAMMARIAN: 'So that great and God-inspired man rejoiced in writing and recognized those things as his own, so that he marvelled and uttered praise, and began with this statement so worthy of hearing: "*Let the heavens rejoice and the earth leap for joy*" (Ps 95: 1).[50] Truly did he rejoice in this word, and did not know how he might employ that rejoicing.'[51]

And how might he rejoice by the betrayal of the faith, as you have described it, and by huckstering of words? For we ourselves should blame him and bring an accusation through your words. For how was it that he accepted the Easterners' document in which (as you have alleged) there is an indication of insanity because acknowledgement of one nature of the Word incarnate is absent from it, and since it therefore offers 'an evil suspicion of heresy' (as you wish to call it), namely the excommunication of Nestorius on whose account (as you have said) he was acknowledging that there was one nature of the Word incarnate? (p. 222) So then, why do you introduce him as rejoicing, when he should have been feeling ashamed? Thus in due course your own words are turned back upon your stupid head: for we too pronounce against you these things of your own, which run as follows: GRAMMARIAN: 'You try to show us a father of orthodox teachings who is in fact changeable, different at different times, and one who destroys his own building. For who is there who acts so entirely impiously that, in order to gratify other people, or rather to injure them as well, he drags himself as well into the pit and removes[52] faith from the faith? Who out of those people who understand things aright arrives at such a pitch of haughtiness as to separate himself from God, so as to be at one with human beings?'[53]

Do you understand how senseless you are, and into what ludicrous emptiness of mind the silliness of your lamentable and ignorant words plunges? As for you, now, receive dishonour because of this – and absolutely rightly so! But Cyril, wise in spirit and in no way pliant, who neither took a bribe nor sold the faith for the sake of human friendship, but who was a wise physician and teacher who was glad about the Easterners' confession, in that they acknowledged one and the same Son, Christ Jesus, and the holy virgin as Mother of God without having added 'mother of man' – as Theodoret, who was sick with the same things as Nestorius, was anxious to say (along with those who were in communion with him) in the complaints he wrote about the Twelve Chapters, and slanderously affixed to them a defect – (this Cyril) was glad about these things and rejoiced because they declared 'for the union came about of two natures',[54] and not 'through equality of title' nor 'through equality of honour' nor 'of one person and one (p. 223) sonship'. But since they allowed for an intermediate position in respect of confession of the union, they provided a place for drawing towards a true and hypostatic union by interjecting those things which he written to them, (the phrase) 'out of two natures', and clearly and openly proclaiming and declaring: CYRIL: 'For the Lord Jesus Christ is one, even though there be recognized the distinction of the natures out of which we affirm that the inexpressible union has been effected.'[55] For from now on, the nature of the Son incarnate and made man is fully perfected as being one, such that only by means of fine contemplation and distinction in thought, and as it were by refined imaginings of the mind, may we observe that there has been a union of two natures; yet after recognition of the union, as if the distinction of the two natures which is (perceived) by thought has already been removed and dissolved, the distinction of those natures which have been brought together into one is not confused – because they have been established in composition and not in the individual property of their subsistence. Let us believe and truly accept one who is out of two natures, both God and Son and Christ and Lord; and let there remain in duality that which, after the confession of the true union, is indeed a thought of those things which are covered in darkness and which affirm that the same entity is both united and not united. {This argument is supported by a citation from Cyril's letter to Eulogius.}

(p. 224) To whom of those people who are mightily famed for intelligence, or who are impudent, are these things not known or made plain? The things which are joined together are recognized as one thing and another only in respect of difference of essence; and the things which concur into one entity are different in kind, and not of the same substance, and they no longer subsist separately, nor are they in their proper substance to be spoken of as one thing and another; for there exists one Christ out of the two of them. For the teacher plainly stated as much, repressing the difference which was whole and entire, and establishing it as a difference in respect of substance:

CYRIL: 'The body is not consubstantial with the Word; but if it is not consubstantial, there is always one nature and another out of which the one and only Christ is recognized.'[56] In the same way, too, I have introduced him in the notes above as saying this: 'So then the diversity in these things makes clear to us only the distinction between the nature of the Word and the nature of the humanity; for the one Christ is recognized from the two of them.'[57]

So when those who were assembled at Chalcedon repudiated the definition 'one Christ from two natures' which alone forbids division of any sort, where then, O grammarian, does presumption provide a place for you (p. 225) to introduce talk of 'one thing' and 'another thing', so as to affirm two natures after the union, and to devise a pretext for distinction in substance so that you may divide into two him who is constituted as one from two, and cast him into a duality of sons and Christs? For (the view) that those things out of which Christ exists are 'one thing' and 'another thing' we have heard that even Gregory the Theologian wrote to Cledonius.[58] But if we dissolve the formula 'from which' by declaring two natures after the inexpressible union, we import natures which subsist separately and apart; then no longer are found 'one thing' and 'another thing' from which exist one nature and hypostasis of the Son who was incarnate and made man, but one being and another being, God and man, who are separate as regards hypostases.

For in the same way the wise Cyril rises up even against Diodore, who devised a pretext for total difference and complete separation in regard to the diversity of the natures which were assembled into one, out of which Emmanuel exist (as we also have noted above). [Two citations from Cyril's work against Diodore of Tarsus follow.]

(p. 226) How then is it, O most wretched man, that alongside diversity of attributes you drag in a difference of substance – and this on the grounds that those things different in kind which concurred into one in a manner beyond all expression are separated by reason of natural quality, so as to perfect one nature and hypostasis incarnate of the Word out of two (natures) – and affirm two natures after the union, and write concerning the holy Cyril exactly as if what you were writing were sound, but without knowing what you are saying? GRAMMARIAN: 'Nor did he refuse to affirm the two natures; for the one is of the Word, and the other of the flesh.'[59] For this man is entirely removed from refusal to speak of two natures, as he indeed says: a union not of two things only, but of many which differ in nature from one another is referred to as a 'conjunction'; and those who say what I have said, and the Easterners, understand that the union of the two natures came about in this way. For when what is composite is separated by the mind alone, it yields to the understanding the two things out of which it is put together as one; but when the union has been acknowledged, we no longer separate the things which have been united, nor do we speak of them as two; otherwise we fall into darkness by defining the same thing as both united and separated in hypostasis. This is what happened to the Easterners, who were covered in darkness in respect of the formula and on the one hand acknowledged a union of two natures (p. 227) while on the other they left it covered in obscurity. For this is the darkness of the formula which he dissipated when he wrote to them. CYRIL: 'For the Lord Jesus Christ is one, even though there be recognized a difference of the natures out of which we affirm that the inexpressible union was made.'[60] Now that phrase 'out of two' is characteristic of the hypostatic union; and the final end of this is the one nature of God the Word incarnate.

But if, as the grammarian says, Cyril had wished that we should acknowledge two natures after the incomprehensible union which were united and not separated, he ought to have said: 'But, once the union has been acknowledged, no longer are those things which are united separated from one another, but already constitute one Son; and his two natures are united and not separated.' But now he did not say this – never and in no way at all did he say it; but when separation into two has already ceased, as it were, after the reckoning of the union, he declared: CYRIL: 'But when the union has been acknowledged, no longer are the things which were united separated from one another, but there is already one Son and one nature of him as of the Word who was incarnate.'[61] And as I have many times asserted, nowhere at all can anyone show that St Cyril wrote: 'so then after the union we declare that there are two natures united'; but everywhere he says that the two are recognized by thought alone and by theoretical distinction; and that those things which were joined together are distinct in substance; but after the reckoning of the union, one nature was perfectly formed and it subsisted, that of the Word incarnate, yes, rather, one Christ and Son and Lord out of two, divinity and humanity.

But the grammarian, who thinks he is crafty and difficult (p. 228) to refute, twists to his own impious use those very matters which have been asserted correctly, and produces a statement as it were out of topsiturviness and declares: GRAMMARIAN: 'But perhaps they will say: Behold, as regards the formula they were in darkness. But if it had been correct to speak of Christ in two natures, he would not have said that they were in darkness.'[62] Now then, you wicked man, who knows nothing else at all but how to act impiously and to be openly without sense and to lie, prove that the Easterners affirmed that Christ is recognized 'in two natures' as the Synod of Chalcedon defined! But you cannot prove it, since this alone did they declare: 'the union was of two natures', as a result of which the teacher said that the one Christ was perfected from two (natures) – and not, as the Synod which was at Chalcedon agreed, one Christ recognized 'in two natures'.

Text 7 *Contra impium Grammaticum, Or.* II.17

Translated from *CSCO* 58: 151–6

For you exalt the duality of the natures, which divides the one Christ into two, to the level of 'substances' according to the common signification of that term; and you affirm that those have been united in hypostasis, that is, 'hypostatically', to use your own expression again. Explain to us, then, how these 'substances' – I mean what is common property of the divinity and what is common property of the humanity – are 'hypostatically' united and are compounded to one another and are perfected as one hypostasis: for thus you have declared above when you produce a definition: GRAMMARIAN: 'Therefore when the Fathers put "nature" on its own without adding "of God the Word", then they understand "substance".'[63] And furthermore, in the statements which precede these matters – indeed, straightaway with the introductory words of this astonishing pamphlet, you said things like these: GRAMMARIAN: 'So, therefore, when St Cyril says "nature" on its own without adding "of God the Word", he is pointing to the common property of the divinity.'[64] Therefore when we follow your eleven definitions, we understand these expressions of yours, and are not voluntarily silent. But when you assert (p. 152) without definition and without any addition that those two natures of yours were hypostatically united, we understand what is the common property of the substances, as you ordered. Again, we ask Your Intelligence: how is what is common property of the divinity (which is recognized in the Trinity) compounded with what is common to, and the whole substance of, the humanity? For composition is the union which takes place in the assumption of the humanity, and which is also designated as incarnation. For you wrote: GRAMMARIAN: 'When we affirm "two natures hypostatically united", they keep silent of their own will and erase from our confession this (expression) "united hypostatically".'[65]

Behold, with open ears we have heard these (statements) of yours, and we accepted 'natures' when they were mentioned without definition as referring to 'substances' and what is signified as common, that is: the holy Trinity as concerns the Godhead, and the whole family of human beings as regards the humanity. And you are caught up in your snares, entrapped in those things which were written by us in the letter to Maron in these words: SEVERUS: 'For they shall not advance to this madness, so as to declare that they are using the terms "natures" instead of generic signification – I mean signification of substance. For if, as is acknowledged henceforward, the holy Trinity is one nature, and the whole of humanity is of one nature, then (to say something which is more than ridiculous) the holy Trinity will be found to have assumed as human nature the whole of humanity, that is to say, the whole human race! But the holy Scriptures teach us otherwise. They teach that God the Word was incarnate and assumed human nature as only one out of three hypostases, since "the Word was made flesh, and dwelt among us" (Jn 1: 14).'[66] Since you read these things, my good man, how was it that you did not guard against ridicule, (p. 153) but go on to say that the hypostatic union is out of two substances according to common and generic signification? And this alone remained – that you should change the wickedness of your senseless opinion so as to put it (as it were) in the form of an objection, and try to dissolve it by means of the most deceitful ideas which you had incorrectly built up, and again rely in tottering manner on things which had been dissolved. So then, this objection, and the clever dissolving of the objection brought about by your subtle erudition, shall be set forth: GRAMMARIAN: 'But if you affirm that the Christ has two substances, it is also necessary to affirm that the Father and the Spirit and (as we may say in short) the holy Trinity himself assumed the flesh of the whole of humanity, that is, of the human race. Such are the objections of the people who oppose us. For they suppose that the substance of the divinity exists divisibly, and that some of it is seen in the Father, some of it in the Son, and some of it in the holy Spirit, such that each single element is recognized from the hypostases in part, but not in all those things which are the property of the divinity. But we have not reached such ungodliness as to suppose that there is division or partition in the divine substance; but we affirm that each designated hypostasis possesses without diminution all the marks of the divinity – goodness, operation, and all those things which are of uncreated nature. For likewise we affirm the Trinity consubstantial, such that the same substance is recognized perfectly in three persons. For indeed the Father possesses the perfect substance of divinity, and also the Son and the holy Spirit in the same manner; hence the Father is perfect God and the Son is perfect God and the holy Spirit is perfect God. The proclaimer of the truth, Paul, is the defender of these (p. 154) when he states, *"for in him dwells all the fullness of the divinity bodily"* (Col 2: 9). For he does not say that the Father was incarnate, but that the whole divinity in three hypostases was without diminution in the Father, in the Son, in the holy Spirit, since he is in each one of the hypostases completely according to the word of our Saviour which he uttered: "all things which are the Father's are mine", that is, all the marks which belong to the substance of the Father belong also to God the Word, even when he was incarnate, not as if the Father is the Son, or as if the Son is the Father, for these titles signify that there is a relationship of the one to the other. So how, then, shall we not affirm that the substance of the divinity was in Christ without diminution, when we assert that he is perfect God? And how, when we confess him as perfect man, shall we not acknowledge that the whole substance of humanity was in him? For he did not assume part of it[67], as Apollinaris claims – flesh without a rational soul – but the whole substance, which is flesh ensouled with a rational soul and with understanding: for this is properly called "substance" when it perfectly exists in general in each and every human being. For each of them is distinguished from one another not by substance, but by those characteristics which are in accord with them, by size and by colour and, generally speaking, by the individual characteristics of personal marks.'[68]

So then, in regard to these things we state as follows: the holy Trinity is neither subjected to the limitations of nature, nor confined by the preferences of our mind, because what it is in terms of substance is not known; and it is above all things and above all intelligence, and is not apprehended even by the motions of our mind; but it surpasses in a manner incomprehensible every intellectual imagining, and it overflows and lies concealed. (p. 155) For in the second theological discourse, Gregory, who has the name of Theologian, declares: GREGORY: 'For one kind of limitation is also comprehensibility.'[69] For this reason, the thoughts most refined in accuracy and considered and profound elevate it[70] above substance and above nature. For this Theologian himself declares, in fact in the discourse *On the Unity of Monks*: 'The best of those things which exist and the most elevated is God, unless one wishes to elevate him above substance and to place within him every existent thing out of which other things come to be.'[71] And in the discourse in which is written the words 'to those who had voyaged from Egypt' he wrote: 'I recognize two different principles in the things that exist: authority, and slavery, things among us which neither arbitrary rule has torn asunder nor poverty has put asunder; but they are things which nature, if it pleases one so to call it, has defined: for what is first is also above nature.'[72]

So then the Trinity, which is before all things and more perfect than all things, is above substance and above nature, and is not subject to these designations. But, as the teacher states in the aforementioned discourse *On Theology,* because 'our mind toils to depart from corporeal things and to be joined to incorporeal simplicities, as long as in its weakness it observes things which are beyond its strength',[73] of necessity we dare through the thoughts and poor pretexts that beset us to draw near to divine significations, that from thence we may receive obscure intimations of understanding, small though they be.

Hence even about the holy Trinity, which is incomprehensible and which no-one (p. 156) may approach, we have used the word 'nature' and 'substance' and 'hypostasis' and all these terms which are similar and approximate in sense; and we accepted the word 'substance', which is indicative of generic signification concerning the holy Trinity; and we affirmed that the one substance is three hypostases of the Father and of the Son and of the holy Spirit, that is, of the one God. For the Father is God, and the Son is God, and the holy Spirit is God, just as one might say that Peter and Paul and John are one humanity. For human beings exist equally in species and in substance, but are distinguished by the individual signs of hypostases. Therefore every one of the hypostases which are under species and substance and under common signification (for this 'common signification' is the defining substance of many hypostases) share in those things which appear in the general species equally. For example, Peter shares in what is common property of humanity and of substance, which is rationality, mortality, receptivity of mind, and ability to learn; in the same way also Paul and John, distinct with individual characteristics and not mixed up one with another, are also sharers of this substance which is held in common, since they are rational and mortal and receptive of mind and capable of learning. For neither rationality and mortality and receptivity of mind and ability to learn are established for each one of the hypostases which subsist distinctly and separately, because substance too is patient of division: for the division of substance is what may be one of diverse substance out of hypostases, whether irrational or immortal or not receptive of mind or not capable of learning; for it is drawn from the substance and generic class, and separates what is common to hypostases of the same class when it does not possess similarity in every respect.

Text 8 *Contra impium Grammaticum, Or.* II.22

Translated from *CSCO* 58: 184–8

(p. 184) *How the formula 'Christ is acknowledged and affirmed out of two natures or hypostases' allows both the contemplation of the difference of those things which without deficiency are brought together into one to be observed in their composition by thought alone; and, after the reckoning of the union, avoids any duality which is introduced by the wicked, be it duality of substances, or of persons, or of natures, or of hypostases.*

Now when we affirm that he exists out of two natures or hypostases, separating as it were by thought alone those things from which he exists or is assembled by nature, we mean this: (p. 185) for it is not as if first of all there existed a duality of hypostases which was thus gathered together into one hypostasis, for this is both ignorant and impossible. For how can those things which subsist individually and separately, and exist in duality, be combined into one hypostasis? Now that which subsists as one entity as a result of being compounded without change from things differing from each other in kind and in substance – such as a reality of the sort that a human being represents, of soul and body – exists indeed in one hypostasis, but by means of reason alone allows those who make distinctions to perceive that he is assembled out of two natures, while he does not subsist in two natures or hypostases. For it is not possible to see each entity as it subsists in its own particular subsistence, but only what arises out of the composition of the individual entities, which is perfectly formed as one hypostasis.

Now once again Cyril, wise in spirit, at the same time illuminates and confirms the matter for us; since he demonstrates that, when by subtle contemplation alone we distinguish those things out of which exists the one and sole Christ, we affirm that there was a natural coming together of two natures or hypostases; but when with distinction and division (perceived) as by contemplation we accept that union, we no longer affirm 'two' after the reckoning of the union, because they do not subsist separately and in their particular subsistencies, but out of the two exists one nature and hypostasis of the Word who is incarnate. [This is substantiated by citations from Cyril's letters to Succensus and from his letter to Acacius of Melitene.]

(p. 187) Is it not known to everyone who hears these things that the person is indeed one, that is, one and sole is the Lord and God Jesus Christ, and one is the nature and hypostasis incarnate of the one himself who is the Word? And if one considers those things out of which Christ exists or is naturally composed – as is possible in this matter also through acute contemplation alone and as is lawful to see with the eyes of the mind and by means of reason – he will perceive and gather the difference of the entities which have been assembled together. He sees the natural essence of the two natures and hypostases; and when, at the same time, he is enlightened by the power of the union and finds that those particular subsistencies do not even subsist in composition, but perfectly form one hypostasis and one nature of the Word incarnate, he cannot affirm that those things which are seen by contemplation are two in hypostasis.

For the reckoning of the union turns aside and restrains the power of the separateness,[74] such that the two may no longer be two, but one entity in an inexpressible manner is perfectly formed in composition through the two of them. And the natures, indeed the hypostases, out of which he is assembled appear no less and without change in the union; but it is not possible to recognize either one of them as a person because they do not subsist separately either in the particularity of their subsistence or in duality; but there exists one hypostasis out of the two of them, and one person, and consequently one nature of him who is the Word incarnate.

Behold, we have plainly demonstrated how, when we make the statement 'out of two natures', we do not understand these natures as substances according to the general signification[75] (p. 188) that they hold together many hypostases – in such a way that it be found, according to your wicked humbug, that the holy Trinity was incarnate of the whole of humanity and of the whole human race; but one hypostasis of God the Word which by contemplation alone may be separated, and one hypostasis of flesh rationally ensouled and assembled from the virgin Mother of God, are to be acknowledged without alteration in composition, and that they indeed remained what they were, but not in the particularity of (their) subsistence, as we have declared on many occasions; and they subsisted in the duality of their natures, but by a concurrence into one entity they formed perfectly one nature and hypostasis of the Word incarnate and one person.

Text 9 *Contra impium Grammaticum, Or.* III.14

Translated from *CSCO* 45: 241–52

(p. 241) But it is plain that those people,[76] by keeping silent about proper opinions, erroneously ascribed to these formulae the effect of mixture and confusion, and the folly of the lie of the two natures before the union; since they understood what was said to Nestorius by St Cyril – 'Leave off from separating the natures after the union',[77] and again elsewhere: 'But after the union, when separation into two has already as it were been taken away, we believe there to be one nature of the Son, as of one, but of one made man and incarnate'[78] – as if (these things referred) to an arrangement in some temporal sense. Now that matter is not, as the noise and invective of godless persons would have it, to be associated with the time before the incarnation, as if, before the Word of God had been united (p. 242) to flesh ensouled with a rational soul, there had been two natures and hypostases of Christ; for the very terminology demonstrates this as being the height of godlessness and folly. Rather, it is said as if having regard for the understanding of one who diligently searches for the difference of the natures out of which the one Christ exists, who actually pictures to himself in contemplation and thought these two things which concur into union; but after the reckoning of the union, it is no longer possible to speak of two, because out of two there is one hypostasis and nature of the Word incarnate and made man.

Now St Cyril's voice, loud and clear, shows more clearly than the sun that the matter is so – the voice which proclaims these things just adduced as having formerly been declared in the letter to Acacius, the bishop of Melitene: CYRIL: 'And so as it were in thoughts we take hold of these things out of which exists the one and only Son and Lord Jesus Christ, and indeed believe that the two natures are united; but after the union, as if the distinction into two has already been removed, we believe the nature of the Son to be one as of one, but one incarnate and made man.'[79] AND AGAIN: 'So when the manner of the incarnation is diligently investigated, the human understanding sees, in short, two things joined one to the other inexpressibly and without confusion in the union; however, when they have been united, it does not in any way separate them, but believes and unshakeably accepts that there is one God and Son and Christ and Lord who exists out of the two.'[80]

These things, moreover, we have already stated fully in the preceding paragraphs. But the people who were gathered in Chalcedon determined to reduce to folly the lawful expression of the holy Fathers that 'one Christ is to be acknowledged as one nature and hypostasis out of two, out of divinity and out of humanity', (p. 243) and 'one nature of God the Word incarnate', and added to it this piece of fiction that 'there were two natures before the union and the incarnation', and likewise that there was confusion and mixture; and thus they anathematized the latter. For if this had not been maintained by them, they themselves would also have acknowledged the formulae 'out of two' and 'one is the nature incarnate of God the Word'. For according to those same people, who affirm two natures after a union made up of a title which is fabricated, it is necessary for two natures to be allowed also before the union; and rightly do they think that it is a fable to affirm that there were two natures before a union of this kind and to fabricate one nature after the union. Thus the hypostatic union is set far aside by this lying fable which godless men have dared to add to it out of their own impure teachings. For he shows himself as one who is single and having no part in the flesh before the union with flesh endowed with soul and mind, and before the complete assumption of humanity; and even when he became man he showed himself as one who exists out of two, divinity and humanity; he subsisted exceptionally in an exceptional fashion, and is separated[81] by thought alone and acute mental contemplation. For he is composed in such a way that with the mind's sharp eye we may observe that the joining together[82] is that joining of two sorts of things, different and in no way consubstantial with each other. Furthermore, at the same time he admits the indivisibility of the union, lest we should henceforth speak of two (natures) after the reckoning of the union. For one out of two is the nature and hypostasis of the Word incarnate, which is complete and subsists beyond all wonder.

Now the following matters plainly demonstrate that the filthy squadron of Nestorius was deceitfully adding to these proper expressions the same blameworthy things, (p. 244) which the Chalcedonian synod also added, when it was fighting against the holy Cyril. In fact, at once Nestorius himself, too, asserted these things in memoranda invented by himself at Ephesus, to which he appended a title as follows: *Concerning the matters which came to pass at the Synod of Ephesus, and concerning the cause which gathered it together*: NESTORIUS: 'Is not this believed by some of the followers of Apollinaris or Arius, in the same way that they also mix together the duality of the natures into one nature?'[83] And in the treatise which has the title *On Faith*, or *Explanation of the Faith*, whose opening clause reads: 'We confess the dogma: of the same substance', he wrote as follows: 'But if these theopaschites, reinforcing the party of Apollinaris, say "after the union, there was seen one nature", we must turn our face aside from them with great indignation, because through this, by co-mingling and confusion, they have godlessly removed both natures from their characteristic qualities; and, because it is a matter of concern to themselves, they then allow them to remain in something which is neither divine nature nor human nature, such that through co-mingling and confusion each nature in fact falls away from its own substance, and completely crosses over into another. Now if they assert that the natures are neither co-mingled nor confused, then necessarily there is not one nature, but they are forced to allow that there are two natures of Christ, impassible and passible, and the dogma affirming Christ to be consubstantial to the Trinity in respect of divinity stands firm.'[84]

Now the Chalcedonians, and the people who brag about this cause as advocates of the impassibility of the Godhead, have asserted these matters in a tone agreeing with these same words, as follows: (p. 245) THE SYNOD OF CHALCEDON: 'Now those who introduce confusion and co-mingling, and foolishly imagine that there is one nature of the flesh and of the divinity, also falsely affirm that the divine nature of the only-begotten is passible through confusion.'[85] But they would better have preserved the unchangeableness and impassibility of the Godhead, and we should have known that they had asserted these things against people who confuse into one substance the elements out of which the Christ exists, if they themselves had acknowledged that there is one nature of God the Word incarnate, and had not evidently cast aside this, namely, that the one Christ is affirmed 'out of two natures'.

But it escapes no-one's attention that they have been prepared for battle against these formulae. For Nestorius lays bare the whole form of the hypocrisy, and shows that their entire fight is against those who acknowledge one nature of God the Word incarnate. For in the work which has the title *Against the Theopaschites or Cyrillians,* in the form of a dialogue, he wrote these things which we have already cited in matters examined earlier: NESTORIUS: 'The theopaschite declares: "And how shall we be accused of joining together the duality of the two natures, we who affirm that Christ is one nature of God incarnate?" The orthodox says: "Do you imagine that this very thing of which you are accused constitutes a defence of the things you are accused of? For you have acknowledged the position adopted by yourselves, that Christ is one nature out of the incorporeal and a body and a single-natured hypostasis of the divine enfleshment. Now this represents a confusion of the two natures, since these natures are stripped of the hypostases which they individually possessed when they are mingled one with another."[86] Moreover, just as his mad fiction demands, he introduces above the theopaschite, who says these following things: 'Therefore the nature of the flesh is passible and mutable and recently created; but nonetheless it is so characteristic of the divinity that both subsist in one (p. 246) and the same nature.'[87] For St Cyril, in the fifth book against the blasphemies of Nestorius, adduces that wicked man as writing these things: 'In this place I would wish to learn from the heretics, who co-mingle the nature of the divinity and the humanity into one substance, who is the one handed over to the Jews by the traitor. For if a mixture of both natures has been effected, both at once would have been detained by the Jews, both God the Word and the nature of the humanity.'[88]

See how they construct a complete misrepresentation of co-mingling and confusion against those who affirm one nature of God the Word incarnate, and slanderously assert that one nature, namely the one hypostasis out of two without confusion, is one substance, as if the substances of the divinity and the humanity out of which comes Emmanuel had been confused and co-mingled into the same entity. Moreover, the godless Theodoret as well proceeded along the same path as Nestorius, and wrote to the Nestorians of Constantinople after St Cyril had received the Easterners into communion. [Four citations from Theodoret follow.]

(p. 248) Is there any need for divination and guesswork about those matters, which are plainly declared? For when these man-worshippers began the battle against St Cyril (or rather, against this truth), they were keeping quiet about the formula 'out of two'[89] and were tearing away the word 'incarnate', and by this means were introducing the slander of change and confusion into acknowledgement of the one nature. For behold! the man who wrote these complaints declared in the Twelve Chapters that the poison of such a charge was a reality. And who, among those who follow godly conduct, shall not shrink from the daring falsehood of such a person? For where, in these Twelve Chapters, does there come forward any suspicion of change or confusion or mixture of substances? Furthermore, where, in the individual writings of this man, is it not plainly excluded – not even excepting the third letter to Nestorius, in which the wise Father wrote the Twelve Chapters relating to those matters? But in truth the godless slanderer, who in those (Chapters) stripped the phrase 'one nature' from this statement which is publicly proclaimed as 'out of two not consubstantial with one another, which were inexpressibly gathered together into one' and proclaimed 'incarnate', openly and insolently displayed his deceitful impiety in his filthy discourse, and barked like a dog at these things: THEODORET: 'Then how is the dispenser of life one who is mortal? How then does he who was handed over to death revivify the dead? But, you will say, he rose up, before other men. This also relates to change! Thus he endured a second change: on the one hand, he became a dead man from being God; and then he became God once more from the dead!'[90] AND AFTER OTHER THINGS: 'And they discover some new refuge in the face of the teachings of the truth: for we believe, they declare, in one nature incarnate.'[91] [Citations from the Antiochenes Alexander of Mabbug and Andrew of Samosata follow.]

(p. 251) These slanders against St Cyril – who used to acknowledge Emmanuel as out of two natures and who used to proclaim one nature of God the Word incarnate – Nestorius and supporters of Judaism and of his filthy opinions had devised: 'change; confusion; he made the very Word of God passible; in fact he adds two natures before the union; but he makes one nature after the union by co-mingling, and mixes and confuses the natures.' The Synod of Chalcedon as well added these invectives to the same words when it openly refused to accept that Christ should be truly declared as 'out of two natures'; and in no way upheld writing 'one nature of God the Word incarnate' in its definition. In fact, it shares in the slander with those people, inasmuch as it openly wrote down their objections in the matters which were published by it; but it estranged itself from the perfect confession of St Cyril which set aside the vacuity of their objections. And when it refused the formula 'out of two natures', and when it tore away,[92] and also when it made mention of St Cyril's letters, it did so for the purpose of deceiving and seducing the simple, a matter indeed of amazing cunning, and something especially fitting for censure by the wise.

Text 10 *Contra impium Grammaticum, Or.* III.23

Translated from *CSCO* 50: 20–5

(p. 20) But the grammarian – a Moabite and an Ammonite, and a foreigner to the laws of Israel, for whom indeed it is not lawful to enter into the assembly of the Lord, into the revelation of the teachers which accords with the virtues and into the sincere observance which is opposed to heresy, which preserves the spiritual harmony which is one and the same as the doctrine of the church – declares internal war, and through mindless ignorance he foolishly presumes to find fault with things which are in the sermons that I wrote to Nephalius, as follows: OF THE PATRIARCH FROM WHAT (WAS WRITTEN) TO NEPHALIUS: 'Again, after the sentencing of Nestorius, he is under an indictment that he affirmed that Christ was two-fold, since he declared: NESTORIUS: "I distinguish two-fold natures within

Christ: on the one hand two-fold in respect of nature; on the other single in respect of authority."[93] Now because of this Cyril, in his letter to Nestorius, also seems to be saying: CYRIL: "Now as regards the expressions concerning our Saviour which are in the Gospel, we distinguish (in them) neither two substances nor two persons: for the one and sole Christ is not two-fold, even if being recognized out of two elements he was assembled as a unity without division, in exactly the same way as a human being is recognized (as being) soul and body, and is not particularly two-fold, but one out of the two of them."[94] And again in those writings which are against the blasphemies of Nestorius, he says in the second volume: CYRIL: "For it is not the case that the Word who is from God, in assuming flesh, went forth as a man like us, and for this reason he is dubbed 'two-fold'."[95] And Gregory of Nazianzus, in the sermon concerning the Nativity of Christ, seems not improperly to have treated of the Word himself when he declared: GREGORY OF NAZIANZUS: "Now he was sent, but as a man; for he was two-fold."[96] When he said a little earlier on: "Now when (p. 21) God went forth with the assumption of human flesh, the things which were contrary (to one another) became one out of two." '[97]

Concerning these matters the grammarian is just as we ourselves have stated, in that the disease of Nestorius preceded him – for none of the Fathers nor of the divinely inspired Doctors declared Christ to be two-fold – since he is crazed with the folly of wickedness and ignorance in the same manner as the Greek who is mentioned in the holy Gospels, who was shattering chains and fetters, and was running about among the tombs (cf. Mk 5: 2ff.), running in vain and daring to affirm Christ as two-fold and the Fathers as witnesses of these things. But it is easy to say to that man: 'My good fellow, if you were attentive, you would plainly recognize that this very thing about which you toil and sweat in vain is present with you, already written by us. For when we publicly adduced Gregory, we brought forward with him all the teachers who hold these same opinions, who acknowledge Christ out of two natures, and therefore entitle him two-fold without blame, and not like Nestorius, in the same way that they also acknowledge a man as one person out of two elements and one nature and substance; for without any censure they entitle him also as two-fold. The two-foldness which is applicable to him is perceptible through contemplation, as Gregory himself acknowledged in the homily *On Baptism,* when he writes these things: GREGORY OF NAZIANZUS: "So then, since we are two-fold, I mean (consisting) of soul and body, and the one nature is indeed invisible, and the other visible, the cleansing also is two-fold, I mean by the water and the Spirit, the one assuredly received visibly and corporeally, and the other incorporeally and invisibly happening at the same time." '98

So also the holy John, bishop of Constantinople, in the sermon which has the title *Concerning the Veiled Character* (p. 22) *of the Old Testament,* whose opening expression is: 'The ploughman truly rejoices', declared: JOHN OF CONSTANTINOPLE: 'For this human life is two-fold, since it is compounded of two substances, the one from what is perceived by the senses, the other intellectual – I refer to the soul and to the body – and it has affinities both with heaven and earth: for on the one hand, through the incorporeal substance it has communion with the hosts that are on high; and on the other, through what is perceived by the senses, it is joined to the things which are on earth, since there is a certain, genuine conjunction of the two created orders.'99 AND AFTER A FEW MATTERS: 'Therefore out of two substances has God established us.'100

So then, my fine fellow, show that the Synod which was in Chalcedon defined the one Christ to be out of two natures, so that like those holy Fathers we may learn that 'two-foldness' had been acknowledged and affirmed without censure only as it were by contemplation of the difference of substance of those things which have been joined into one. But if it refused to admit that Christ be spoken of as 'out of two natures', and preferred to define him 'in two natures' neither separated nor divided, it is clear to all that that (synod) knows and understands him as 'two-fold', like Nestorius, who said in the treatise which is entitled *Statement of the Faith* as follows: 'So then, in the two natures we await the Son and judge of us all, at once the same, visible and invisible: visible, that is, insofar as when he assumed our visible substance, he consented that it should be his continually without separation; but invisible in respect of the divine substance in which no human being at all sees him, nor can see him, in accordance with the saying of the divine Apostle (cf. 1 Tim 6: 16).'101 And St Cyril quotes him in the first volume against his blasphemies,102 to the effect that he writes these things as well: (p. 23) NESTORIUS: 'We preserve the one-ness of the sonship in the divine and human nature,'103 AND AGAIN, IN THE SECOND BOOK:104 'The Son is two-fold, not in rank, but by nature.'105

So then why, O grammarian, do you suppose that you will escape agreeing with Nestorius's opinion, inasmuch as you affirm that you acknowledge Christ in two substances? For behold! he himself also (as you yourself observe) expounded the phrase 'in two natures' as 'in two substances'. But if you take refuge in the generic signification by which we understand 'substance' as a compendium of many hypostases, then by the vanity of your reasoning you will be imprisoned in such folly and wickedness as to declare that the substance of the holy Trinity was incarnate in the substance and in the whole *genus* of humanity, a matter which reason by much testing has proved. And these sayings of Gregory the Theologian and the holy John which have been quoted will teach you concerning the composition of our humanity as regards one hypostasis compounded out of two elements, namely, these substances out of which this one entity comes together: not so much to indicate generic things (because composition of things generic does not occur), as to indicate the single soul and the single body out of which one living thing subsists; and it possesses affinity with those things which are in any respect whatever of similar *genus* and similar substance. For he said: JOHN OF CONSTANTINOPLE: 'This living creature man is two-fold, since he is compounded out of two substances.'[106] For they used to employ the generic term 'substance' for the signification of a particular; and whenever the Fathers are accustomed to speak of one particular hypostasis they speak of one substance; and this matter we have demonstrated above in extended discourse. (p. 24) Now we have said these things without restraint, to show that those who affirm that Christ subsists in two natures or substances designate him as two-fold, like Nestorius does, but not like those orthodox teachers who were before him, who acknowledged him 'out of two natures' as the Son who was incarnate without change and perfectly made man; because after St Cyril's refusal we always and in every way abstain from speaking of Christ as 'two-fold', just as he also in the same way rejected the term 'conjunction' which had been properly employed by the Fathers, so that he might restrain absolutely the violence of Nestorius's way of thinking. For he rejected it in general, and also wrote about it in similar fashion and without any restraint: CYRIL: 'For it is not because of the fact that, when he took flesh, the Word who is from God the Father went forth as man, that he should be for this reason designated also as two-fold.'[107]

But the valiant grammarian, who crawls over divine words with unwashed feet as if he were doing something difficult in order to find them, publicly brings forth the arguments of Gelasius, who was bishop of Caesarea, which designate Christ for us as 'two-fold'. Now, then: was this not because the same Gelasius calls Christ 'a God-inspired man', when he wrote as follows in the treatise against the Arians? GELASIUS: 'Thus that God-inspired man, whom it befitted to endure the pain of death voluntarily for the benefit of mankind, both received (on the one hand) the crown of victory (cf. 1 Pet 5: 4), as the word of Scripture says, the splendour of authority; and (on the other hand) gained a magnificence which had not been his beforehand.'[108] Shall we make into a matter under dispute the general refusal of the wise Cyril, who decreed that Christ should in no way be styled 'a God-inspired man'? And shall we wait for you, a godless yet ingenious investigator, to enlighten us in (p. 25) what sense Gelasius on the one hand, and then Nestorius on the other, designated Christ as 'God-inspired'; and how Cyril did not fall into danger so as to become one dishonouring his father, by waging internal warfare and strife against the teacher who preceded him? But every God-fearing person turns away his face from you as from an unclean and senseless man, and shuts his ears to the words of your humbug, and grasps as a norm the refusal of the renowned Cyril which he proclaims universally and plainly in the fifth of his apostolic chapters: CYRIL: 'If anyone should dare to say that Christ was a God-inspired man, and not rather that he is truly God as one Son, and that by nature, inasmuch as the Word was made flesh and partook of blood and flesh in the same manner as ourselves, let him be anathema!'[109]

We therefore hold fast to the refusals of St Cyril as to some sacred anchor, and designate Christ neither as 'God-inspired man', nor as 'two-fold', nor as anything else of this kind. For also the holy and ecumenical synod which was in Ephesus, truly permitting the things which had formerly been declared by the teachers, and seeing that these concurred with the same sense as that of St Cyril, accepted the precise rejections of these same words, so that the wholeness and piety of doctrine might be preserved; and that through the introduction of such words there should in no way be introduced by force any of those things which the people of Nestorius's faction believe. Therefore, also those things which were written against the wicked Nestorius it both ratified and signed and crowned with the crowns of orthodoxy, in such as way that the spirits of the apostolic teachers who were before it rejoiced and, at the same time, gave their decree.

Text 11 *Contra impium Grammaticum, Or.* III.37

Translated from *CSCO* 50: 233–6

(p. 233) Again, when Gregory the Theologian in the discourse *Concerning the Epiphany* wrote about God and our Saviour Christ as follows: GREGORY OF NAZIANZUS: 'Now he was sent, but as man: for he was two-fold, inasmuch as he was weary and hungry and thirsty and he struggled and wept in accordance with the habit of the body',[110] the stupid grammarian, inheritor of foreign humbug, lacking knowledge and having no sense, after falsifying the statements of the teacher, cited them as follows: THE ALTERATION OF THIS SENTENCE OF GREGORY ABOVE, WHICH THE HERETICS CHANGED AS FOLLOWS: 'Now he was sent, but as man: for there was in him a two-fold nature. Thus from then onwards he was weary and hungry and he struggled and wept, (p. 234) in accordance with the habit of the human body.'[111] Who, then, will ever call these people Christians, and not children of the devil, who invented the first falsehood? Who *did not stand in the truth*, according to the Saviour's saying in the Gospel: for *'when he speaks falsehood'*, he declares, *'he speaks of his own'* (Jn 8: 44), *'and not from the mouth of the Lord'* – for indeed this saying also we may adapt from prophetic discourse. For if the sacred writings of the holy Fathers assist them, why do they attach to them things which they did not say, and write along with them expressions which are pleasing to themselves? Furthermore, let Isaiah the prophet declare to them as he shoots (forth words) skilfully (saying): 'Your hands are involved in sins, and your lips have uttered sin, and your mouth schemes iniquity.' (Is 59: 3). For they ought to be in awe of this homily of St Gregory *On the Epiphany,* which is renowned among all people and preserved among all people without falsification; and indeed they ought not shamelessly to stretch out against it a defiled hand which is even ready to invent anything at all. See, now: we ourselves have shown at length in matters examined earlier how the Fathers spoke of Christ as 'two-fold', as one about whom there is 'two-foldness', namely contemplation and reason: who, while he exists as God eternally, at length was incarnate for us without change, inasmuch as it is also affirmed that he was sent from the Father – this, indeed, since as God he fills all things. And therefore we quoted the most eminent apostolic teacher Athanasius, who declared as follows: ATHANASIUS: 'So then, this is the sense and design of the divine Scripture, as we have said on many occasions: in it there is a two-fold signification concerning our Saviour. He was God, and is the Son, and is the Word and Wisdom and effulgence (p. 235) of the Father; and at length for our sake he was incarnate when he assumed flesh from Mary the virgin Mother of God.'[112] Since Gregory the Theologian himself also thought things which were in accord with these matters, he declared as follows: GREGORY OF NAZIANZUS: 'He was indeed sent, but as man: for he was two-fold',[113] when he forbade the foul Arians to ascribe the humility and condescension of his being sent to an earlier order of incarnation and to an existence of the Word who is before the ages, as if he were a creature and not the creator. For then, when he was incarnate and was made man, Gregory says that that corresponded to the fact that he was sent by the Father, when he accepted that according to the habit of the body he should be hungry and be thirsty, and things of this kind. For in no way did he acknowledge Christ as two-fold after the inexpressible union, as if he subsisted in two natures; which is what the argument of these wicked men maintained. For he proclaims him as one out of two in this same homily *On the Epiphany,* when he states as follows: (WORDS) OF GREGORY: 'Now God was born by assuming one of two things which are contrary to one another, flesh and spirit: of these, he deified the one, while the other was deified. O new mingling! O glorious blending! The one who exists comes into being; and the creator is created!'[114]

Therefore since Emmanuel from then on exists and is one out of two natures without confusion, and is one hypostasis and nature, that is, the Word wholly incarnate and made man, the same was acting in divine fashion and in human fashion; the same was speaking as was befitting God and man, and was using two-fold words and actions. Therefore, in this regard, contemplation about him is two-fold: but Gregory did not divide Emmanuel on the basis of the different sort of words and actions into a duality of natures and forms after (p. 236) the union in such a way that the one should do and speak things relating to the deity, while the other should do and speak things relating to the humanity, which is nothing other than a duality of Christs and Sons. And we have plainly shown in those things (he wrote) to Theodoret complaining about the fourth chapter in its blasphemy: CYRIL: 'But I say that it is better and far more learned rather to apply the human expressions not to another person who is acknowledged as Son separately and by himself – to the form of a servant, as it is their custom to assert – but rather to ascribe them to the conditions of his humanity. For it was necessary, since he is God and man at the same time, that he should behave in accord with both principles.'[115] [The citation from Gregory is repeated.]

TEXTS 12 AND 13

The following two texts from the *Adversus apologiam Juliani* deal respectively with the claim of Julian of Halicarnassus that Christ was impassible (Text 12), and with his coinage of the term 'non-different difference' (*diaphora adiaphoros*) to avoid differentiating even in abstract contemplation (*theoria*) between the divinity and the humanity in Christ (Text 13).

Text 12 *Adversus apologiam Juliani*, ch. 3

Translated from *CSCO* 301: 183–8

(p. 183) *The statements of Julian, which lead to godlessness and proclaim uncleanness, to the effect that the body of our Saviour was not passible in sufferings, and which deny that he existed in a state of passibility, on the grounds that he suffered neither on account of his own sins, nor against his will – since no man among those whose religion is orthodox would say these things which have been slanderously manufactured to introduce error – and the refutation which was set up against them by the holy Fathers.*

Why, then, O most shameless of men, by darkening the truth do you imagine that you disturb religion, and write as follows? [JULIAN]: 'So then, we acknowledge that in truth the Lord suffered voluntarily and died in the flesh which is his own and ours and is consubstantial with ours; while we do not acknowledge that it was by natural necessity that he humbled himself to this state. For Peter says: *"Christ suffered for us in flesh"* (1 Pet 4: 1). But he who suffers for us is himself not subjected to suffering; for he would not be setting others free, if he himself were in subjection'.[116] And further: [JULIAN]: 'As to this saying, *"Christ suffered for us in flesh"*: – the person who hears these words *for us* should not consider that he suffered on behalf of his own self. Now if, by compulsion of nature, he had been subjected to sufferings and death, he would by every means have sought his own freedom, and not that of the others with whom he was experiencing danger'.[117]

Now what do you know from us, who (as the teacher said) rightly acknowledge that Christ, in a body suffering like ours, voluntarily endured the trial of innocent sufferings – you, who have blasphemously declared in the manner of your own folly that he suffered and died inasmuch as he was subjected to the debts arising from his own sins, and not rather on behalf of the human race (p. 184) did he himself offer the sacrifice and offering to God, even to the Father, as Paul says? (cf. Heb 5: 1; 9: 14). Now when, by means of arguments which appear to have the sense of introducing your ungodly doctrine, you seek to affirm as in a fable that God and Christ our Saviour suffered in impassible and immortal flesh, by such means you slander religion and the approved teachers who have taught it. Then you say that whoever affirms (as the venerable Proclus affirms) that he voluntarily endured the sufferings which were fitting as to nature, is affirming that he suffered of necessity for himself, and not on our behalf; but that when he was condemned to death on behalf of his own sins he was nailed to the cross, which he ascended in order to nail our sin along with him and to tear up the bond which existed by reason of our sin (cf. Col 2: 14); and also to abolish the authority of the prince who holds power, as Paul proclaims (cf. Heb 2: 14; Eph 2: 2); and by this means that he might be exalted below and draw up to the height those of us who were below (cf. Eph 4: 8–9) – and to ratify his word which he uttered when he voluntarily approached the cross: '*Now the ruler of this world is being cast out*' (Jn 12: 31); '*and I, if I be lifted up from the earth, draw all men to myself*' (Jn 12: 32).

Now do not deceive yourself, and do not suppose that when you go out from the place of struggle you will unbind those toils from which you cannot flee. For see! You have heard those things on whose account Proclus has evidently enrolled you in the company of the Manichees, since you do not acknowledge that he suffered in flesh like us with natural and innocent sufferings; but with sufferings voluntary and free from all blame, Emmanuel redeemed the whole human race, his family in flesh, that is to say, our flesh. Now first: by means of the expression 'incorruptibility' you have concealed the impious doctrine, and you have written: [JULIAN]: 'Incorruptibility was constantly present with the passible body of our Lord, even when he was suffering voluntarily on behalf of others'.[118] Then, afterwards, I mean after my *Refutation,* you renounced even the very word 'passible', and in the *Additions* you wrote without shame: 'We do not affirm him as (p. 185) consubstantial with us in respect of passibility, but in respect of identity of substance; insofar as he is impassible and incorruptible, he is consubstantial with us in respect of identity of substance'.[119] And in this *Defence* which recently arrived, where you took hold of a pretext and acted as accuser of the Manichees and of the fantasies of Eutyches's party while disseminating these views of yours with loud noise, by means of which you suppose that you are concealing the impiety of your teaching, you state: 'For the multiplication of the loaves symbolizes through this kind of provisioning nothing other than the power of impassibility in the sufferings of the Lord's body';[120] and further: 'On account of the natural incorruptibility which belonged to the first-born as a result of the union which was with God the Word'.[121]

Who, then, is there who on reading this does not clearly determine that you are opposed to the Fathers and to the Spirit who spoke in them and instructed them, those Fathers who affirmed that the Word was partaker in the flesh with natural and innocent sufferings, and who handed on the tradition that he was passible in flesh, until the time came when it was proper for him to suffer, he who voluntarily on our behalf applied himself to sufferings and who accepted that he should undergo their trials? And hear what Athanasius, who imitated the Apostles in word and deed, wrote in the third treatise of the writing *Concerning the Holy Trinity against the Arians*. [Citations from Athanasius follow.]

(p. 186) Do you have understanding ears, so as to hear; and is your sense of hearing utterly deaf? For look, as the preacher of the truth (sc. Athanasius) has said: 'Just as we affirm that the body is his, so also the sufferings of the body were affirmed as being his own, even if they had not been possessed by his divinity'.[122] And he has granted us to reckon and to acknowledge openly that, as Christ is one without division, he is impassible and passible: in his divinity, (p. 187) which is impassible and not susceptible of any suffering, sufferings are predicated of him; but in the flesh, which is passible, he the same truly suffered through the fact that he was made man. For he declared: 'As for the one to whom there happened the business of his being condemned, of his being scourged, and of his being thirsty, and crucifixion and death and those other weaknesses of the body, to him belong both uprightness and grace'.[123]

Therefore, by means of the body, which naturally accepts the weakness of sufferings, there came about for us the uprightness and grace of God the Word who was incarnate, who displayed the great extent of his power in the weakness which he accepted of his own volition. And when he rose from among the dead, as was fitting for God, and when he put death to death, we rose with the one who suffered for our sake and died and rose.

Observe, now, if you will, how the one who said these things acknowledged as one and the same Emmanuel who divinely and sublimely performed magnificent deeds. Through the trials of his sufferings, he displayed his flesh as passible, when he added these statements also: [ATHANASIUS]: 'For it was granted them to see how it was the same one who both performed the wonderful deeds, and it was the same one who also displayed a passible body, by allowing that he should weep and be hungry, and that in him there should be seen those things which are proper to the body. For through things like these he is acknowledged in that, although as God he is impassible, he assumed passible flesh; through the mighty deeds, however, he showed himself as the Word of God who now was made man'.[124]

Now indeed the truly wise Cyril also, who was fighting against the madness of Nestorius who used to divide Christ into two natures after the divine and inexpressible union, when he was combatting the complaints of the impious Arius in the *Defence of the Eleventh Chapter*, quoted these same words which he recognized as being completely accurate.[125] Since he followed the footsteps of the apostolic teaching and of the other Fathers, the Doctors, he too acknowledged Christ as the same, passible and impassible, not in the same way as you do when you act wickedly in your madness; but he acknowledged Christ (p. 188) as impassible inasmuch as he is God before the ages, and passible inasmuch as he voluntarily became man for our sake. For no-one at any time among the Doctors of religion declared the flesh to be impassible in sufferings in such a way as to indicate that Christ suffered in appearance.

Text 13 *Adversus apologiam Juliani* ch. 19

Translated from *CSCO* 301: 279–85

(p. 279) *Refutation of the unlearned and spurious accusation which most boorishly alleges that I divide the one Christ into two particularities, because I affirm the body as passible and mortal while the Word of God is impassible and immortal; and that I acknowledge the difference of these things inasmuch as it is specific to them or as in respect of natural signification, which preserves for what is without division those things out of which the union without confusion arises, and reveals the wicked folly which Julian speaks of as 'a difference which is not different'.*

But since you are so miserable and defiled with the scab of the Manichaean heresy, and in every respect deny the truth of the redemptive sufferings and death of the only-begotten Word who was incarnate without change, you declare that I need your help; and that I agree with the views of Nestorius; and that I divide Christ into two natures both in their own operations and properties. It will be good, then, for us to laugh at you, and to add words from the inspired Scripture, and to say: '*Let not the hunchback boast, as if he were of upright stature!*' (3 Kgs 21: 11). For since you are bent towards the ground, bowed down under heretical burdens and hunchbacked, how do you bring help to those who stand upright? For since you write these things (p. 280) to make me turn aside to these many old women's prattlings of yours, you address the other false accusers like this: [JULIAN]: 'For the false accusers, attempting to introduce the abominable and polluted teachings of Nestorius, and seeking by every means to set up division by making judgement about the duality of the properties, set corruptibility and passibility and mortality against incorruptibility and impassibility and immortality; and they lead him who is one into two Christs and two Sons, since they falsify the inexpressible and incomprehensible union.'[126]

Now (in reply) to these things we shall say, in short, one simple, true word: show us that we have written somewhere that Christ exists in two natures and in two properties. But you cannot say so. For in every place each person discovers that Our Lowliness anathematizes those who divide the one Christ in a duplication of natures and of their operations and their properties; but Our Lowliness, like the wise Cyril, acknowledges that Christ exists out of two natures, out of divinity and out of humanity, and recognizes their difference and their character as it were in natural quality. Now natural quality consists in the fact that the essence of those things which are assembled into the union without confusion and without division is not the same. For the divinity is of one essence, and the humanity of another, out of which the Word who is before the ages became indivisible and was called Emmanuel. And the quality inheres in the nature which constitutes the difference of the essence; and the difference of the quality represents the inequality of the *genus* of the divinity and the *genus* of the humanity. But this does not divide the one who has inexpressibly come into being through the union (of the two) with one another. For it is certain that Christ is one out of two (natures), consubstantial with the Father in respect of the divinity, and the same consubstantial with us in respect of the humanity; and for this reason he is not divided into a duality of natures. For he who is God for everlasting at the end of days became man, without changing what he was (p. 281) in what he became, and without having altered what he became into the essence of the divinity.

But because you have lost your senses, you have written: 'Let us say concerning Christ that the difference is not different', since you are drunk in your mind, and you confuse the divinity and the humanity out which exists the one Christ – one person, one hypostasis, one incarnate nature which is of God the Word himself. For if you call the difference itself a 'non-difference', then Christ would be proclaimed (as your vapid talk prefers) as consubstantial with us in respect of divinity, and consubstantial with the Father in respect of humanity; that is to say that these (the divinity and the humanity), according to your opinion, would alter and be changed continually, the one into the other; and the flesh for its part would change into the essence of the Word itself, while the Word would be changed into the essence of the flesh itself. Thus we laugh at you, because of your 'non-different difference'.

How, then, do you consent to write against those who confuse the natures, when you yourself do not know what you are saying, but fall into their own pit as you lead the blind astray (since you are blind in your sense because of your reasoning) as the book of the holy Gospel says (cf. Matt 15: 14)? Indeed, like one who is covered over with a veil, you also accuse them of the very ideas in which you yourself are held fast! For whereabouts has the truly wise Cyril spoken of 'non-different difference', or any other of the God-inspired Fathers, or Gregory or Diodore or Timothy, if (as you allege) it is these men you are following, these men whose names you also defile with your impure mouth while you alter their teachings and terminology? For the wise Cyril – of whom Dioscorus and Timothy are pupils, who in the things they have written have quoted testimonies from him as if they came from holy Scripture – in the *Second Epistle to Succensus* wrote these things: [CYRIL]: 'For although affirmation is made by us of the one only-begotten Son of God who was incarnate and made man, it does not involve for this reason a matter of confusion, as they suppose (p. 282); furthermore, the nature of the Word did not change in that of the flesh, nor did not that nature of the flesh at all alter in itself. But each nature, while remaining at the same time and being apprehended in the quality which corresponds to its nature (according to the account which has just now been given by us), the inexpressible and incomprehensible union has demonstrated to us as one nature of the Son but, as I have said, of the Son incarnate.'[127]

Now consider, you foolish man and full of all ignorance, how when he said that he acknowledged one nature of God the Word incarnate, he stated that the quality which corresponds to the nature of each (sc. the divinity and the humanity) was not disregarded by him as being not divided, but as enduring and at the same time being recognized. Now what out of the two (sc. the divinity and the humanity) endures and at the same time is recognized is in no way divided, since it is combined in a natural union: it is one without alteration out of two elements, and is not divided into two. For the fact that soul-enfleshed flesh animates the flesh, and in the same way the Word animates the Word without undergoing alteration, does not introduce duality either of the Word in respect of the flesh, nor of the flesh in respect of the Word. For the one nature and hypostasis of God the Word which is without alteration was incarnate, which does not accept division into God the Word and man, but displays God and man the same without division, that is to say, God who is incarnate. [This is supported by two citations from Cyril's work against Diodore.]

(p. 283) Now then, tell me: are you saying that this wise teacher preaches the opinions of Photinus, of Paul, and of Nestorius because he does not speak of the 'non-different difference', and does not confuse the things out of which the one Christ exists; but affirms that their proper character be recognized according to nature, to the effect that there is a natural difference of those things which lead to the union, namely a natural difference of divinity and humanity? For he is the same, invisible and visible, impassible and passible, subject to time and before the ages, but not by natural change or alteration such that the divinity leaves behind what it is in its invisible essence, not (bound up) in time and without coming into existence, and such that the ensouled body endowed with mind which was hypostatically united to him abandons its existence in visible essence and in subjection to time and falls into tangibility, according to your 'non-different difference'. For while the divinity and the humanity out of which Christ existed subsisted in essence, the invisible became visible, and the impalpable became palpable, and the impassible became passible, by union with the body which was visible and passible and palpable.

Now this teacher, who is a minister of the holy Spirit, wrote in the third homily, that is, in the *Commentary* (p. 284) when he explains: '*For we have not a high priest who cannot suffer with our weaknesses*' (Heb 4: 15), as follows: [CYRIL]: 'But you will say, in what sense does the one who knew no suffering suffer? In respect of this very question I myself address you by bringing as witness apostolic words. For Paul said: "*O the depth of the riches and of the wisdom of God, whose judgements no man has searched out and whose ways cannot be sought out. For who has known the mind of the Lord?*"' (Rom 11: 33–4). For because his suffering was salvation for the world, he humbled himself. Now he was and is impassible as God; but he became flesh according to the divine dispensation, that is, he became man – not by change of nature, nor by undergoing transformation, nor by leaving off being God, but rather by making as his own flesh taken from the holy virgin through a union according to the divine dispensation; in order that, when he reckoned as his own the suffering through which he was able to suffer, he might bring death to an end by the resurrection from among the dead, and take away sin from the world. For the most wise Paul, when he was considering something similar to this, wrote: "*For since by man came death, by man also came the resurrection of the dead.*" (1 Cor 15: 21). For because it was right that the suffering which befell Christ should bring corruption to an end – for the Word who is from God the Father is life and giver of life, whose flesh which died and overcame the bonds of death was his own – he arose, as I have said, while leading human nature to what it was from the beginning. For he had been fashioned for incorruptibility and life.'[128] [This is supported by a citation from Cyril's *Scholia*.]

(p. 285) If it pleases you, fasten on these words as well like a rabid dog, and accuse him because he has set passibility against impassibility, and as if he were making of him who is one two Christs and two Sons, and alleging that impassibility is characteristic of his sublime nature. For you imagine that those who do not preach the fantasy of your own stupidity divide the divine dispensation itself.

5

HOMILIES

Homily XIII (Text 14), which Severus delivered in late January 513, celebrates Emperor Anastasius's abolition of the levy known as the *chrysargyron* or *collatio lustralis* in 498. While piety may have been a motive in the removal of a tax which was felt to be oppressive, the reform needs to be seen as part of Anastasius's overhaul of currency and taxation policies (Whitby 2000: 185 n. 147). The homily itself, which does not survive in its entirety, presents the emperor, and by association the Empress Ariadne, as an *exemplum* of compassion and munificence some fifteen years after the event, and is a good illustration of the esteem in which Severus held the eirenic Anastasius (Allen 2002: 714–15). There is no indication in which church the homily was preached. Homily XXIV, delivered on Ascension day, 16 May 513, also commemorates the emperor's munificence, manifested in his gift of a purple garment to the church of Antioch.

Homily XIV (Text 15) was delivered in the church of the Theotokos in Antioch (Downey 1961: 659) on 2 or 3 February 513 on the feast of the Hypapante, several days after Homily XIII. It survives in a more extended Coptic version, presently being edited by Youhanna Nessim Youssef, and in some Greek fragments. Here Severus presents his mariology (Allen 1996: 168–70), in which Mary is given her pedigree at the outset: she was praised by prophets, apostles and martyrs; indeed, she herself is prophet, apostle and martyr. She is superior even to the apostles because she is the origin of the proclamation of the Gospel, and she has put a stop to the heresy of the Manichees, Julianists, Eutychians, Apollinarians and Nestorians. In the course of his exposition, Severus gives a classic statement of one-nature christology (§ 17) and the place which Mary occupies within it, a place which is always subordinate to that of the pre-existent Logos. Mary still, however, basks in reflected christological glory, being connected with the refutation of many heresies.

Among Severus's Cathedral Homilies are two on the feast of the Forty Martyrs of Sebaste in Armenia, whose cult was one of the most popular in late antiquity and the Byzantine period. Ephrem Graecus, Basil of Caesarea,[1] and Gregory of Nyssa – and on the Latin side Gaudentius of Brescia – also preached on the Forty. Basil's homily is referred to by Severus (Text 21 below) as a classic on the topic. Homily XVIII (Text 16) was delivered on Saturday, 9 March 513, and Homily XLI on Saturday, 8 March 514, after the homily from the previous year had been read out again, as the congregation had requested when it was first delivered (Brière 1960: 54). Although, as we know from *SL* I.42, there was a chapel of the Forty Martyrs in Antioch, it is more likely that both homilies were delivered in the church of the martyr Barlaha (Downey 1961: 489), for we read at the start of Homily LXXIII on Barlaha the following:

> I seem to see the holy old martyr Barlaha direct a piercing glance at me and fiercely accuse my silence – and not just fiercely, but with justice. This is his accusation: 'As for you, do you not hear the apostle Paul affirm that there is no respect of persons with God (Rom 2:11)? How come that you have twice made such a rich encomium of the Forty Martyrs, who share this holy temple with me, and you have paid no attention to my struggles?'[2]

Severus also composed five hymns on the Forty (Brooks 1981: 614–20).

Homily LXXII, on the deposition of the relics of the martyrs Procopius and Phocas[3] in the Church of the angel Michael (Text 18),[4] was delivered on Monday, 1 June 515. It affords glimpses into the thought-world of Christians in Antioch at the time, some of whom objected to the idea of giving martyrs' remains a resting-place in a church dedicated to an angel. In the course of dealing with this objection, Severus denounces the pagan practice of worshipping angels, and launches an attack on artistic representations of angels which depict them as kings or princes in royal purple. The homily is evidence of a developed angelology in the first quarter of the sixth century (Allen 1996: 170–4).

Text 14 Homily XIII

Translated from *PO* 38/2: 392–7

(p. 392) *Concerning the liberality of the gift of the devout emperor, which he handed over on his own authority, consisting of certain residues which were taken from the taxes and the monies of the public treasury.*[5]

1   Great and difficult to contemplate is the depth of the dispensation which the Word of God and the Saviour Jesus Christ demonstrated towards our race by his advent in the flesh; and all this is so clear to us that we praise him alone as benefactor and perceive him as (our) maker and therefore worship him as the one who, after we had been made, fashioned us anew for that which is excellent; and with the eyes of our mind cast downwards we behold and praise in silence him, the one who is beyond all thought and discourse.

2   For who is there who would not be amazed to see the king of the heavenly hosts paying taxes to the kings who are on the earth, and like one subject to taxes and under tribute also being enrolled along with those other people, even (what is indeed a still greater thing) while he was a babe in the womb of the virgin Mother of God (cf. Lk 2: 1–5)? And that very thing appeared somehow to be a matter of humility and consonant with the condition of his self-emptying and voluntary poverty. For the fact of his being submissive to the enrolment doubtless appears truly human through that same thing which is visible; and yet he is in complete conformity with God.

3   For the one who was in the *form of God*, even on account of love for mankind, took the *form of a slave* (Phil 2: 7) in which he became man, without change: for this expression, 'he is', shows the unchangeableness of the divine essence and the steadfastness which inheres in the one who is and who always exists, when he willed to put an end to our servitude which had reduced us to slavery through sin: when he was enrolled for tax symbolically like one of those who had been made a subject; when he broke the bonds of that subjection and tore up the promissory note (cf. Col 2: 14) which was contrary to our race – who then was there who was competent to set this right? He who by nature is free. Now who is the one who by nature is free? The only-begotten Son and Word of God . . . .[6]

(p. 394)

20   . . . he has for provisions. And he looks at the old coat which covers him, and wants to bring it to the merchants to fill his wretched belly; and he plans to sell his children as they sell slaves, and to acquire provisions for the price of his own flesh and blood. There sits the proud creditor, who is more wicked and severe than any wild beast, making mock of the wretched man, declaring

as it were by his mockery of neediness as if there were no such thing – while he moves his fingers and counts up the interest and calculates the time left for the bond to run and reads it out in a loud voice, and threatens to hand him over to prison and (so that he may increase his income) to punish him with harsh and intolerable things if he does not repay quickly what he owes.

21 Or again sometimes, when there is a poor stranger, he throws him out of his house when it is in the middle of the wintertime and drives him away and immediately demands payment of him. But at once this wretched man, being withered by cold and seeing that the poor and cheap clothing which he had acquired and his rags so vile are worth only a few coins of the sort they throw down in the market-place, and seeing that the debt is required and that he has nothing to pay it with and that he is as it were harassed from every side, sheds warm tears about his sufferings; and there is no one to put an end to his neediness.

22 How then, O man, shall you say to God with confidence: 'Forgive me' (cf. Matt 18: 21–35), when you yourself have nothing, when you are liable for huge debts and ten thousands of sins, and when you have shown to your kindred and your brother the harshness of a stony compassion? But why am I concerned with the business of debt? Many times it is a matter of abuse or insult or other harsh thing which is most contemptible whatever it be, that we do not agree to forgive our neighbour: then, as if we had been shamefully treated in regard to our honour and had undergone all ills, we sharpen the goad of wrath in the manner of scorpions, and like camels we keep hold of the grudge in our mind and do not rest until we pay back some evil in return for this dishonour, we do damage by (our) actions, even though we have suffered injury in words only, as we admit.

23 How then shall we say this with confidence: 'Forgive us' (cf. Matt 18: 21–35)? For Oh! (I am going to say the same thing many times): where is the upright man, that we may obtain that thing of which we ourselves have not made our neighbour a partaker? That is indeed also what the Sage said, when he said in wonder: *'Since he himself is flesh: he stores up his anger and begs healing from the Lord'* (Eccl 28: 3, 5).
(p. 396)

24 But let us remember the day of judgement; and since we have need of mercy, let us prepare in advance mercy for ourselves. And let us forgive liberally, so that we may deserve a forgiveness which is more liberal. And through the gift of the devout emperor, let us

turn ourselves to philanthropy; and for him and for the empress who is a peacemaker and lover of Christ let us pray, saying: 'Redeem your king, O Lord' and also her; 'and answer us on the day that we call upon you'. For to you are due the praise and the glory and the power, now and for ever and to the ages of the ages. Amen.

The end of Homily XIII

Text 15 Homily XIV

Translated from *PO* 38/2: 400–15

(p. 400) *Preached in memory of the holy Mother of God and ever-virgin Mary.*

1 It is fitting and just that we should offer praise composed of words to all the saints: and let us honour them with laudatory sermons and with festivals as those who have truly served their Lord and have contributed faithfully towards the dispensation of our redemption. And let us on the one hand praise the prophets as those who by their own excellence appeared sufficient to preach in advance the great mystery of piety (1 Tim 3: 16); and on the other hand, let us praise the apostles as those who proclaimed this (mystery); then the martyrs as those who affirmed the prophecies of the former and the proclamation of the latter with their own blood – hence they also have received this title because of their affirmation, for it is the custom to call witnesses 'martyrs', those who by their voice give credibility to things which are not demonstrable or which otherwise are in some way or other not credible.

2 Now the voice of Christ's martyrs is the shedding of their blood which followed the first and divine outpouring of blood which the *Lamb of God who takes away the sin of the world* (Jn 1: 29) shed for us, he who has borne witness of himself before these others. For in truth he was not at all in need of anything – he who witnessed a noble confession before Pontius Pilate (1 Tim 6: 13) (as the Apostle Paul said) – and very justly so: for of what other witness who might be more faithful than he should he have need, who is himself the truth (cf. Jn 14: 16)? But since he accepts the devotion of the will of his own servants, he makes them partakers in this title which is his, and makes them to be called martyrs.

3   Now how shall any one not honour the Mother of God and the truly holy and ever-virgin Mary as prophetess, and as apostle, and as martyr? As prophetess – in accordance with Isaiah's prophecy, which says about her: (p. 402) *'And I came to the prophetess, and she conceived and gave birth to a son. And the Lord said to me: "Call his name 'Swiftly-plunder-and-suddenly-pillage"', because before the child knows how to call "father!" and "mother!", he will take the might of Damascus and the plunder of Samaria before the king of the Assyrians'* (Is 8: 3, 4 LXX).

4   But who is the prophetess spoken of in the holy Scriptures, who has given birth to a son who is called *'Swiftly-plunder-and-suddenly-pillage'*, who immediately on being born, and *before he knows how to call 'father!' or 'mother!'* plunders the warriors and pillages them, if it is not the Mother of God, the virgin who has given birth to Emmanuel who, from the beginning of his birth in the flesh, overthrew the Slanderer by taking the *might of Damascus* and carrying off the spoils of Samaria?

5   Now these words represent figuratively by a kind of antonomasia[7] the worship of idols: for, on the one hand, Damascus is to be interpreted as 'bloody', while, on the other, Samaria is the one who forged the calves of gold and removed from among them the true service and the worship of the one who alone is God (cf. 1 Kgs 12: 26–8). Now it is known to all men that in these two things especially the worship of idols is to be recognized: by the fact that we name and worship as gods things made by hands, and by the fact that we offer sacrifices with blood and holocausts. Therefore Emmanuel took the plunder from this as soon as he was born in flesh, first when he was leading the Magi to worship in swaddling-clothes the age of his infancy, and next when he was going to Egypt on account of the slaughter of the children by Herod and shook his idols[8] (cf. Is 19: 1), just as Isaiah prophesies. And he was doing this and was taking this plunder before the king of the Assyrians – for the prophecy calls the Slanderer *the king of Assyria* in many places, and that he is so named one can discover in general, so to speak, everywhere among the prophets (cf. Is 10: 12 LXX).

6   Such is the child that Mary the prophetess has borne for us: he who from his infancy and straightaway from his birth has torn down the fortress of the Slanderer's tyranny: and, says Isaiah the prophet: *'Do not marvel'* (Is 8: 4 LXX), for this child was himself *'the mighty God, the angel of mighty counsel'*, as one who in himself makes known and signifies (p. 404) as it were the living Word,

the Father who is the Mind that is over all things. He was himself the *marvellous counsellor* (Is 9: 6) as the one who, together with the Father, made the intelligible world and this visible world, and who heard (as being his counsellor and his equal in glory): '*Let us make man in our image and in our likeness*' (Gen 1: 26). He was himself the *prince* (Is 9: 6) as the one who is the power of the invisible Father, for Christ is *the power of God and the wisdom of God* (1 Cor 1: 24); and again he was the one who rightly heard: '*Your throne, O God, is for ever and ever: a sceptre of integrity is the sceptre of your kingdom*' (Ps 44: 7). He was himself the *prince of peace* (Is 9: 6 LXX) as the one who has joined together the earthly things with the heavenly, and has pacified everything by the blood of his cross, as Paul says (Eph 1: 10; Col. 1: 20). He was himself the 'father of the world to come' as the beginning and as the one who was broadcasting the seed of the life which is to be and of eternal endless hopes, that is to say, the kingdom of heaven which he was preaching.

7 Because of this, the virgin and mother, as one who gave birth to a child such as this (who is at the same time both Lord of the prophets and Lord in his own right) was prophesying after Elizabeth's salutation when she says: '*For behold, from henceforth all generations shall ascribe blessedness to me, because the one who is mighty has done great things for me, and holy is his name. And his mercy, to every generation, is for those who fear him*' (Lk 1: 48–50).

8 But one may truly call her apostle and, one might rightly say, higher than all the apostles: for from the first[9] she herself was even counted together with the apostles, as the Book of Acts also records when it says: '*These were assembled together and continuing in prayer with Mary the mother of Jesus*' (Acts 1: 14). Besides, if what they heard from our Lord as '*Go, teach all nations*' (Matt 28: 19) is what constituted them apostles, what nation is there that this woman has not taught and brought to the knowledge of God, and that, moreover, when she was silent, through her giving birth in such a renowned, exceptional and sensational manner, and through her celebrated conception which made her the mother and origin of the Gospel proclamation?

9 Furthermore (one should not be reluctant to say it) she is in many respects a martyr: as when she bravely bore Joseph's opinion of her when he was under the impression that her conception had taken place as a result of adultery, (p. 406) before he knew the mystery of the birth as a result of the angel's revelation (cf. Matt 1: 19f.); and also when (because of Herod's senseless rage) she

113

fled to Egypt (cf. Matt 2: 13); and again when (through fear of Archelaus) she returned from Egypt and departed to Nazareth (cf. Matt 2: 21–3); and when she was passing every day with Jewish murderers, and was living a life which was close to death.

10 How, then, shall we not deservedly honour this woman, whom the spirits of the righteous honour at this time?[10] On the one hand, the patriarchs honour her as the one who fulfilled for them the hope expectation which was awaited from time long past, and who brought the blessing of Abraham's seed who is Christ, which has passed over to all the peoples and all the uttermost parts (of the earth). On the other hand, the prophets honour her as the one who enlightened their prophecies, and who has given birth to the *Sun of Righteousness* (Mal 4: 2) who has revealed hidden things, both secrets and things not known. Again, the apostles honour her as the one whom they recognized as the beginning of their proclamation. The martyrs honour her as the one who was the first to bring to them the exemplar of their own struggles and victories.[11] Then the Doctors of the church and the shepherds of Christ's rational flock honour her as the one who has stopped up the mouth of heresy and who has poured forth for us, in the likeness of a drinkable and pure spring, the rushing tides of orthodoxy and – foremost and absolutely the best of all things – has expelled the darkness of the Manichees.

11 For when the Word of God became incarnate of her without change, he showed that the maker and framer of our created state is one. For if, according to the stories of the blasphemous fables of those men, on the one hand the good God is the maker of the soul, yet on the other hand the evil principle and ungenerated darkness are the makers of the body, how was the Son of the Father and the good God destined to come in our likeness, as it is written: 'He was made a *partaker of blood and flesh*' (Heb 2: 14)? But since they do not tolerate the lowliness (of the incarnate Lord) thus expressed, they run towards and take refuge in the illusions which the filthy Eutyches received and inherited as a paternal heirloom. For they say rather that he appeared in fantasy only, and that in truth Emmanuel himself was not a human being, thus contradicting the holy Scriptures and the sacred book of the Gospels, according to which the holy virgin by manifesting herself as the medium of the mystery of the divine assumption of flesh and blood, dissolved the whole fiction of their rantings.

12 Accordingly because of this he (the Word) did not take as the servant of his dispensation the sort of gift that might be a shadow

and illusion, but a true flesh, (p. 408) even equal in substance to us whom he was in earnest to heal and renew. For if he had willed to be an illusion, where was the need for Mary? And furthermore, where was the need for his taking up residence in the womb, or the nine months' pregnancy, or the birth? for the swaddling-clothes, for his mother's breasts, for the milk, for his tender years and his upbringing? Indeed, all these things this uncreated one took upon himself on our account; and he voluntarily subjected himself to those laws of human nature which he himself established, and passed through all these conditions of ours *except for sin* (Heb 4: 15), so that when he appointed for us all the freedom which is his own and the blessings, he blotted out the sin which was contrary to our race and the servitude which arose from it, and the curse.

13 Indeed, this is what Moses also has made known plainly, Moses, the opponent and enemy of the most wicked Manichees. For he saw a bush which was on fire and which was not consumed, which was symbolizing figuratively in advance the indivisible union of God the Word with the human creature, a union which was something undertaken for the sake of love of mankind and (was effected) without change. Now the bush is a thorny plant, which shows that he was made a partaker (except in respect of sin; cf. Heb 4: 15) of the nature which is thorny and under sin on account of Adam's transgression of the commandment, so that he might indeed send us power against sin, because he was named second Adam and became the beginning of the new creation, just as he was of the first creation.

14 Now this virgin also drives away and expels from the holy courts as something polluted the stupidity of Apollinaris, who alleges that our Saviour Christ is lacking a mind. For since this virgin is a rational living creature capable of receiving reason and knowledge (for such is the nature of humanity), she has given birth to God as an infant, rational and endowed with reason, who took flesh without change to confer perfect redemption upon us rational creatures. For in truth the charge of (his) lacking a mind would have been brought against God the Word, if he had left his own image (that is, our faculty of reason) without healing in withdrawing it from the divine union, by taking flesh without reason and deeming this alone worthy of redemption.

15 On the other hand, the virgin Mother of God in no way consents to tolerate the insanity of Nestorius. For how is she not the mother of God, she who bore as child *the mighty God, the angel of mighty counsel, the wonderful counsellor, the prince, the prince of peace, the father*

of the world to come (Is 9: 6 LXX)? On the contrary, he (Nestorius) asserts: 'It is not the natural property of a woman that she should give birth to God.'[12] Now if (p. 410) you mean (God) without a body, I myself affirm this too, along with you. But if you mean him who was incarnate, have no doubt about the miracle. For in truth a woman cannot give birth at all to a mere soul without a body besides; but when it is joined with a body and becomes a single unit in one simultaneous creation, it is born at the same time as the body, and she is therefore rightly and truly called mother not simply of the flesh, but of a human being endowed with reason. Reckon this same thing also in regard to the birth of Emmanuel in the flesh, for thus the holy book mystically instructs us when it says: *'Therefore because the children have been partakers of blood and flesh, so also he in like manner was made a partaker in the same things'* (Heb 2: 14).

16 For God the Word did not obtain the beginning of his divinity from Mary, since he was without beginning and the maker of every age and time. But when he chose to become incarnate and to be made man, that is, to unite to himself hypostatically the flesh which is consubstantial with ours inspirited by a rational and intelligible soul, the virgin supplied at the same time those things arising from her own created nature, all those things which are the property of a woman, so that at one and the same time there entered into him what was of her nature. And the holy Spirit – since there had not been intercourse with a man – acted effectually and brought the birth to completion. Thus God the Word himself, when he had been conceived and born in the flesh, showed Mary the Mother of God to be the one who had given birth to the Word endued with a body; and it was in accord with what is better and wonderful that she was named, since the mystery itself consisted in this – namely, the kingship of what is better, and the lifting up of our race from this place, and its transformation into something better.

17 Therefore the one who was born was also named Emmanuel, since he is one indivisible and without confusion, out of two natures, both divinity and humanity. This one who, since he possesses all the unique and indivisible qualities, namely, his incorporeal generation from the Father and the very same divinity (for he alone was begotten of the only one, even God from God) and his birth from the virgin (for he alone was born in the flesh of a woman not joined in marriage and the only one of her kind), did not violate his mother's virginity – how was this one, after

the inexpressible union, prepared to be divided and broken by the duality of the natures, as the Synod of Chalcedon has taught since it followed the foolish teachings of Nestorius? But he is in all respects one and unique. Because of this, he has also called us, who were separated from God, to one-ness and to peace, since he is the *mediator of God and men* (1 Tim 2: 5).

(p. 412)

18 This is why we honour also the holy Mother of God and ever-virgin Mary with honours which are surpassing great, inasmuch as she is the one who is able, more than all the other saints, to offer up supplications on our behalf, and since we too make our boast of her as having acquired her as the adornment of our race – the rational earth from whom the second Adam, who is neither fashioned nor made, fashioned himself in flesh (cf. 1 Cor 15: 44, 45) – the plant of virginity from which Christ the heavenly ladder was prepared in flesh by the Spirit, so that we ourselves might be able to ascend to heaven when we fix our footsteps firmly upon it (cf. Is 9: 36); the intelligible Mount Sinai which is not covered in smoke, but which shines with the *Sun of Righteousness* and which bestows not only the Law of the Ten Commandments, but the lawgiver himself when he was *seen on earth and held converse with human beings* (Bar 3: 38), and gave instruction in the Gospel and with persuasion captured not one people Israel, but every people and race.

19 What honour, therefore, shall we render to the Mother of God, or rather to God who was incarnate of her for the redemption of our souls? For it is there that he finds honour and sacrifice and whole burnt offering. For how is it not a good thing that through his advent in the body the earth should become heaven, such that even the angels might dwell on it, as he himself also said in the Gospel: '*Amen, I say to you, that from now on you shall see the heavens opened, and the angels of God ascending and descending*' (Jn 1: 51)?

20 But we ourselves – we who are obliged to demonstrate a way of life which is worthy of heaven – do we not even do those things which are fitting for earth, but are suitable for Sheol and the pit of destruction? And since it was right for us to occupy ourselves with virginity and to observe it because of God who was born of a virgin, do we not even in chaste marriage bridle the lusts which the cross of Christ has blunted and made easy to overthrow, because the cross has blunted *the sin which is the sting of death* (1 Cor 15: 56)? Rather, we dishonour the temple of God by fornication, and become '*stallions lusting after mares*', as the prophet says (Jer 5: 8).

21 But I beseech and earnestly entreat you: do not let us make this brief pleasure, which as soon as it is fulfilled passes away and brings distress, into a flame which cannot be quenched and a torment without end. But *'let each one of us possess his vessel in holiness and honour'*, as says Paul (1 Thess 4: 4) (p. 414) who is wise in all things, so that we may be esteemed worthy of those good things of eternity through the grace and philanthropy of our great God and Saviour Jesus Christ, to whom is due praise with the Father and the holy Spirit to the ages of ages. Amen.

The end of Homily XIV

Text 16 Homily XVIII

Translated from *PO* 37/1: 6–23

(p. 6) *From the same St Severus: A sermon on how there was an enactment of the holy canons enjoining that we should make remembrance of the holy martyrs during Lent, and of the Forty Holy Martyrs.*[13] *The sermon was preached on the Saturday.*

1 Let none of you be surprised that I have made you come out to this temple of the martyrs, famous in their victory, on the grounds that our fathers instructed in the beginning of the canons that during these forty days of fast we should hold no assembly (to commemorate) the victory of the martyrs. For even if we have met together, it is not that we are acting in contradiction to the laws, for it is lawful on Saturday and Sunday, even at the height of the fast, to offer the bloodless sacrifice, and to make remembrance of the holy martyrs.[14] Nevertheless, I would argue that one interpret a law not according to its letter, but according to its intention. And as for the intention of this law, it is this: commemoration of the martyrs will not cause us to fall prey to appetite, or make us resort to the tavern or to gluttony, that we should interrupt our abstinence for the fast. For those who establish a law do not only enact what belongs (strictly) to the law, but also anticipate . . ..[15]

2 For nothing is more appropriate to the fast than the heroic deeds of the martyrs, and it is not at all surprising that the martyrs love the fast, the deprivation of food and these other acts of self-denial, which are good training exercises for their struggles. Indeed, they would welcome it and be glad if we celebrated all their festivals with an abstinence like this. But because we would be resistant to

the disciplines of virtue, and not many would be eager to meet for the martyr's celebration if they were instructed to fast on that day as well, because of this, (our fathers) have permitted us to rejoice and hold a festival in commemoration of their struggle, (p. 8) out of consideration for the weakness of our nature, and imitating their Master who bore the cross so as to bestow freedom upon us.

3 Again, the fact that we should rejoice and keep festival in memory of the martyrs is not outside the laws of the Spirit either. For, before we received the sure hope, or rather the pledge of the resurrection, that is, the resurrection of Christ from the dead after three days, death was death, and the mourning which followed from it brought no comfort whatsoever. But when he who is God and Word appeared for us by means of his coming in the flesh, and completed the dispensation which is on our behalf, and loosed the bonds of Sheol, death itself has become a sleep, and departure from (this) world has become more a festival than an occasion for mourning. And he who threatened the faithless Jews by means of the prophet and said: '*I will change your feasts into mourning*' (Amos 8: 10), has turned our mournings into festivals, and (this applies) especially for those who, like the martyrs, by means of a good and virtuous way of life, have prepared themselves for the resurrection. That is why joyfully and full of gladness we celebrate the death of the martyrs in the annual cycle, dancing and singing with the prophet David, and saying with true faith: '*Precious in the sight of the Lord is the death of his saints*' (Ps 115 [116]: 15).

4 So we ought to recognize both the intention and the words and the spirit of the church's canons and laws. And thus we will understand whether what we do or say is in agreement with the legislation, and we will not become blind like the Jews. And should we rely only on the letter (of the Law) and cling (to it), and cover our eyes from the beauty of its inner meaning, (like the Jews) who found fault with our Lord and God and Saviour Jesus Christ on the grounds that he was breaking the Sabbath because he saw fit to heal those infirm and sick on that day, although they lacked exact knowledge either of words or of the spirit of the Law?

5 For in fact the Law, when it gave instructions concerning the Feast of the Passover, and commanded being at leisure during these seven days of festival, as well as on the Sabbath, said in Leviticus: '*You shall do no servile work*' (Lev 23: 7, 8). But in Exodus and Deuteronomy, as if to show the meaning of this instruction,

it says as follows: '*You will do no work during (these days)* (Ex 12: 16 LXX), *however, whatever things are done (for the good of) the soul, these alone are you to do*' (Deut 16: 8 LXX). In consequence, it should be clearly seen that a '*servile work*' does not refer to (an activity) leading to the profit or healing of the soul, but to the satisfying of a fleshly pleasure, a luxury, or the performance of a profession, whether in agriculture, (p. 10) or in trade, or in any other similar (profession) in which we spend our life – this is what it was really forbidden to do on the Sabbath.

6   But how does healing paralysis or leprosy not aim at the health of the soul, pitifully bowed down in bodily pain? For just this reason, Jesus, lawgiver and healer, who knew better than they his own (law) which he established and laid down, questioning the foolish Jews to their confusion said: '*I ask you, what is permitted on the Sabbath? To do good or to do evil? To kill the soul or to save it?*' (Lk 6: 9; Mk 3: 4).

7   And so may no-one Jewishly accuse us, because we celebrate the memory of the holy Forty Martyrs during these days of fast. Although in fact we are not permitted to do so for other martyrs, nevertheless this is legitimate concerning these Forty Martyrs. For they are the offspring of these forty days of fasting, for each day has brought forth for us an athlete and martyr.[16] For in fact, it was in those (days) that they struggled, and grew strong through their saintliness and courage, and became equal to a contest such as this. So it is right that the Fathers should rejoice over the contests of their children, and we should not do them an injustice, and assign the memorial of these men to other days.

8   Let all learn that the discipline of the fast knows how to train and instruct children towards martyrdom, and not (just) one or two, but a whole congregation (*ecclesia*) in its entirety and a company of soldiers and a troop of men armed with the entire spiritual panoply, those, in fact, who appeared in public when the judge at the time summoned them and made them appear before him, differing as they were in race and physique, but equal in spiritual stature and *arrived at the perfect man*, according to the saying of Paul (Eph 4: 13).

9   For just this reason they were equal in readiness and discipline in the conflict like armed men, as well as in vigilance, like brave men who knew the rules of combat and how one should attack enemies, (men) who have learned in the way of the Apostle to make every thought captive to Christ (cf. 1 Cor 15: 27) and have

transferred (their) experience of battle and applied (it) to spiritual conflict.

10   And when they were speaking to the man who was presiding as tyrant, they made two of their number their spokesmen, having placed them as it were at the head of the whole troop, while they arranged themselves behind them, and thus gave their support to what was said. One was named Kandios and the other (p. 12) Kurion, and both were instructed to lead soldiers in spiritual matters.

11   On the one hand, whenever the judge used flattery, they made especially firm replies, fearing lest the flattery itself should dissolve the firmness of their bravery. But whenever he changed to become cruel, working himself up with threats, at the same time adding incurable wounds, even instructing that their faces be struck with stones, then these men in their turn, again rising to the occasion, made their replies with a seemly gentleness, imitating our God and incarnate Teacher, him who said to the servant who struck him on his cheek: '*If I have spoken wrongly, bear witness of the wrong; but if well, why do you strike me?*' (Jn 18: 23).

12   O model of patience, who is able to inspire imitation, but who surpasses all imitation! For even if someone were to imitate him exactly in everything, the palm would return to him, because he was God, and submitted himself voluntarily to things such as this.

13   Therefore, we too, having learned the martyrs' tactics, let us stir ourselves up against debilitating fornication, (and), in the face of the passion which turns us savage like wild beasts, let us train ourselves to calmness. For, if we wish it, there is even now an opportunity for martyrdom.

14   Well then, after the judge realized that neither brutality terrified the martyrs, nor did flattery distract them, but that they saw through his wiles, and laughed at (his) machinations, and called him Agrikolaos, which is a word in the Latin language, with the result that he was very aptly named in the Greek language, being wild and a flatterer, then, inflamed with fury, he listed all the varied and usual instruments of torture. But, seeing that they were all equally laughed at and disdained, he resorted in his mind to an innovative method of torture, so as from this to weave a double crown for the martyrs, one from the fact that conventional tortures seemed insignificant in the face of their heroism and excellence, and the other from the fact that they endured an unusual punishment with fortitude and strength.

15   For they were ordered to pass the entire night in the open air and stripped, bitten[17] by the blast of the north wind which was especially sharp, and covered by frost and powdery snow. (p. 14) They remained steadfast in the lake, pounded by the waves. Immobilized by the frost, every (suffering) drove them towards certain death, any one of them alone being able to carry them off to total destruction and corruption.

16   But on the snow and the lake these heroes imagined themselves as if they were on a soft bed. And, although the extremities of their limbs were snapped off and burnt by the cold, and the warmth of (their) bodies fled deep inside them, they sent back to the exterior the fervour of (their spirit), and wrapped (their) dying bodies with it. The warmth of faith increased in proportion as (their) bodies chilled, and strongly warmed the athletes. They represented in their minds that gnashing of teeth which was a threat of everlasting torment, and they took no account at all of the sharpness of a (merely) temporary chill.

17   And if, by chance, one of them was driven by pain to sorrow or to groan, he heard his neighbour respond ascetically in the face of pain with psalmody and prayer, and at once he chanted with him, and responded ascetically together with him, and turned back towards grace. So they sustained one another, these good soldiers and companions in arms, and maintained intact their joint support, as if in battle rank.

18   From heaven, the Master of the Games watched them, while at the same time a choir of angels rejoiced, and prepared to meet them, and rehearsed hymns of victory for the athletes. And a light, descending from on high, picked out and illuminated the stadium of their contest, similar to that light which our Lord showed on the mountain to the disciples, when *his face shone like the sun and his clothes became white as lights* (Matt 17: 2), for he loves to glorify his true servants like himself.

19   And in fact, crowns also descended for the combatants, equal to their number, but lacking just one. For one of them, having fainted under the torments and submitted, rushed towards the nearby bath-house. And at once, the moment he felt the heat from the bath, he died with his flesh broken in pieces. So he died a double death, one, the first, of sin which is eternal, and in which the soul dies, the second, that which sets free from this vain and temporary life.

20   His comrades in arms groaned; (p. 16) troubled by distress, they did not rejoice at the sight of the heavenly light, nor did they

rejoice at the presence of the crowns; but as disciples of Christ who love their brothers (cf. 1 Pet 2: 17), they wept at the departure and loss of their brother, and at the mutilation of (their) company and of the honourable number of forty.

21 But the fathers[18] who love their children, I refer to the forty days of the fast, discovering themselves capable of some great feat because of God who was incarnate and fasted during them, were not indifferent to the pain and misery of their children, whom they had conceived through the frost and snow, but immediately they conceived and brought forth another, and substituted him for the one who perished.

22 For spiritual childbirth is like this: before (there can be) still birth, suddenly conception together with childbirth (take place), and again it travails many times over at the same time. It was like this with Paul, who wrote to the Galatians: *My children, for whom I am again in travail, until the likeness of Christ is formed in you* (Gal 4: 19). Likewise the prophet Isaiah shows forth this kind of travail, which is completed very quickly, when he said: '*Through fear of you, Lord, we have conceived and been in travail, and have brought forth the Spirit of your salvation which you have created upon the earth*' (Is 26:17, 18 LXX).

23 But let us see what this wonderful travail of the days of the fast was, which consoled the martyrs. A man was sitting outside and remained steadfast in guarding this bath-house. He was looking towards the shrivelling arena of the athletes, so as to receive any fugitives from the struggle who might desert (their) station for the comfort of warm water. He was thinking about that, and carefully keeping watch, when he saw the light and observed the crowns which were descending. He was smitten within his soul and completely overcome by the beauty which was appearing. Then, proclaiming himself to be a Christian, he threw himself into the middle of the martyrs, remaining with delight in the lake and the ice, and, so to speak, desiring an addition of the cold which was even more acute; he was awestruck, (and possessed by) something of a chaste frenzy to be devoured by a pious death, thinking of these words of Paul: *The sufferings of this present time are not worthy to be compared with the glory which is to come, which will be revealed in us* (Rom 8: 13). Hence, he, too, was deemed worthy of (his) divine desire, and, when he had been dipped and made perfect in the contests of piety, he flew[19] a martyr with the martyrs and swiftly saw him whom he had so ardently loved. (p. 18)

24 Now is the time to chant the (verse) of David: *This is the change of the right hand of the Most High* (Ps 76 [77]: 10). For how was there not a change when he who took such trouble in (providing) the laxity of a bath, and was a cause of weakness, became a competitor in a feat of endurance? Behold, he who sought to receive the deserters is numbered among the heroes. Moses too will sing on this theme, saying: '*Your right hand, O Lord, is to be praised for its strength*' (Ex 15: 6). And Christ is the all-glorious right hand of the Most High, which is the agent of such great wonders.

25 But let us alight for a moment on the blossom of this bath-house, like diligent bees, that when we gain some profit from it, we may skilfully prepare a spiritual comb of honey from it.[20] For this, then, is what the judge contrived by a wicked device, namely that in the vicinity there should be the comfort of a bath-house as a lure, which would demonstrate even more the extent of the martyrs' endurance.

26 For, on the one hand, the man who has despaired in his mind, and who has no concern for any bolthole, indeed, who perhaps has no desire for one, will endure and persist in afflictions; on the other hand, the man who, having a place of refuge close by, if he should wish to change his mind, and chooses suffering for himself rather than ease, that one is truly steadfast, but not the one who leads an ascetic life in spite of himself, through absence and lack of opportunity (for falling).[21]

27 For this very reason, there is no excuse whatever for anyone to say: 'We must go to the show of the horse-races,[22] because we have recently been given permission'. For show me your perfection this very hour. If, from the absence of merriment you were not a spectator of evil previously, I am grateful to the absence at that time. But as for you, even when you do not see the race, I know you love the shows and on each occasion you provoke God by your desire, and, a fearful matter, this is during these holy days of the fast, at a time when we should be restrained and live in remorse because of him who suffered in the flesh on our behalf. For I pass over saying that we should lead our whole life like that.

28 But now we, on the one hand, recite the liturgical prayers; on the other, the theatre screams piercingly, and pours out its din before us even until night, with flutes, cymbals and lascivious and satanic songs. One would have to be more insensible than stones not to ask why God abandoned the flood. (p. 20) For is (God) not

beloved, given that when we act like this, we still live and see the sun?

29   But let us turn back to the martyrs. For they are able, by their prayers, to turn even us from wickedness, to water the earth with rain, and to drive from our soul and bodies every sickness and harm. For these men, these (heroes), after they had competed in a great contest, and with a leap[23] had been made perfect, and had departed to Christ in their spirits, that God of spirits and all flesh, (their bodies) were commanded by the judge to be burned with fire, for he grudged us the blessing (which would come) from their holy limbs. So servants brought all the bodies of the saints on a cart, except they left just one, who was (still) just breathing, after all these afflictions, imagining that they might make him recant his good intention.

30   But his mother, when she saw what had happened, anxious, forgetting woman's weakness, scorning the harshness of the persecutors, and contending for just one thing, loss that he not to lose her son – for she judged it a loss that he remained in this life – when she had lifted him with her hands, and placed him on her shoulders, she ran to the cart, and threw him on top of his companions saying: 'Let the cart bear also my ear of corn,[24] which I carried within my womb, and brought into this world, but now, having carried him upon my shoulders, I have sent him to resurrection. I will see him there in a little while, and he will not leave me again when he inhabits the heavenly tabernacles'. Let mothers who love the flesh, but do not love (their) children, hear, be chastened, and learn the hope of a mother, a manly hope, and as is proper for Christians, and let them hasten towards the things to come.

31   But, in such a manner that the martyrs might sanctify the entire visible creation, an especially drastic and severe decree of the persecutor instructed that the ash from the flames and what remained of their half-burned bones should be thrown into a river which flowed nearby. After they had been thrown in, the waters which received them kept them safe, and, like a ship, showed them to a certain known place as soon as they were collected together, these precious remains which had been scattered, (the waters) which also, at an earlier time, when they parted, allowed Israel to pass on dry land, and which curbed their turbulence and natural course for the crossing of the ark.[25]

32   It is to this precious ash of the martyrs that we should apply the saying of the prophet Isaiah: *If you pass through the fire the flame will*

not (p. 22) *burn you, and the rivers will not overwhelm you* (Is 43: 2), ash, indeed, which, once divided, has crossed every border – if someone should find that he possessed even a tiny part of it, for example a tiny grain, he would have within his home the Forty Martyrs themselves, directing a seasoned and formidable gaze against the demons – ash which is a means of healing to the weak, an instructor and teacher for those who are in need of teaching, a reconciler for those who are at enmity one with another and set in (their) anger, calming and kindly to those who ask for and pray that they might receive their intercessions. For they have made themselves *all things to all people* (1 Cor 9: 22) since they wish to benefit all.

33 Wise and great Basil, teacher of the whole church beneath heaven, similarly gave praise to these (martyrs), when he was composing eulogies for the athletes of his own region. Beyond doubt, he brought to light both excellent teachers and martyrs when he took up this blessing from God. So, coming to what has been said by the teacher, take delight in it.[26] For we, too, have said these few words under that man's influence. And since you are grateful and glad, praise Christ who is the fount of all knowledge and wisdom, to whom with the Father and the holy Spirit be praise and power now and for ever, from age to age. Amen.

The end of Homily XVIII

Text 17 Homily LXXII

Translated from *PO* 12/1: 71–89

(p. 71) *Concerning the deposition in the Church named Michael's of the sacred corpses of the holy martyrs Procopius and Phocas.*

1 Mighty is the power of Christ's coming in flesh and of his divine epiphany; and the whole experience itself has shown that it is so strong and true that, from the facts themselves, even strangers to the faith cry aloud with Paul by way of confessing: '*Great is the mystery of piety!*' (1 Tim 3: 16). For one will discover also among the Jews – from those things which are related in the form of a history in the divine Scripture which is still read among them, but which is not understood – that before the manifestation of Christ in the world they often lapsed into idolatry; and instead of (p. 72) God's honour and will, they chose those of evil spirits, and were

often chastened by the violent irruptions and maraudings of their neighbours and of the barbarians who were outside their borders, and they did not convert nor repent of their error. Now after Christianity appeared and took control and was gloriously spread abroad – Christianity, which was religion in the authoritative and true sense – they were ashamed in comparison with us; yet still they unseasonably run towards the book of the Law and towards one God when the mind and spirit of the Law demonstrate that he is to be acknowledged in unity and in trinity – the former because of identity of essence, the latter because of the differences and non-confusion of the hypostases – in such a way that they always appear to be in accord with what is written: *fighting against, and standing opposed to, the holy Spirit* (Acts 7: 31).

2   Now among the Greeks also it is easy to observe the most wise of all their philosophers who were renowned in the most ancient times, who particularly introduced in public religious services and rites which were obscene and expressed in symbols, and all those things which led to polytheism and the veneration of images; but those (p. 73) who sprang up after the religion of the Christians blossomed and flourished, while they were ashamed at our splendour and purity on account of the filth of the things which were celebrated in initiation rites and worshipped among them, by ludicrous contrivances and different explanations consequently took pains to cover up the obscenity which those who had preceded them affirmed – but without being able to keep control of the magnitude of this obscenity, even in moderate fashion by persuasive sophistry. For they attempted to take from the truth which belongs to us some images as a support for their own private, futile, and unstable opinion and for their error.

3   Therefore, when the divine Scripture states that there are angels and archangels, virtues and powers, thrones and dominations, and other titles of the intelligible orders which are not given names by us now, but which *in the world to come* (Eph 1: 21) are also destined perhaps to be named and to be known – according to the state of readiness and purity which each person possesses when he has first been purified by deeds of virtue in the here and now – they supposed that they had found a defence of the polytheism which is held in repute among them. Since they are covered in shame because of these allegories, and because of those people from among human beings they have made into gods, they have a hidden (p. 74) wickedness and conceive within themselves the destroyer who also devours them like the bellies of vipers which,

when they give birth, destroy their offspring. For they worship the angels like gods; and again, without moderation, they go forth beyond lawful boundaries, and as the outward garment of piety they possess the covering of demon-worship. Thus it is also the case that many of those who acknowledge themselves as Christians are sick, because they conceal a pagan mind under a sheep's skin, and do not recognize the excellent greatness, yes, indeed, the high sublimity of our mystery.

4   To so great a degree are we removed from those who worship angels and attach to them the glory and worship which are due to God alone that we also choose war without truce against the Arians, who declare: 'There was a time when the Word of God was not' – he who is in the beginning and is with God who is God (cf. Jn 1: 1); and in the same way they also hold the opinion that the everlasting and holy Spirit was established in time after the Father and the Son. For everything which does not belong to the uncreated nature or essence is not God, even if it was (p. 75) possessed of existence before the other creatures. For we also hear the prophet when he declares: '*Let there not be among you a new god: and may you no longer worship a foreign god.*' (Ps 80: 10). Now '*new*' refers to one who does not exist for all time, but who has been made in time, or in some portion of the age, and in a moment more or less short, like one who is temporal. For Paul proclaims: '*In the last days, the Father has spoken to us by means of the Son, by whom also he made the worlds*' (Heb 1: 2). How is he not one who exists for all time? But as one who does not exist in time, he took up existence in some particular point in time.

5   So, then, we too acknowledge that the angels and all the powers in heaven which have been recounted have been made by God, but are not gods: '*For to us there is one God the Father from whom are all things, and we are in him; and one Lord Jesus Christ, in whom are all things, and we in him*' (1 Cor 8: 6). And David also, the most divine among the prophets, sings in declaration to the God of all: '*He who makes his angels spirits, and his ministers a fire which glows with flame*' (Ps 103: 4). And also in another place he says: '*Bless the Lord, all angels (p. 76) of his who are mighty in strength and carry out his word, so as to proclaim the voice of his words. Bless the Lord, all his hosts, his ministers who perform his will*' (Ps 102: 20–21).

6   To these it is pleasing to add as well what was said by the Apostle about them: '*Are they not all ministering spirits, who are sent for the service of those who are destined to inherit salvation?*' (Heb 1: 14). So then, they are created spirits, and intelligible and incorporeal

creatures, whose business it is that they should praise God and receive the divine commandments, and perfectly perform those commands with swiftness and power. For they possess the power which is appropriate for what they are commanded, since it is given to them from above to perform such things, both when they are sent for the service of our salvation, and when they share in the primal, uncreated, and essential light which is seen in the holy Trinity; and from there are they illuminated.

7   For this reason, those who also fulfill the duty of equerries, who bear spears and carry arms, are also named 'angels of light', not because they exist in outward forms such as these (for what is separate from the denseness of the body is also in every respect without outward form), (p. 77) but because they appear and are understood in this way through notions of the spirit, namely, through their designations and actions which are known to us, so that they show forth the kingly power and universal authority of the one who rules, who is indeed entitled both Lord of Hosts and Lord of Sabaoth: for 'Sabaoth' is to be translated as 'Hosts'. Therefore Luke also states that *a multitude of the heavenly host* appeared to the shepherds *and said: 'Glory to God in the heights, and on earth peace; among men, good pleasure'* (Lk 2: 13–14). For let no-one judge these things about them from those visions in which they have appeared from time to time to holy men; for these are diverse, and appear differently at different times, according to the appropriateness of the need which is determined, and in such outward forms that they might be seen by the eyes of sensible beings. Therefore there appeared indeed to Daniel – who was consumed within himself by the depths of wisdom and the intelligible beauty of divine visions, as a result of which it came about that he was called (and quite properly) *'man greatly desired'* (Dan 9: 23; 10: 11, 19) – men diverse, various, and differing in outward appearances at different times, because of the variety and difficulty (p. 78) of the explanation of the revelations. So, on one occasion he saw Gabriel like a man who flies, who made him recognize by what he said that the outward appearance of a bird is a sign of swiftness. For he said: *'At the beginning of your petition the word went forth; and I have come to inform you of it'* (Dan 9: 23). Again, on another occasion, (he saw) *a man who was clothed in linen, whose loins were girded with gold of Uphaz, and his body was like chrysolite, and his face was like the appearance of lightning, and his eyes like lamps of fire, and his arms and his feet like the appearance of glittering bronze, and his voice like the voice of many people* (Dan 10: 5–6). Now all

these things demonstrate the difficulty of the interpretation and the difficulty of comprehending the visions; and they show that the variety of outcomes divides the times which are in the future among several kingdoms; for the variety of the materials, and the confused and uncertain voice of many people, refer to this matter. Therefore he had need of further understanding about what had been said, and heard (the words): *'Understand the words which I am speaking to you'* (Dan 10: 11).

8 But if we suppose that the essence of these beings also corresponds to the appearances which are seen in (p. 79) them, it is also necessary to suppose that they are diverse and material, and that that is the case, indeed, when they are immaterial and simple since they are incorporeal. *For are they not all ministering spirits, sent to minister on behalf of those who are destined to inherit salvation?* (Heb 1: 14). And was not Gabriel like this, who was sent for the annunciation of Mary the Mother of God for our sakes who are destined to become *heirs of God and co-heirs of Christ* (Rom 8: 17), and henceforward to be saved by the redemption? Why is it not in the same way that the ones who appeared to the women by the sacred tomb, and who were the first to proclaim the resurrection, were ones who – as also befits the light of God's knowledge which shone after them – were seen in white and dazzling robes?

9 Shall we not then regard as blessed those who are in this sort of state, who delight and rejoice in the illumination from on high, and who carry out the divine commands? Indeed so, I say; for I too am greatly confident of it. So let us honour them to such a degree, as much as we know them only as the true ministers of the good God and Lord and as the good stewards they are, and to the extent that they greatly exult and rejoice about our salvation. For *there is joy* (p. 80) *in heaven over one sinner who repents* (Lk 15: 7), Christ, God the Word, has decreed. So then, it is known that the host of heaven rejoices. For taking up the matter again, he speaks more clearly as follows: *'I say to you that there is joy before the angels of God over one sinner who repents'* (Lk 15: 10); and again: *'See that you do not despise one of these little ones. For I tell you that their angels in heaven always see the face of my Father who is in heaven'* (Matt 18:10). And again it is written: *'The Seraphim hide their face'* (Is 6: 2), because the glory of God cannot be seen.

10 But from this it is certain that, corresponding to the doctrines contained in it, the divine Scripture makes use of our own customary (expressions), shaping the account of its teaching. So then, through the Seraphim and the hosts which are swift and

valiant above all others and rapid and lofty and exalted (for the great number of their wings clearly demonstrates this), it makes known that this lofty glory is entirely inaccessible and invisible. Then, through the angels to whom has been entrusted the guardianship of those who are considered the least among us, who always see the face of the heavenly Father, it makes known the vastness of their philanthropy and their gentleness, (p. 81) because of which the angels are considered as possessing all the confidence of those who are personally conversant with the most sublime princes. And as regards us human beings, we find that the scriptural word shapes itself in similar fashion. For on the one hand, fearing the awesome visitation of God, the prophet cries aloud: '*Turn your face from my sins*' (Ps 50: 11); on the other, in attracting peace to himself, he says: '*Make your face shine upon your servant; and do not turn away your face from your servant. Because I am afflicted, answer me swiftly*' (Ps 68: 18).

11   For one must consider the 'face of God' in differing ways corresponding to these sorts of senses (sc. described earlier), and not as a type and a corporeal icon and as a human likeness, which is indeed alien to a nature or to an incorporeal essence. Thus the angels are said always to see the face of God (cf. Matt 18: 10) when they earnestly take pains to guard us, and perhaps also when in some measure they use supplications on our behalf. Something of this kind the angel who spoke to Daniel also acknowledged, when by some kind of personification and hint he foretold the liberation of Israel's captivity, (p. 82) declaring as follows: '*There is not one who helps me against these, except Michael your prince*' (Dan 10: 21). For the angels are given as guardians even to peoples and to cities and to each human being, and especially to those who fear the Lord, in the likeness of faithful taxiarchs and soldiers who are from the great king. For Scripture says: '*The angel of the Lord will encamp around those who fear him: and he will deliver them*' (Ps 33: 8). For '*will encamp*' means that the help of a single angel possesses the power of a whole camp and battle array.

12   But in mistaking their rank as soldiers and stewards, let us not, therefore, through pagan error, dishonour them by honours which are beyond the limit (of what is fitting). For everything which is offered to the glory of the one who alone is God is for them a dishonour. Thus the angel who spoke to Manoah said: '*And if you make a whole burnt offering, offer it up to the Lord*' (Judges 13: 16). This is what these stewards Barnabas and Paul did, men who were also as faithful as the angels, when the demon-worshippers

131

in Lycaonia presumed to sacrifice to them as gods. For they cried out: '*You men, why are you doing this? We too are men, subject to the same passions as yourselves,* (p. 83) *who declare to you that you should turn away from these vanities and turn back to the living God, who made heaven and earth and the land and the sea and everything that is in them*' (Acts 14: 14).

13   By contrast, the pagans used to employ a multitude of devices and shake every rock to merit a sacrifice and to be regarded as gods, on the grounds that they had performed in some city a favour benefitting human beings or had performed a good deed. For as such they regarded those who preceded them who were falsely considered by human beings to be gods. But the ministering, intelligible, and heavenly spirits are not of these kinds. For they have within themselves such an intense fear that they are near to God, and they tremble at his awesome sublimity. For they also call to mind the fall of the Slanderer who formerly belonged to their own order; and who, as it is written, '*acted haughtily against the Lord, and strove against him in dishonour*' (Job 15: 26). But the presumptuous hand of the painters, being a law unto itself since it condones the fictions of pagan illusions regarding idolatry, and planning everything for profit, clothes Michael and Gabriel in the manner of lords or kings (p. 84) with a royal robe of purple, adorns them with a crown, and places in their right hand the sign of rulership and universal authority. For these reasons, and ones which are like them, those who so senselessly honour the angels depart from the church and transgress her laws: those who ordered and set in place the holy canons have placed these people under anathema.

14   So then, we too, adhering to the accuracy of the latter, and blocking the hidden entrance-ways of demon-worship, consecrate churches which have been built under the dedicatory title of the angels with the bones and sacred limbs of the holy martyrs, or with their victorious dust which has all been bravely burned and has become a sacrifice: by this very deed we proclaim that they, too, like the angels, are mighty powers. For they also have become, as David says concerning the angels, '*mighty ones in power who perform his word*' and '*his ministers who do his will*' (Ps 102: 20–1) – and this when they were bound in the flesh. Now from this they turned away their faces like a stranger, and lived incorporeally and performed many miracles. But not even on that account did they forget their status as stewards. Do not (p. 85) suppose, therefore, that even the angels are anything other than

ministers and stewards. For this is the teaching and the doctrine: that the martyrs are united with them. God acted also in this way towards the Israelites who were prone to idolatry, since he permitted them to offer sacrifice, but to none other than himself alone; and he mingled with the sacrifices the symbols of rational and evangelic ministry, and left behind some small element of ancient custom to draw them towards the truth, and to rob those to whom some of this custom had been left and in some way to equip himself with this custom. Therefore we teach and give instruction to the effect that the martyrs are joined as one with the angels, so as to distance ourselves from erroneous doctrine, since the former as well as the latter have only one duty, namely to praise God and to minister to him in respect of our salvation.

15 For also in heaven their habitations are with one another. And Paul is a witness, writing *to the myriads of the angels and to their festal company*, referring to *the church of the first-born who are inscribed in heaven* (Heb 12: 22–3). Now the latter are those who, by faith and the laver of re(p. 86)generation, have been made rich by adoption as sons, and have partaken of the spiritual birth through which no-one is of inferior birth, but all are first-born on account of a single fulness of grace and of equal honour. In this manner speaks also Gregory the Theologian in one of his treatises: 'There will be a general festal assembly of the heavenly and the terrestrial hosts; for I am persuaded that these exult together with us and keep festival with us on this day, if indeed they be lovers of humankind and lovers of God'.[27]

16 In this sense we bring together the martyrs with the angels, as being the faithful stewards of the one Lord, and since they are a single festal assembly which loves humankind and loves God. For we do not drive out the angels (in the manner of pagan error) by means of the holy limbs [of the martyrs] on the grounds that they died of necessity. For if this were so, the angels would not have stayed and lingered by the tomb of the crucified one in the way of the spear-bearers at kings' palaces; and they would not have said to the women: '*You seek Jesus of Nazareth who was crucified. He is not here: for he has arisen, as he said*' (Matt 28: 5–6).

17 Now then, you men who lack sense: those who honoured the one who was crucified, how shall they (p. 87) then honour those who suffered and wrestled in combat for him? And how shall they turn away their faces from the ashes of those limbs which conducted themselves in purity and chastity and with virtue – ashes which continually effect cures of every kind, which drive the demons

out? It is possible to see these wonders in Palestine, in Caesarea itself, which Procopius performed; those in Pontus, which Phocas performed, Phocas who openly appeared to those who were in trouble on the sea and who sailed together with them, and who placidly and peacefully accompanied those who were almost about to be swallowed up by the waves.

18 The angels are close to the limbs of those who have been laid to rest in this place; and they love them and praise them together with their spirits. For they honour those who went about in the body incorporeally and in the same manner as themselves; and by no means do they turn their face away from the mortal nature of those who have lived in virtue. And what is amazing, if this should be so in the case of the martyrs? (It is just) as when God was ordering the Israelites to take up the dead body of Joseph as they were hastening from Egypt towards the promised land (and said): '*Behold, I am sending my angel before your face, so that he may guard you on the road*' (Ex 23: 20). Or rather, he himself was also going (p. 88) along with them, since Moses was saying: '*If you yourself do not go with us, do not make us go up from here*' (Ex 33: 15), when he replied: '*Indeed I will do for you what I have said, for you have found favour before me, and I know you better than all human beings*' (Ex 33: 17). And this happened at a time when whoever came into contact with a corpse was considered an abomination according to the childish commandments of the Law, which were instructing and teaching us allegorically that we should keep our distance from the dead works of sins.

19 It is also said that Michael himself attended to the tomb of Moses's body when the Slanderer was acting as opponent, since God allowed it, and wished through what was being seen to display what was not seen to those who at that time were observing but little, and who were much inclined to senselessness: that after (our) deliverance from the here and now, the Slanderer and the evil powers which are with him rise up in opposition to our souls as they journey towards the heights, because they wish to block the way through. And they prevail over those who have done evil, but are overpowered by the righteous through angelic assistance; and this, indeed, Antony perceived, Antony who is mighty in asceticism and in the angelic life. (p. 89) Now the sacred Scripture has it as follows: '*And Michael the archangel, when he was speaking to the Slanderer in contending about the body of Moses, did not dare to bring against him a charge of blasphemy, but said: "The Lord rebuke you"*' (Jude 9).

20 So then, since we have been counted worthy of these mysteries and of benefits which are like them, let us praise Christ, the God of the angels and of the martyrs, since we know him thanks to all these. To him is due all praise, and glory, and authority with the Father and the holy Spirit, now, and always, and to the ages of ages. Amen.

The end of Homily LXXII

6

LETTERS

The following letters have been selected for their chronological spread and the variety of topics which Severus addresses in them. They also reflect the wide range of his correspondents.

From the time of his patriarchate (512–18) we have letters to Bishop Nicias, the metropolitan of Laodicea (I.6), who is known to us from other sources (Honigmann 1951: 13, 15, 35–6), the prefect Timostratus (I.8), a well-known official in the East (*PLRE* 2: 1119–20), the abbot of the monastery of Simeon Stylites at Qal'at Siman (I.43), and a certain Stephen the reader (VIII.1). From Severus's exile there are two of his letters to the noblewoman Caesaria (Letters 98 and IV.10), one of his frequent addressees (Allen 1999: 392 and nn. 21–2), to the new parents Ammianus and Epagathus (III.2), and to the noble young woman Georgia (X.8). The so-called *Defence* to the emperor was composed in 532 and sent to Emperor Justinian; the Synodical Letter was written on the accession of Patriarch Theodosius to the see of Alexandria on 26 July 535.

The letter to Nicias (Text 18) betrays one of Severus's recurring concerns in *SL*, namely the canonical ordination of priests and bishops in a turbulent period which often saw clergy changing from the monophysite to the dyophysite position, and vice versa. Here the specific concern is that two men have travelled out of their jurisdiction to seek dyophysite ('Nestorian') ordination. The obligation of the city-church to its clergy, and the fact that ordination is not a meal-ticket are addressed in the letter to Timostratus (Text 19), who at the same time is made aware of the poverty of the patriarchate of Antioch, presumably in the face of the Persian wars and the upheavals of the Chalcedonian controversy (Allen 2001: 365–6). The letter to the abbot of the monastery of Simeon Stylites (Text 20) for its part provides us with important information regarding the respective roles of the patriarch and the abbot in the administration of monastic

136

establishments, the process of a church law-suit against a monk who had introduced dyophysites into a non-Chalcedonian monastery, and the protocol involved in dealing with the miscreant. The issues raised by Stephen the reader are of a quite different order (Text 21), for he displayed his dissatisfaction with Severus's Homily XXX on Simeon Stylites because of the paucity of biographical facts which it contained on the saint. In the course of pointing out that encomia on saints are read in various churches in the eastern empire, Severus gives us information on contemporary liturgical practices, at the same time advising Stephen to omit the first few paragraphs of Homily XXX if he is reading it in a Chalcedonian church. The two letters to Caesaria show the deposed patriarch exercising pastoral care towards a noblewoman from his place of exile. In Letter 98 (Text 22) he defends himself of the charge made by a third party that he subscribes to the doctrine of *apokatastasis*, adducing Patristic quotations from the Cappadocians, John Chrysostom and Cyril to support his arguments; in IV.10 (Text 23) he addresses her moral and canonical concerns regarding taking part in Chalcedonian liturgical events, providing her with a nuanced answer tailored to her high rank. The letter to Ammianus and Epagathus (Text 24) reveals Severus personally involved in choosing the name of a new-born child, and disapproving the request that the parents had made to the patriarch to be sent viaticum by him: the validity of the sacrament is not enhanced by the rank of the priest who dispenses it. Also personal in tone is the letter to Georgia (Text 25), in which the patriarch counsels a young woman whose parents are sad and angry at the fact that she is still not married. Text 26, an extract from a letter to John the hegumenos, which survives in Greek, has been included because it contains the formula 'a single activity of the God-human' (*mia physis theandrike*). This was adapted from ps.Dionysius the Areopagite and was to play a significant part in the monenergist and monothelite controversies in the following century.[1]

Of quite a different order is the letter which Severus wrote to Emperor Justinian in 532 (*CPG* 7070 (3)), which is preserved in the anti-Chalcedonian *Church History* of ps.Zachariah Rhetor (IX.16). The document (Text 27) is a defence or apology for the fact that Severus did not accept the emperor's invitation to attend a doctrinal dialogue in Constantinople which was designed to end religious conflict by direct negotiation (Grillmeier 1995: 343–7). The patriarch makes much of the offer of safe passage which Justinian gave him, and of the difficulties and slanders which he is suffering because of the ascendancy of the Julianist party in Alexandria. Parts of his doctrinal dispute with Julian are also rehearsed. In 535–6, Severus finally acceded to the imperial request to go to Constantinople, only to be condemned by the synod there.

The Synodical Letter of Severus to Theodosius of Alexandria on the accession of the latter to the patriarchate (Text 28) was written in reply to the letter which the new patriarch sent to his colleagues in order to demonstrate his orthodoxy. The fact that Severus was the recipient of such a letter even though he had been deposed seventeen years before is a testimony to his stature amongst other non-Chalcedonians. He stresses his belief in Nicaea, Cyril's Twelve Chapters, and the *Henotikon* of Zeno, while denouncing Chalcedon and Leo's *Tome*.

Text 18 Letter to Nicias

Translated from *SL* I.6: 42–3

(p. 42) *Of the same (Severus), to Nicias the bishop*[2]

An evil and unlawful deed, and one which is at war with the laws of the catholic and apostolic church, has come to our hearing: namely, that some of the men who hail from the village of Minidus and Ouaris[3] have boldly ventured to sail to the west, and to receive unholy ordination from people who are of the same mind as Nestorius, and divide our Lord and God Jesus Christ after the inexpressible union into a duality of natures. Now this is an ordination which is invalid not in one way only, but in many ways, and is to be considered as if it had not happened at all; since even if those who laid audacious hands upon them had been orthodox, it was not for them to perform an ordination in another part of the world, or rather in one outside their boundary, resulting in the dissolution of proper (p. 43) order.[4] And they did that thing, while we, by the grace of God, are guilty of not even one heresy! For the holy canons clearly proclaim this in both intention and in words. Now, therefore, may your love of God make known the sense of the sacred laws to all who are in the environs of their part of the world; and may you publicly pronounce them stripped of every priestly and diaconal honour and degree; and may you forbid from contact with these men those who are in communion with us, or rather with the orthodox faith; so that they may not have a share in the wickedness, and call upon themselves the wrath which comes from God.

The end

Text 19 Letter to Timostratus

Translated from *SL* I.8: 45–8

Of the same, to the Prefect Timostratus

It seems to me something worth praying for and delightful that I should converse with Your Greatness through letters, and that I should offer a salutation which is owed to you as a debt, as if repaying an obligation which is in some sort necessary, and not the fortuitous outcome of this event (p. 46) about which I am, in truth, embarrassed to write. For although I was happy to come across what was lately sent from Your Excellency, I left off the reading of it with sadness. For I found the cause or *hypothesis*[5] of the letter burdensome when examined (as it were) in the theological sense – difficult, rather, and impossible and (to speak in the manner of Scripture) *according to the flesh* (2 Cor 1: 17), and something determined in accordance with the senses. For while the holy Apostle, or rather, Christ who is speaking in him, restrains and with a certain threat prohibits the gift of ordination and says: '*Do not lay your hand suddenly upon any man, nor be a partaker in others' sins: preserve your soul in purity*' (1 Tim 5: 22–3), by many people ordination is considered an activity like some craft of the manual sort, that of the metal-worker, so to speak, or of the carpenter, or as some occupation to which pertains the benefit of means of support, and a pretext for *dapane*,[6] that is to say, for travelling expenses and relief of poverty – as if it were unlawful for us here to procure the necessities of life from any office other than this.

Now the good people (concerned) do not know that it is essential for a man to pass through all the ministerial orders of the church, and that he should first be instructed in the particular manner which pertains to priests, and so be counted worthy of ordination either as priest or as deacon. And these things are so because the function is difficult and not common, in accord with the enactment of the law which has previously been quoted, which states: '*Do not lay a hand suddenly on any man, nor be a partaker* (p. 47) *in others' sins*' (1 Ti 5: 22), and which also adds the statement: '*Preserve your soul in purity*' (1 Ti 5: 23). And each of the additions rehearses the awesomeness of the enactment of the law, and indicates that it is proper that the hand should be stretched out only with a certain sort of serious great necessity, and not willy-nilly, over the head of those who are for ordination.

Now as regards our expounding the first reason why ordination is an awesome thing, these brief observations are sufficient for us. But I shall add a second reason as well, which looks at a consideration which the senses can appreciate. And this is what it is: namely, that our holy church is truly indigent and in want; and it is so entirely chafed and made dependent upon a burden of interest-payments that it dare not scarcely even lift up its head, but loans upon loans are added to it, and interest upon interest accounted to it. Now all those who live in the great city of Antioch are witnesses of these things; and I suppose that there are not many even of those who dwell beyond its borders who have not heard of the matter. Even so, men who come from the royal city and others from its vicinity, being pestered by certain individuals, do not give up continually (so to speak) writing to Our Lowliness and requesting ordination, supposing that this is not something which makes us indignant. Indeed, this passion for ordination has made some persons behave so foolishly as even to display themselves lusting after the vestments which particularly make up the (p. 48) priestly apparel, while not, on the other hand, seeking also to receive provisions. And when once they had been counted worthy of this thing they had laboured for, when the time of distribution came, they reached out their hands before all the others, so to speak, so that not only those who made a game of these sacred things because of their deceit and knavery were made objects of ridicule, but also we ourselves, who had been deceitfully deluded.

Now I have been constrained to write these things to Your Excellency since I sorrow within myself, and because I know that I am sending this to Christian men, and to those who are able to sympathize with me and can also maybe stretch out a hand to me because I am weary, and like a man who is being throttled by men who lend on interest and compelled to be sustained in need, when there are no resources nor yields which are sufficient to meet the size of a request which is pious indeed, but difficult because of its frequency.

The end

Text 20 Letter to the Abbot

Translated from *SL* I.43: 134–7

Of the same, to the abbot of the monastery of the holy Lord Simeon

Because Nonnus, even before he came to the monastic community of the holy Simeon, was on many occasions called upon to defend himself against those indictments and accusations which were being brought against him, and did not obey, but even when he was under an order issued by the devout[7] legal representatives of the church set this at naught with a boldness which was like that of a man who was entirely accustomed to scorning holy things; and when, on one occasion only and covertly he made an approach to me at night, as if he were doing things which merited night and darkness, he supposed that this was enough for him to have his case overlooked.[8] And in the end, when at the hand of Your Reverence he received an unequivocal letter, he impudently persisted in the same way, I tolerated it, and was not stirred up into a righteous commotion; but rather, when (p. 135) I had given him a time-limit of ten days, I permitted that limit to be doubled for him. And he (in no small way indeed) set himself as if he had not been called, since he excused himself with pretexts consisting only in sins; and he returned answer through Your Reverence, asking that the clergy should not be present at his court-case, because it is clergy who have suffered wrong through him, and from them he was in the habit of taking the unholy and polluted profits.

For he acted in the same way as those who have stolen, or committed adultery, or done murder, and then declare that there should be present at their court-case neither those who because of theft, nor those who because of adultery, nor those who because of murder have been outraged and have suffered wrong. And it is no wonder if he spits out things such as these, when he is guilty of wicked deeds which are of this sort. For what shall those people say, who *hate justice and distort all right things, and build Zion with bloodshed and Jerusalem with wickedness* (Mi 3: 9–10), as a certain one of the prophets has declared somewhere? For how should a person fail to say that full of blood are the hands which have sold the gifts of the holy Spirit, which he had neither authority to give to people, nor to remove from those who possessed them? For this is what is amazing about his sacrilege: that he would conceal himself as it were insidiously (in hypocrisy, I mean), while at each ordination service he would be listening to the execrations and fearful curses (p. 136) which I was making against unlawful profits of this sort, and he would shut his hearing, *like the deaf adder which blocks its ears, which will not hear the voice of the charmer* (Ps 57: 5–6), as the prophetic Psalmist declares.

But now, so that I do not drag the letter out with superfluity in saying many things, I am making him this second and third summons through Your Reverence, or rather (which is more true to say) one which possesses the force of the tenth and twentieth summons; for one might deservedly consider them equal in number to the summonses of the days that have passed! Because I wish, even if later in time,[9] to urge him to make a defence when pious bishops, according to the express will of the holy canons, are present and ready to undertake the court-case, when the holy Gospels are set in the midst, and the dreadful threat which is from those Gospels hangs over those who turn aside what is upright. But if he is rash and is tardy even after this letter, the judgement and the decision which is appropriate shall go forth against him, the same divine laws of ecclesiastical order.

For we on our side did not wish that these facts about him might in any way be disregarded by the illustrious magistrates of Antioch; but as far as possible we even brought them to their knowledge. And we would have encouraged them, and some of the skilful orators, to be judges of the matter, (p. 137) except that we were deterred as we were considering the regulation of the holy canons, which require that church law-suits be tried by pious bishops, and which excommunicate those who abandon these and turn to the civil courts, putting them to shame. But on account of this very same reason we sent the God-fearing deacon Eusebius; for we do not agree, after the course of so many days, to detain the pious bishops here, who need to return to their familiar flock.

The end

Text 21 Letter to Stephen

Translated from *SL* VIII.1: 440–42

Of the same, to Stephen the reader

I admit that I was very glad when I received the letter which was sent to me by Your Reverence through His Excellency Sergius who is the head of the 'second people' of Syria,[10] for two reasons: both because it was yours, and because the things written there are as they are. For I have found by experience that the man is of the sort that you indicated to us by your words; and for this, many thanks to Your Reverend Self. But because – after you received the sermon which was preached by us about the pious Simeon – you request that another should also be composed by us as a biographical account, you appear to me to be acting in the same way as a greedy and exact moneylender! When he sees that the one who owes him money is unproductive, he wants to take back the principal only; (p. 441) but when he has taken it, and has seen the gold in his hands, he is enticed also to make demand for the interest which, before he took back the principal, he scorned, deciding in charitable manner that only what belonged to him should be returned, without profits.

But know this absolutely plainly: that we took pains in that sermon, even when we were addressing ourselves to a style which is festal and expressive of praise, that we should not disregard the historical and narrative style either, so that the sermon might have the two things together. Then the reader might be the more delighted, when he receives a narration which is decked out with blossoms of praises, and indeed is something which does not fall short of ecclesiastical dignity.

Now the fact that the praises of the saints are also read out in the churches is witnessed by the sermon of the wise Basil concerning the Forty Martyrs, which is read out to the people in the city of the inhabitants of Beirut[11] and also by that of the holy Pamphilus,[12] both in that city and in that of the men of Caesarea which is the metropolis of Palestina Prima. And we know as well that the eulogizing sermon which was preached about Gregory the Wonder-worker was read out in many churches, and in the royal city itself, and, in the same manner also, the sermon about Basil the Great.[13] For it is proper that we who are examiners of the laws should disable you, and so restrain your avaricious hearing.

Now I suppose that the preface of the same sermon (p. 442) which was written by us on the holy Simeon will be troublesome to you, inasmuch as it is not acceptable to the Byzantines (sc. anti-Chalcedonians). But it is easy for you to use the three or four sections which are placed at the beginning, to leave out those things which are troublesome, and to read out in connected narrative the things which remain.

Now we have heard from other people of the confident speech of Your Reverence – or rather, that we should speak more truly, of your witness on behalf of orthodoxy. And you are blessed both in the praise which is here and now, and in the recompense which is awaited, which is promised to those who have striven well.

The end

Text 22 Letter to Caesaria

Letter 98, translated from *PO* 14/1: 200–13

From the fifth letter of Mar Severus, from the fourth book which was composed after the exile, which was written to Caesaria the hypatissa

Now as to the question which Your Excellency's great honour has asked me by letter, I return a ready answer: never have I admitted or approved those who talk of *apokatastasis*[14] and an end of the sentence of the severe punishments which are decreed for us in the world to come; and he who claims that he holds letters of mine which teach this doctrine is clearly lying. For this reason, I applauded your greatness so befitting the love of God, in that you asked that the letters of this sort should be shown to you: letters which the one who devised was necessarily forced to show deceitfully as having been manufactured by me. But since those who espouse a doctrine like this wish to fulfill their desires, as if it arises in fact out of opinions which they espouse with conviction, they employ words which are tailored for those who listen to them, (p. 201) saying that it is not proper or worthy for God and greatly distant from his compassion that one who has sinned for fifty years or a hundred in this world should endure severe punishments for ages which have no end, because this leads them astray. For the laws of God, and those which exist among human beings, judge it right to repay sins according to the will which motivates the sinner; and it is possible to hear even wise men out of doors who are talking about people who have committed disgraceful acts and things which are not lawful, saying: 'This man ought to die not once, but many times'.

But when someone, like us, hears that God became incarnate, and without change became man for our redemption; and that because of this he came down from heaven, and clearly decreed *a fire which is not extinguished and a worm which does not die* (Mk 9: 44), and yet despises all these things – how shall he not be counted worthy to be condemned in double measure (if it be possible to say so) to everlasting fire and to severe punishment without end? For even if he should live a hundred years or more than this in this world, and pass all of his time like this in vanity; it should be known that if he were able to live (p. 202) without end, remaining without dying, he would not desist from avarice and lasciviousness and licentiousness and a disgraceful life which consists of lusts. How, then, will a man who is like this not be punished endlessly corresponding to his will? Now even those who introduce *apokatastasis*, that is, an end of judgement, say about sinners that they will be severely punished for many years and for long drawn out periods, as one might say, and for prolonged ages to come. And then, afterwards, they will be cleansed and find mercy and be esteemed worthy of the blessedness which has been promised.

But those who say these things forget that according to their human thoughts (p. 203) they are thus showing also that injustice and unrighteousness are of God. For if a man lives while he sins for fifty or eighty years more or less, is punished with harsh sentences, and bears severe punishments for many prolonged ages, again it would seem, according to their reasoning, that this is not worthy of God's compassion, nor again is it fitting for the love of humankind which is found in him, because the time of their severe punishment is not equal to the time of their lives which was spent in sins. For it would be right that if God approved the opinions of those who think these things and followed and complied with their beliefs, that he who sins for fifty years should bear punishment for only fifty years; and it should not be as they assert, that the moment prolonged for many ages be a long drawn out sentence for him, and (p. 204) his torture continue for ages. For also our Lord and Saviour Jesus Christ in the holy words of his Gospel, when he was separating the just from the sinners said: *'These shall go to eternal severe punishment; but the just to everlasting life'* (Matt 25: 46). And he made pronouncement concerning the two sorts, the former and the latter, in the same parable in terms of an equality without variation, when he ordained that expression 'for ever' without variation in respect of the two groups. And Basil the Great among the teachers of the truth shows this plainly in the homily which was composed by him in the section of question and answer directed to the brethren of the monasteries.[15] [Basil's discussion of Lk 12: 47 follows.]

(p. 207) Since these things are acknowledged as being so, it is fitting to know that the statements *'he shall be beaten with many blows'* or *'he shall be beaten with few'* (Lk 12: 47) indicate, not that there is an end to severe punishment, but variation within it. For if God is the true judge, and renders to every man according to his works, it is possible that one person should be in the fire which is not extinguished, and that another should be in fire which is more moderate, or stronger; and that another should be with the worm that does not die, and another in bitter miseries; and there may be one who is in torments which are more tolerable, and one who is in pains stronger than they, each man as he deserves. Furthermore, it is possible to perceive in Gehenna a difference in the torments of those who are being punished, and again in this (place) one recognizes what is called *'outer darkness'* (Matt 25: 30; Lk 17: 10), (p. 208) different from the former, since it is a darkness which is in the midst of it. Then there is a place of punishment in which a man weeps on his own, and again one where he is in gnashing of teeth because of the mighty pains of the bitter sentence. And what is said in the book of Proverbs: *'he brings down to the depths of Sheol and to the foundations of the pit'* (Prov 9: 18), informs us that there are men being tortured in Sheol, but not in its depths; and there are those who are in the pit, but not, as it were, in its foundation. All these are things by which is made known the variety of punishment which is contained in the sentence passed on those who are punished as their deeds deserve, either by means of a harsh sentence, or by a punishment in which there is a respite corresponding to their actions.

These things are seen hinted in the case of diseases which befall human beings in this life which they live. For there is one who burns (p. 209) with the fever while he lies with other sicknesses; and there is another who is in a fever only, and one which is more moderate than the former; and another who, while he has no fever, is buffeted by other sicknesses of every variety; and yet another, whose diseases appear either more moderate or more severe than those of his colleague. Now what is said by our Lord with reference to '*many blows*' and '*few blows*' (Lk 12: 47) is in line with our manner of speaking, corresponding to the common usage which is observed among human beings. And many other expressions are like these. For many times do we see that this kind of language is taken up also by a person who is afflicted by one disease or brought low by a sickness. In what way? As when we see a man who is in a fever only, or is seized by a pain in the eyes, we are amazed at how much he has suffered and how many adversities he has borne. So then what is said about '*many blows*' or '*few blows*' (Lk 12: 47) is to be taken in the sense I have stated: not with reference to extent of time (p. 210) which has an end, but as referring to variety of punishment which was inherent in the sentence prepared. [Testimonia from Gregory Nazianzen, John Chrysostom and Cyril are adduced to support this view.]

Text 23 Letter to Caesaria

Translated from *SL* IV.10: 306–9

Of the same, to Caesaria the hypatissa

Because you have asked (out of the devoutness which loves doctrine) if some of the orthodox are acting properly when they do not communicate with the heretics, but only hear the reading of the holy Gospel, or even remain at the time of the eucharistic prayers but do not communicate in those things which are being confected: the reply is absolutely clear to those who are not ignorant of the divine laws. For John the Evangelist, speaker of divine things, wrote: *You are our letter, written in our heart, and known and read by all people* (2 Cor 3: 2).

If, therefore, one should not even offer an ordinary greeting to those who bring another doctrine and do not (p. 307) teach the orthodox faith, how could anyone take part in the prayers and lections or in anything else of this kind, with people who are like these? And that wise man Paul also commands that we should turn away our sight from those who serve the work of heresy, when he writes thus to Titus: *A man who is a heretic after one admonition and two avoid: knowing that such a man is perverted and sins, being self-condemned* (Ti 3: 10). Therefore, the one who assembles with the sinners makes himself liable to the same verdict. But the holy canons of the church have also plainly rejected the notion that a person might pray with the heretics. For the 135th canon says: 'It is not lawful to receive the blessings of the heretics, which are not blessings, but rather non-blessings'. And immediately next to it is the 136th canon, which states: 'It is not lawful to pray with the heretics or schismatics'.[16] And these matters are stated with some exactitude.

But when I (lowly individual that I am, in accordance with my lowly knowledge) observe the extent of the Scripture inspired by God, then I find that those who are in ministerial appointments or in high offices of state and who are required to be near and follow around those who hold power, are counted worthy of a dispensation; so that when they go in with them and hear the lections and the prayers, they may preserve their integrity. By this I mean that they do not participate in the communion from which they are divided. For observe this: in the Fourth Book of Reigns[17] is written something along these lines. (p. 308) A man, captain of the army of the king of Syria (which is Damascus), whose name was Na'aman, and he was a leper, went to the prophet Elisha and was counted worthy of cleansing from his disease. And as a result of his being healed, he acknowledged the one and unique true God of Israel, even the maker and creator of all; and he spat out the gods which were false in name, and his ancestral worship, and idolatry. And when he was about to go back to his homeland, he said to the prophet that he would not again give heed to foreign gods and empty demons. He said: 'But even if the king of Syria goes into the temple of the demon who is called in their land Rimmon, and I go in with him too (when I show honour to him and support him with my hand), I will do obeisance to the true God in my own mind, and him alone will I acknowledge; but I will not participate with the king in the idolatry and bow down with him to the demon'. He said: 'Only pray for me, that God may indeed pardon me in this affair, because (I act out) of necessity'.

And the prophet was silent, and neither gave praise nor found fault; but pursued something of a middle way through silence, and gave him a dispensation. And when he had said farewell to him, he let him go away. And it is good that we should also quote the words of the divine Scripture which Na'aman uttered to the prophet, which are along these lines: 'Your servant will never again make burnt offering or sacrifice to other gods, except to the Lord only. And because of this thing, may the Lord pardon your servant when my lord goes into the house of Rimmon to bow down to him there, since he (p. 309) will be supported by my hands. And when he bows down in the house of Rimmon, I will bow with him, but to the Lord God. And may the Lord pardon your servant because of this business. And Elisha said to Na'aman: '*Go in peace*' (4 Kgs 5: 17–19).

Since, therefore, Your Illustrious Honour is aware of these things, I pray that with a faith pure and clear you may travel along the Lord's paths in deed and word. For along with these other outstanding qualities of yours, I am amazed also at your reading and meditation in the divine words which your divine-loving letters bring forth as flowers and fruits, and which gladden those they reach.

The end

Text 24 Letter to Ammianus and Epagathus
Translated from *SL* III.2: 262–7

Of the same, to Ammianus and Epagathus

I am in wonder at the generosity of Your Excellency that – after such expenditure that arose on account of myself (who deserve nothing like this), which you have paid out through the love of God – you have thought it proper to confer these things upon me with greater plenty and (p. 263) further honours, even when I am far away . . .. (And after other matters) . . . But I was mightily glad, and sent up prayers of thanksgiving to Christ, the God and giver of all good things, who, outside all human expectation, has indicated that a boy child be born to you, the Christ-loving Ammianus.

Now since you have left pending on my decision the imposition of his name, as a consequence of the abundance of faith which you possess, and because you make me bold insomuch as you press me to speak and do things which are over and above the measure that is proper for me, I have decided that it is good and right that he be named John. For the holy Baptist and Forerunner was also born to his parents outside of hope and expectation; and I believe that, by his intercession, the boy will live and arrive at *the measure of the stature* (Eph 4:1 3) and profound old age. For consider this! On the very same day that I received your kind letter which intimated his birth to me,

I placed it beside the holy mysteries; and, when I was about to take part according to my usual custom in the divine communion (it being the day of assembly), after the other lections and the priestly psalms of Hallelujah, I began to read the worshipful Gospel. And I discovered that the order of the reading was the narrative that concerns the holy Forerunner and Baptist, and his divine martyrdom and consecration, when his head was cut off for the sake of the Law of God. So I thought as a result of (p. 264) this thing, which had happened so by chance, that also Jesus, the God of the sacred Gospels, had decided and approved the imposition of the boy's name which I had ascertained. I beg you, then, that you do not defer the business even for the matter of one day, but that you lay hold of the convenient time that has been given us by God, and that you offer the child to the God-loving father Ze'ura for the divine laver of regeneration.

But since you have no timidity[18] of this sort, you ask that from my humble self communion (that is to say, the oblation) be sent to you: how is it that this matter is not good, and one which provokes Christ our Redeemer and our God? For it is necessary to send it to those who are entirely destitute of divine communion, for when the faith is one, the holy communion (p. 265) also is certainly one, and not a thing other and different, even if one of the priests who offers has a heavenly and exalted way of life, while another has one which is low and wretched. For it is not the man himself who offers the sacrifice, but Christ confects it by means of the formula[19] of the one who is offering, and changes bread into the flesh and the chalice into blood by the power of his Spirit and inspiration and grace. For on account of this it also happened to Elijah the prophet, at the time when the famine was holding all the land in its grasp, and he was living in a wadi called the Torrent of Kerith: the ravens would bring to him everyday, at the command of God, bread in the morning and flesh in the evening (1 Kgs 17: 1–7), the Word thereby making it known in figurative manner that although there may be men who, in the manner of the ravens, are not clean, they are nonetheless intermediaries through whose hand the divine food is given and committed to us. And they do not besmirch with any injury those who receive the sacrament; nor do the uncleanness and negligence in way of life of those who minister the divine grace lessen in any way those who are being nourished when their faith is known to be orthodox and sound. (You are not, of course, unaware that the Law lists the raven with those which are not clean among birds (cf. Lev 11: 14).)

Furthermore, (p. 266) the theologian Gregory, who was bishop of Nazianzus and teacher of all who are beneath the heavens, teaches in the sermon which concerns holy baptism that there is not one bit of difference between the divine laver of regeneration which is administered by a priest whose way of life is slack, and that which is granted by a priest who is resplendent with the ascetic life and other such virtues. This he indicates when he sets forth the matter like this, using figure and example: just as two seals, one of which is made with refined and pure gold, but the other of lead, having incised upon them one and the same device which does not vary in any respect, will both imprint on wax one and the same image without it being in any way different; and none of those who has not seen the seals can distinguish between the wax which was imprinted with the gold seal or that which was imprinted by the lead seal: in the same way, even if a particular individual priest be a man of gold because of the purity of his way of life, while another be one who has the blackness and contemptibility of lead because of the laxness of his life – just as they possess equally and in every respect the one seal of the orthodox faith which is not at all counterfeited by heretical teaching, so the two of them effect one baptism and one eucharistic oblation of exactly the same power (p. 267) and honour, and one which is not in any way deficient.[20]

So then it is right for your understandings which are in the Lord that you should draw near with full assurance to the divine communion of the pious bishops who dwell with you and of the God-loving presbyters who confess in every respect the same faith as we do, and declare it with confidence, and not shrink from fear, nor counterfeit it through cunning, as the Apostle says: *'For it is a duty to remove oneself afar from men who are like these, just as from open heretics'* (2 Cor 2: 19). Rather, to state the facts in accordance with God, you have an abundance both of bishops and of genuine presbyters, in whom there is nothing counterfeit.

{Not the end}

Text 25 Letter to Georgia

Translated from *SL* X.8: 512–15

Of the same, to Georgia the daughter of Anastasia the hypatissa[21]

Never in any way do I treat carelessly matters concerning Your Honourable Dignity; but with great zeal I am anxious for your salvation, as of a beloved daughter. And I gaze upon God's profound judgements, and I understand through the facts themselves that you are supported by the great help which is from above, and diligence which is good watches over your life. For the fact that you have arrived at the prime of age and have not yet been yoked in marriage – this, to your honourable parents and to those who love a tendency which is worldly might doubtless be considered something of a vexation, and at the same time distressing. But I consider it a great help, and determine that it is indeed so. For what was said by the wise Paul to the Corinthians also pertains to this idea, I suppose: '*If anyone supposes that he is put to shame by his virgin who has passed the prime of her age, so also ought it to be*' (1 Cor 7: 36). For what he has said means in fact something of this sort: 'What is considered by some to be a matter of shame – I mean that a virgin attain to great age – this I consider to be useful and advantageous'.

For just as the fruit of a tree, when it is taken before the proper time, produces no pleasure through its taste (p. 513) because it is devoid of the sweetness which makes it agreeable, and also hurts the teeth because of its sourness and astringency, in the same way also a virgin who has not up to now matured in her time (so to speak) but possesses a sense of the flesh which is incomplete and too tender, hurts and yields no advantage to the one who marries her. For her behaviour is not firmly established and, since her time has not yet come, it is mobile and is not fixed; but it is also of a kind which is readily provoked and results in puerile anger, and is perhaps afflicted by depression and unreasonable sorrow.

For how is it not disgraceful, that, when an athlete does not go down to the rough and tumble of the wrestling-arena . . . into the order of battle, except he has been well trained in matters of warfare? But should a virgin be brought into the partnership of marriage, and transfer over into the headship and management of her husband's house, when she has not been fully instructed in her parents' house, and does not know how it is proper for her to manage the house, and in what way or otherwise she should approach each one of those who are under her authority? For many times those who are not mature and established in their behaviour, when wicked men have taken them in marriage – they have turned them into their own wicked sort, and like something on wax they have imprinted on their tender sense the manner of their own wickedness. As a result, when they have been filled and cannot . . . souls . . . (p. 514) your modest mother in your father's honourable house, and through a long period of time has been taught knowledge of stewardship, and has been completely instructed in profitable disciplines like these – and at the same time, you have also abounded in wise behaviour – you will arrive at your husband's house like some carving and bronze statue which is perfect in beauty and not lacking in anything.

And you will be to him *a help-meet like him*, for indeed the woman was created by the one who said from the beginning: '*It is not good that the man should be alone: let us make for him a helper like him*' (Gen 2: 18). For in truth, a harbour for a man is a woman who is instructed and wise in managing a house for a husband: she is both understanding and a diligent helper in the hardships of the world. For when a man has gone out to . . . in the court of law, either because he is doing wrong or is being injured; or, indeed, often he is inflamed to wrath, and wilfully abuses or on the other hand is abused in turn, when another's anger blows against him like some whirlwind. But when the time calls and he goes back to his house for food, excited and stirred up by his thoughts, he meets his wife's intelligence: then he finds her behaviour placid and serene, and he repeats what has happened to him in the marketplace. Then she gazes with gentleness like a trained doctor at those maladies which are deep-seated, touching his heart with prudent words, and she learns the reasons for his distress. And when she finds (p. 515) that he has been disturbed for no worthwhile reason, she moderates the fury of his mind when she holds out . . . tranquil . . .

. . . that I have also written these things. And I pray you, my lady, that you do not say to anyone that you have received this letter from me, even if he should be an angel who is from heaven! For you will indeed invite danger for me if you speak about it, and you will grieve God, and you will make many people angry with me, because I did not also write to them as I have done to you. But we also believe that Christ, who is the God of the orthodox – who continually brings to effect the words which say: '*And other sheep I have which are not of this fold. And it is right for me that I should bring them also; and they shall hear my voice, and there shall be one fold and one shepherd*' (Jn 10: 16) – will also make his own your honourable and exalted father.

{Not the end}

Text 26 Letter to John the hegumenos

Translated from *Doctrina Patrum* 309, nr. XXIV: 15–25

Severus of Antioch, from the third letter to John the hegumenos
As we have already written extensively in other writings, we have understood and understand the statement of the all-holy Dionysius the Areopagite, which says: 'But when God became human he performed for us a new divine-human (theandric) activity', as (meaning) one

composite (activity); in our eyes it cannot be understood other than as a rejection of every duality; and we confess that when God became human he performed this (activity) in a new way, both as one divine-human (theandric) nature and hypostasis, just as the one incarnate nature of God the Word.

Text 27 Defence to the emperor

Translated from ps.Zach. Rh., *HE* IX.16; *CSCO* 84: 123–31

(p. 123) *Chapter sixteen of the same book gives information about the Defence of Severus in the letter which, when he declined to come to the royal city, he wrote as follows.*

The Word of the Father who is from everlasting, the Son of God, who in these last days became incarnate and was not changed; and who also perfectly became man by the holy Spirit and the holy virgin Mary, Mother of God; and who truly became like us in all things apart from sin; when he was delivering his teaching of redemption in parables to his disciples, sowed the seed which came forth from it, so that both they, and everyone in the whole habitable world who should receive the Word through them, might lay to account whatever good might spring up from him in respect of righteousness (p. 124) and holy deeds – this not for themselves, but for the power of him who in the beginning sowed as it were by grace; and so that with austere and resolute voices they might send forth their utterances as they were proclaimed among the valleys and sharp rocks and rocky precipices in the desert.

Now in the same way Your Serene Power has also sown the seed of kindness in my low estate, and has caused these letters to spring forth from me (not as the offspring of effrontery): for how was it possible that an answer should not be given by me to Your Majesty's powerful and resolute voice, which was heard by me? For when those who harshly held my low estate in contempt imagined that on every side they had shut the doors in my face without mercy, then, like a miracle unhoped for, you yourself call to yourself by your letters me, a man who is cast out and expelled, as it were, by those who are against him. And this resembles the action of God who, for those who were being pursued by enemies (and) who supposed that they were shut in and caught by them, provided a wide road of redemption which was worthy of his wisdom and mighty power, namely, that which the miracle accomplished in the case of Pharaoh who sent them away after the long period of their servitude. And Pharaoh pursued them so that he might bring them back under the servitude of his harsh yoke, and surrounded them in the desert of the Red Sea with his horsemen, and was shutting up the road whilst, in his mind, he imagines and says: *'Those men are wandering about in the land: for the desert has shut them in'* (Ex 14: 3). But the wondrous God who performs mighty deeds made of the sea a dry path of grace for those who had supposed that they were shut in by the warriors, so that they might cross over it (p. 125) on foot. (He was the one) who commanded Moses to lift up his staff over the sea, and it would be divided. And in (ways) which are similar to these things you, also, with the staff of Your Majesty's tranquillity, have divided the sea which is in the desert which closed me in; and a way which appeared to be impassable you have once more made it possible for me to cross over.

Now the great demonstration of your tranquillity is that you have also composed your letters to me with an oath which is without reluctance, inasmuch as you promise me safety, acting in this manner also according to the standard of God. For he, too, inclining himself to man's infirmity, often sent forth his promises with an oath, as Scripture teaches; and Paul made mention of it when he says: *'When God made his promise to Abraham, because he had nothing greater than himself by which to swear, he swore an oath by himself and said: "In blessing I shall bless you, and in multiplying I shall multiply you"'* (Heb 6: 13–14). But I who am frail presume to say that I have not been in need of such safety, since I put confidence in the word which comes forth from your mouth alone, which for me is perfect preservation, as the wise Ecclesiastes said: *'Keep the king's saying:*[22] *and do not be solicitous on account of the word of God's oath'* (Eccles 8: 2). Moreover, I have confidence through the trial of those very deeds which in truth witness more than the oath to your gentleness, and also your inclination to mercy, which make up a tranquil soul. For immediately when you received the anxieties of kingship, you set free from mourning all ranks which were bound in exile – chief priests, and nobles, and people – since you had regards to him who bestows honour upon men equally through the rising of the sun, (p. 126) and through the rain and the temperate air which he gives, and through the rest of the things which are requisite, and result in life for human beings. But I shall not forget myself, nor be lifted up when I drink of the abundance of this stream, the riches of Your Serenity; but I shall reckon to tell the things which are in my own mind. For I fear that if my humble self were to be seen openly in the royal city, many people might be alarmed; and since in truth I am nothing but a feeble man who is bound to this heavy yoke of sins, I fear that many, on hearing this, might be violently moved and burn with his concern as if from some small coal of fire, so as to annoy and harass even Your Power because of its love towards me; and I think that it will neither seem fitting for you, nor be of any advantage for others.

But I have said this, not as if I were possessed of any strength against the power of Your Majesty – for it is written: *When the righteous king shall sit upon the throne, nothing wicked rises up over against his eyes* (Prov 20: 8) – but because I am convinced that just as this strength is joined to you by the grace which is from above, so are you clothed with understanding and wisdom; and you take pains so that, not by this sword, but by the sagacity which befits the kingdom you take care of many things. Now of this matter we are instructed by Scripture, which says: '*A wise king winnows and scatters the wicked*' (Prov 20: 26). And just as it is easy for those who winnow with the wind which blows to separate the straw from grains of wheat, so too is it easy for Your Serenity, O lord, by means of a heart which considers all things, and by the mercy of a benevolent father, (p. 127) to separate those in subjection to yourself from those who are opposed, so that they may merit mercy in the unity of the church. For I know that because of this you have determined that my lowliness also should approach even to your feet; because when you also summoned the holy bishops of the East, who pray for the salvation and preservation of Your Majesty, and since you considered this worthy of your letters, these men also, when they had written to you what seemed to them to be the case, instructed my lowliness in this your will, that according to the church's custom we might be of assistance in encouraging matters by prayer on your behalf.

But in your great city of Alexandria not one of those things which has been alleged against me in false statements was committed by me. Indeed, it is easy for me to demonstrate the folly of the abusers: for they have held me in contempt, when they say that I stirred up seditious conflict with large amounts of money which I distributed in the city. And this is known to those who hate me exceedingly that, since I am entangled in the suffering of other sins, I do not seek to collect money quickly nor on easy pretexts; but my life is poor as it were by habit, in such a manner that not even the renowned office of bishop has withheld me from this. For in the same way as I carry out the priestly office, so with the same goal I am poor – it is the custom which is proper for priests (cf. Deut 18: 1). For on this account also the Law which was given by Moses commanded that the tribe of Levi which was chosen should have no portion in the land; but that the offering of 'separation' should be sufficient for its necessary provisions inasmuch as it shares in these things along with the widow and the needy and the orphans, because they are accustomed to poverty: as Scripture says: '*And the Levite, who has no allotted part nor inheritance with you, and the alien and the orphan and the widow who are in your towns, shall come, and they shall eat and rejoice, as the Lord your God shall bless you in all your deeds which you yourself perform*' (Deut 14: 28). And since, as it is written, (p. 128) *straightforward lips are acceptable to the king, and he loves just discourse* (Prov 16: 13), Your Power is able to learn from the nobles who were formerly in Alexandria, and now from their rank whom nothing escapes the notice of, whether any such thing even nominally has been done or heard by me in the way that they have told lies about me and slandered me. But I myself say nothing about these abusers, since it does not escape your understanding what sort they are.

Moreover the judgement awaits me, along with them, after we have been separated from the world of toil, before the judgement-seat of Christ, at which we are to give account of idle speech and empty opinion; and we bishops especially, to whom much has been entrusted, shall be judged by however much we enjoy and amuse ourselves here in carnal affairs.

But if people use the word 'disorder' to describe the fact that I wrote to Julian, the bishop of Halicarnassus, who has turned aside to the heresy of Mani and holds the opinion that the voluntary sufferings of the Saviour, Christ the mighty God, were in appearance only, I confess it with ten thousand mouths and tongues: neither do I deny what I have written, as nobody shall quickly order me to deny my faith. For this seems good for your faith too, which is careful for more than the affairs of the world so that it may possess those things which are befitting for the spirit. Nor have I done these things as of my own will, nor of myself, nor compelled by my own self, but I was mightily troubled by him; so I wrote because he had supposed that I am a follower of his doctrine. For when I went through the things he had sent to me (and I was a long way off from Alexandria) I found in what he had written about the word 'incorruptibility' that he was covered with the blasphemies of Mani as with a sheep's skin.

(p. 129) So as to leave aside a lot of material which I shall not speak of, this foolish man, who acknowledges the sufferings (of Christ) with his lips only, while concealing his ungodliness, wrote as follows: 'If incorruptibility was at all times united voluntarily to the body of our Lord, the body passible for others'. [A summary of the altercation between Severus and Julian follows.]

(p. 130) And as for the rest of Julian's error which is contained in the letter in a lengthy discourse, I turn aside[23] from writing them here, since the things which this holy Severus composed against Julian are found in many books. But at the end of the same letter he wrote as follows:

So I entreat you, therefore, and take hold of your feet, as again I repeat the word that you leave behind my humble self, and do not drag me out among human beings again, since I am growing feeble in my body and in my soul, and am therefore infirm. For true is the word of Scripture which says: 'The soul fails because of blows'.[24] And many now are the white hairs on my head which testify to me of death and departure from this weary life; and it seems to be best and profitable for me to sit hidden in a corner and to contemplate the separation of soul from body, as I await the house of my grave, *for the earth is the house of everyone who dies*', as Job said (Job 30: 23). Because the hair of the other animals who live on earth is not changed; but the rational animal nature of this human being, since it is destined to come to judgement and in the world to come is to be asked for an account of its deeds, when it reaches old age, the hair of its head becomes white, so pointing out to him the kind of nature he possesses and urging him to make good his deeds upon his departure inasmuch as it relates to those who are delayed. And Scripture, too, bears witness to it: '*Lift up your eyes, and see the fields that they have become white, and ripe for harvest*' (Jn 4: 35). For the separation of the soul from the body is in truth the harvest, and as it were with a sickle he shears one for the other, and it is sheared. For this reason I beg that your power indeed grant me this request: (p. 131) it is easy for me to dwell in hiding where I am, since I have lived the rest of my days in the world in secret, as if in a corner. For such is the life of a monk.

Christ, God over all things, grant you power over your enemies, with the perfect peace and harmony of the churches, that you may be crowned with this as well. And if in these letters of my request there be any offence or anything presumptuous, I pray that you pardon me as (in) other things. For it is best for a king who loves Christ to overcome evil with good, as the apostle said: '*Because when indeed you show this, rightly are you called victors*' (Rom 12: 21).

The subscription of Severus in the same letter

The only Trinity – for this is our God – preserve Your Faithfulness for many years while you make peaceable the power of the government of the Romans; and bring into subjection to you all the people of the Romans and the barbarians; and grant perfect concord through you to the holy churches in a right faith, and esteem you worthy of crowns in the kingdom of heaven.

Now the holy Severus delayed after this letter up to the thirteenth year;[25] and then he came to the royal city, because the king's letters pressed him.

Text 28 Synodical Letter to Theodosius

Translated from Documenta ad origenes monophysitarum illustrandas*; CSCO* 17: 12–34

(p. 12) *AGAIN THE LETTER OF THE HOLY AND CHIEF BISHOP SEVERUS, PATRIARCH OF ANTIOCH, which was written to the blessed Theodosius, Archbishop of Alexandria, which is also entitled the Synodical Letter. In the thirteenth indiction, in the month Tammuz, on the twenty-sixth day.*[26]

Now before I received the synodical writings of Your honoured and fraternal Excellency, when it was reported to me of your divine election to the evangelic see, I was grieved at the sufferings which befell you on account of matters of religion, as fulfilling the apostolic law which issues the command and declares: '*When one member suffers, all the members suffer*' (1 Cor 12: 26). For indeed I have also regarded you as blessed, in that you have straightway tasted the danger of religion through which you were bound to the mighty power by birth through the breath of the holy Spirit, by which you were born as high priest – through that *breath which blows where he wills* (Jn 3: 8). Now *he wills* where there is Law, while he departs from those who call upon him violently and outside the Law, addressing them in the words which are found in the prophecy: '*When you spread forth your hands, I shall turn aside my eyes from you; and even if you increase your prayer, I shall not hear you, for your hands are full of blood*' (Is 1: 15). Now was it anything of a marvel that these things happened to you, as they did to the great Paul? Who, the moment he came up from the waters of the Jordan when he had been baptized by Hanania, began the labour and apostleship of teaching and (as it is written) was disturbing the Jews who were dwelling at Damascus; and to flee from the hands of those who were seeking to kill him, when the gates of the city were fastened, he was let down from the wall in a basket and made his escape (cf. Acts 9: 10–25). And he became a fugitive: he who afterwards (p. 13) was a performer of many wonderful deeds and powerful acts and many awesome things – as he himself writes and declares, and as examination of his deeds proved. For it was fitting that he should be tested by sufferings, and be struck with the first blows as if with brass (implements), so that in his own substance he might fulfill the divine testimony which Christ had uttered beforehand: '*He is a chosen vessel for me, to bear my name before the Gentiles and kings and the sons of Israel: for I have shown him how much he is to endure for the sake of my name*' (Acts 9: 15–16). So then, as to these difficulties which have befallen Your Perfection, it is right for us to believe that they have been permitted for that trial by the inexpressible counsels of sublime wisdom. For concerning those who are tested in conflicts of this sort, one of the divine wise men says: '*God tried them and found them worthy of himself, and like gold in the crucible he tested them*' (Wis 3: 6).

So then, it is entirely certain that when the holy bishops were standing in the Holy of Holies and laying hands upon your honourable head; and – with sacramental and ineffable words were bringing forth the grace of the Spirit, the lover of men and governor, from on high; they were showing you to be a son of Aaron, that is, a legitimate heir of the priest who departed and passed away to God – for there was no other way by which the priestly garments might be assumed, concerning which the divine Scripture says: '*The garment of holiness which belongs to Aaron shall be for his sons after him, that in it they may be anointed and consecrated*' (Ex 29: 29). [There follows an exegesis of Num 16.]

(p. 15) Now while I was turning these divine judgements and sacred thoughts over and over in my mind, those God-loving bishops and religious clerics arrived who had been sent by Your Holiness to My Lowliness, bringing the writings of your teaching which is fitting for priests and in agreement with canonical and ecclesiastical opinion. And when in happiness I saw these and embraced them, with rejoicing I praised the God of peace, Jesus Christ, and I received the items which had been sent; and when I set them before my eyes I imagined to myself that through them you, the holy shepherd and high priest, were close to me, and that I was seeing you and embracing you in the manner of a brother. And when I was alone, and no-one at all was with me – for it is a thing very dear to me to sit in solitude, especially indeed in labourings in matters concerning divine things – I was reading the writings rather with my mind than with my physical eyes; and from the sense of those things which are written in the holy narratives which I had just recited, I found these narratives also comparing you to the perfect likeness of Aaron! For when the Israelite assembly was disobedient and unwilling to be docile – for the God of all was designating them by these terms, and names like them, and through these things come the fearful chastisements which we experience – and it would not exchange presumption for obedience, but was lifted up in pride against the divine authority of the priesthood, Moses was commanded that from every head of the twelve tribes (for the whole people was divided into and comprised in these tribes) (p. 16) he should take one rod, and set the rods of all of them in the Tabernacle of the Testimony in front of the Testimony, as it is written (cf. Num 17: 4). For these things were as follows: the Ark of the Testimony; and the tablets of stone which were inscribed by God; and the manna which was put in a golden pot. These items were they which, by miraculous means, openly demonstrated and witnessed and brought back to mind (for those who were unmindful and ignorant) the power of God which performs mighty deeds in a manner inexpressible. And for this reason they were also called the Testimonies; and the tent in which they were placed had a name in like manner, and was called the Tent of the Testimony. And in this same sense Paul wrote to the Hebrews and stated: *'When God was bearing witness to them with signs and wonders and differing miracles'* (Heb 2: 4).

So therefore Moses, equipped in mind, and as a revealer of divine things and head of the assembly, did what he had been commanded; and on the next day he inspected the rods as he had been instructed. And he saw the rods of the others, how that they were dry rods, in their natural state; but Aaron's rod had sprouted leaves and produced nuts (cf. Num 17: 8), through which was prefigured for us as in a type Emmanuel, who is the rod of the kingdom and who, as from the root of God the Father, has shone forth and has been born: who is without beginning and without time, and with him and the holy Spirit he reigns over the things which are in heaven and the things which are on earth. And at the end of days for our sake he was incarnate and made man without change; and he the same sprang forth in respect of flesh from the root of Jesse and David, from whom arose Mary, the virgin Mother of God. And he became the high priest and Apostle of our salvation, and in this manner also appeared as the rod of the priesthood, teaching us the vigilance instructed by the Gospel, and making fruits[27] spring forth in those who believe, leaves and fruits of virtue. For those who have also examined these things declare (p. 17) that the rod of the nut-tree, and also the nuts themselves, naturally produce vigilance in those who are accustomed to use them. And God himself declared this to the prophet Jeremiah speaking of prophets metaphorically: *'Jeremiah, what do you see? And I said: "I see the branch of a nut tree". And he said: "You have seen aright, because I am watching over my words to perform them"'* (Jer 1: 11–12).

For in the same way as the exercise of virtue involves the toil and the sweat which precede it – and they are bitter – but its result is light and pleasant, so too is the nut. In the outer shell it displays hardness and tartness, while in the inner part there is set whiteness and nourishment. This rod I have found in your writings, O brother of ours beloved and honourable, as it defines the vocation of the high priesthood and grants it to you. *'For no-one take this honour to himself, but only when he is called by God, as was Aaron'* (Heb 5: 4), as Paul too affirms when he shows to the Hebrews the profundity of the writings of the Law. And did not Isaiah himself tell us this clearly when he declared: *'And a rod shall come forth from the trunk of Jesse, and a shoot shall spring forth from his root: and the Spirit of God shall rest and dwell upon it, the Spirit of wisdom and understanding, the Spirit of delight and of power, the Spirit of knowledge and of proper worship'*? (Is 11: 1–2). For he who is the hypostatic Word and self-existent wisdom of God the Father, the only-begotten Son through whom all things came into existence, being full of might and glory and of all those things which properly pertain to God by nature, and being in nothing inferior neither to God the Father nor to the holy Spirit, emptied himself, while he himself was not moved from the state of perfection. For he remained what he was eternally; but inasmuch as he bore human sufferings according to the divine dispensation, he was a participant in these conditions of ours, and became like us in all things apart from sin because he truly became man, and like a (p. 18) rod he sprouted from the root of Jesse. Now the rod also makes known a germination and conception without seed which arose from the holy Mary ever-virgin. For the property of a rod is that is sprouts naturally from the root, and it is not born as the result of copulation or sexual intercourse. For God the Word himself, the inexpressible might of the Father, as the providence of the mysteries of the Gospel writings demonstrates, rested upon the virgin; and from her and from the coming of the holy Spirit in inexpressible manner, united to himself hypostatically flesh ensouled with reason – when he was united with the condition of the flesh and the course of (human) existence in a manner appropriate for God who is superior to every thought and word. For the existence of the flesh neither preceded the union with the Word, nor was it beforehand apprehended by thought; but from both, from the divinity and from the humanity, which are perfect in their own respects, there came the one Emmanuel, the great and indivisible name.

Truly great is the mighty mystery of the religion which shows us that God the Word, who is superior to every beginning and is before all the ages, undoubtedly assumed the properties of the flesh inasmuch as he became man without change; and the fact that he was the same who was conceived and born after he had completed the full period of gestation is to be acknowledged and truly believed, since the immutability of the divine nature was not impaired: and it showed rightly and truly that in fact his mother, the Mother of God and ever-virgin, did not lose what it is to be a virgin either through the splendour of the birth itself, nor after the birth; and that the holy Spirit was essentially as God in him[28] and also above him in relation to the fact that he became man; for from that same womb, by his Spirit, God constituted his flesh and consecrated it and united it to him, since all these things concurred together without division. That is what he also (p. 19) displayed openly at the Jordan, when he was baptized with our baptism – not that he needed to be baptized, but so that he might sanctify water and lay a foundation for our rebirth and receive the Spirit for us, and not for himself. For all these things were done wisely and according to the divine dispensation for our sake, as it were as the second beginning of our race. [There follows a long passage on the workings of the Spirit and on the voluntary nature of Christ's sufferings.]

(p. 23) So then, those who assert that the flesh of our Saviour, from its very establishment through the womb and the union, was impassible and immortal; and who assign to it the incorruptibility which is recognized in impassibility and immortality (and not simply in holiness and sinlessness); and who foolishly suppose that they honour God with matters of surmise, first, deprive us of healing and strip us of victory over the devil and death, and then defraud him of the honour which is due to him as healer and Saviour and benefactor; and, on the other hand, we ourselves have been the cause (p. 24) of the most wicked blasphemy, to the effect that he mocked us and did not redeem us. For an impassible and immortal body does not admit of sufferings and death, but is considered to have suffered and died only in surmise, and as it were in an illusion of sleep. Now if the sufferings are considered to be false, and Emmanuel did not die our kind of death, then in every respect his resurrection also is to be considered false; and all those things which relate to our redemption, and the hope of resurrection which was promised to us, are lost. Furthermore, we are unavoidably laid under the servitude of death if we were redeemed by nocturnal hallucinations and not in reality by the blood of his cross, and if we were not ransomed and set free from mischief by this divine blood, as the Apostle declares (cf. Col 1: 20).

So then, Your Holiness has affirmed right well and fittingly that the body of our Lord and Saviour was consubstantial with us and suffered natural and voluntary sufferings like us, but *without sin* (Heb 4: 15 etc.). And by this means you have put away those who have dared to assert that he suffered in an impassible and immortal body; and you have shown that they are strangers to the divine sheepfold, since the rational flock of Christians does not recognize an alien voice (cf. Jn 10: 5). For the rod who comes forth from Jesse and David, who is Emmanuel (as we have said earlier), which sprouted from the holy and ever-virgin Mary, the Mother of God, which was cited in Your Holiness's writings, grew green and budded in that flesh which was hypostatically united to the Word, because there was nothing of the ancient sin which made our race wither: for when he became incarnate in a flesh which was of this sort, it was proper that he should draw near to death, and the devil, who was holding the power of death, when he did not find in him any kind of sin whatever, was overcome by a just victory and was displayed as ineffective by the resurrection.

For this reason he spoke beforehand (p. 25) about this war against death which (through the wickedness of the Jews who fight against God) the devil imagined that he would make ready for him, saying: 'The ruler of this world is coming, and in me he finds nothing' (Jn 14: 30). For because the rod was producing the nut and was possessed of the energy of the divine power of awakening, when it was handed over to burial it demonstrated the grave as the place of incorruptibility and of awakening and of resurrection. For his soul was not left in Sheol, nor did his body see corruption; but he raised it in flesh, and he will raise us at his coming, as Paul when writing to the Corinthians shows (cf. 1 Cor 6: 14). And also Daniel, the seer of divine visions, was prophesying in the same manner and declaring: 'And many who rest in the chasms of the earth shall be awakened, some for everlasting life, and others for shame and eternal disgrace. And those who possess understanding shall give light like the beauty of the firmament, and many of the righteous like the stars for ever' (Dan 12: 2–3).

And furthermore one may observe the true pledges of this hope in what Matthew the evangelist related as having occurred when the voluntary and redeeming death was perfectly fulfilled; for he says: 'And many bodies of the saints who were asleep arose; and when they had come out of the graves after his resurrection, they entered the holy city and appeared to many' (Matt 27: 52–3). And also our Lord and Saviour himself, as he was proceding to the glorious cross and approached with longing what he would suffer, named himself 'the green wood' (Lk 23: 31); and he turned to the mourning and lamenting women who were following him and said – while giving woe to the Jews who are destined to suffer things for which there is no remedy because of their presumptuous fighting against God, and because they will not profit from the greenness and moisture (that is, from his incarnation without sin) – '*Blessed are the barren and the wombs which have not borne children, and the breasts which have not suckled.* (p. 26) *Then they will begin to say to the mountains: "Fall on us"; and to the hills: "Cover us". For if they do these things with a green wood, what shall they do with the dry?*' (Lk 23: 30–31).

These spiritual interpretations of the rod set in your writings are proclamations of our true redemption and pledges of the resurrection, to be believed by us. Now the rod of illusion, which deceives and is swiftly and foolishly found by the preachers of deceit, is the dry root which cannot bring forth the blossom of the resurrection. For what will an illusion without a body bring forth, an illusion which began with Valentinus and Basilides talking nonsense, which passed on through Marcion and Mani, and ended up in Eutyches and Julian of Halicarnassus?[29] In the same way the rod of Apollinaris, too, is a dry rod – Apollinaris, who cuts off the mind of the divine incarnation and declares it deprived of the first-fruits of our redemption. For if the Word of God indeed bore flesh of our flesh and a rational soul but, as that senseless individual supposes, abhorred a mind as ruler of the human soul, a mind which is most honourable and great in our creation by which we are made as the image and likeness of God, we have not received healing. For according to their talk, this healing came to what was not united with the one who came to redeem us, as the prophet David sings and declares (cf. Ps 79: 3, 7, 19). And similarly dry and without fruits is also the rod of those who divided into a duality of natures after the inexpressible union the one, our Lord and our God Jesus Christ: how this may be termed 'one rod' by them I am unable to comprehend! For vanity brings them forth as something which appears as two and subsisting separately, and allots separately to the human nature the sufferings and the cross, and separately to God impassibility and the working of the divine signs, in such a way that in man (p. 27) is comprehended the beginning of our hope and our redemption, by which I mean the resurrection. But the fact that the hope which is in man is vain it is our allotted portion to hear from Jeremiah the prophet, when he says: '*Cursed is the man whose confidence is in man, so as to make the son of flesh his arm and to turn aside his heart from the Lord*' (Jer 17: 5). But far be it from us to turn aside our heart from the one God and redeemer Jesus Christ our Lord, and exchange confidence in man for his trustworthiness.

For we acknowledge one rod, the Word which was made man without change, and without illusion and in perfect manner. For he is the one rod, truly and undeniably; and he himself is the same who was performing the divine actions in a way befitting the deity, and voluntarily so; and who, according to divine dispensation and in reality, was suffering the things proper to humanity: and he gave himself as a ransom for the many and suffered in flesh which was capable of suffering and dying, while existing within the bounds of divine impassibility. And furthermore he did not in any respect change what is immutable insofar as he is God, nor indeed did he admit of a single alteration; and thus he remained as one of the Trinity even as he verily suffered in the flesh: and the censure of the theopaschites which is cast upon us he demonstrated as truly ridiculous because of what was said by the divine Paul, that the Lord of glory has been crucified (cf. 1 Cor 2: 3). He did not add a fourth number to the Trinity; and he is the same who in the whole redemptive divine dispensation was speaking as God and as man, because he was truly God, and he was truly man. For if the fact that he would speak in human fashion had brought shame or belittlement to him, he would have been ashamed of it from the beginning of his participation in flesh and blood in our likeness. But it is no shame for the healer in some sort to despise his honour, and to say and suffer something human to save and heal the sick. For from where (p. 28) do we know his self-emptying and his humiliation and his poverty by which he grew poor for our sake even though he was rich, except through the human expressions and voluntary and providential sufferings? For just as we recognize the difference of the divinity and of the humanity out of which Emmanuel exists, so also we recognize the distinction of his expressions and divine and human actions; but all these we affirm of one and the same individual as of God who was made man. For we do not accept that we should assign these things to the two natures; since along with division into a duality there goes necessarily division in every (other) matter. And the great Athanasius and the wise Cyril, the teachers of your rational flock, or rather of the whole flock of Christians which is under heaven, have taught us these things. *'For anything the faithful ones of Israel have set in place* (2 Kgs 20: 18) does not fail', as it is written. For they were faithful guardians of the teachings of the Spirit, since the two of them grew rich with the prophetic and apostolic and evangelic Spirit.

From these rooms Your Perfection has also sent to us the synodical letters; for from of old the honour of sound teaching pertains to that see which holds fast to the Gospel. From that see, those who were legitimately occupying it also used to send forth festal letters to the whole world, and with the indiction of the festival each year used to mingle the purity and accuracy of the faith, a custom which has also been preserved up to these times, and will be preserved, and will flourish under your authority until the consummation of this age.

Therefore if anyone should call your holy church the root of orthodoxy, he has not dropped away from the standard of the truth. For that Athanasius, valiant in his teachings and in his struggles on behalf of religion, used to stand at the right hand of the reverend Alexander of blessed memory, the head of the holy convocation of the three hundred and eighteen Fathers, (p. 29) when he was still counted among the deacons: and at that time he was consulting with the orthodox shepherds and those who were striving for the truth concerning the accuracy of the definition of the faith, that it should not be controlled by any stratagems and inventions of the heretics, and so that he might close up every opportunity open to them. Therefore I am grieved in my heart for the love of the church which is governed by you and by your own shepherds; and I acknowledge it for myself as a sickness made up of praise. For the writings of the apostolic Athanasius and the most wise Cyril, like a spiritual quiver, have supplied me abundantly with arrows against those who presumptuously divide the one Christ into two, and also against the error of those who preach illusion, both in oral conflicts about the Scriptures[30] and with the armoury of ink and pen, as the modest writings of my lowly self plainly demonstrate.

So then, it is right for us to retain this faith, and to acknowledge what the praiseworthy assembly of the three hundred and eighteen Fathers defined; and we should write this single definition of our confession on the spiritual tablets of our hearts to proclaim more clearly than any trumpet that *'with the heart it is believed for righteousness, and by the mouth confession is made for redemption'* (Rom 10: 10), as Paul teaches. This definition also the Synod of the one hundred and fifty Fathers issued in writing as its own, and also the holy and ecumenical Synod which was in Ephesus which cast out the wicked Nestorius and all those who followed his error. So let us set these things around us like a spiritual rampart and an impregnable wall – the Twelve Chapters (p. 30) of Cyril the wrestler, which contain the order of the twelve tribes by which the spiritual Israel is numbered and established; since each separate chapter opens for us a divine door leading to knowledge of the divine assumption of human nature, and shows the way to the lawful and constant entryway to the church – which Ezekiel the prophet saw beforehand when he was mystically carried away to the vision in which was shown to him the temple which was on the mountain, which was possessed of twelve doors corresponding to the number of the names of the tribes of Israel (cf. Ez 48: 30–34). Now these things represent (as I suppose) the divine teaching of the twelve apostles, from which the Twelve Chapters of the wise Cyril send forth breeze like a sweet-smelling ointment. Therefore we, too, anathematize with all our authority those who have boasted and spoken against them, and those who cast forth before them the seeds (that is, the tares) of Jewish anthropolatry – Paul of Samosata and Artemon who preceded him, and Photinus and Diodore and Theodore and Nestorius who openly displayed the impiety of these men and therefore himself provided a name for the heresy;[31] and Theodore and Andrew and Ibas of Edessa and Alexander of Hierapolis, and Eutherius of Tyana and Irenaeus the bigamist (that is, the one who had two wives[32]) and Cyrus and John who came from Aigiai in Cilicia, and Barsauma the Persian who was not only sick with this impiety, but also took pains to dishonour the purity of the life of the Gospel with depraved canons and was condemned along with his commentaries and his depraved life, and if there be anyone else like these persons – these the divine Chapters of our father Cyril refute: these are the things which are proclaimed by the whole church of the orthodox which is in the whole world and strengthen the soul of the faithful, since those (p. 31) who encounter them are enlightened with the light of divine understanding: they have no need of the praise which comes from us.

Now along with these afore-mentioned profane teachers of anthropolatry we must number and anathematize also the Synod of Chalcedon and the blasphemous *Tome* of the impious Leo of the church of the Romans, whom the same Synod called 'the pillar of orthodoxy': for outside the canon of the divinely inspired Fathers, it established a definition of the faith, and after the inexpressible union divided the divine and indivisible incarnation into a duality of natures along with their activities and their particular properties, as the *Tome* itself also indicates to those who read it – since openly and at length it expounds what it means that the one, our Lord Jesus Christ, should be acknowledged as existing in two natures. But we receive and declare praiseworthy the upright confession of the *Henotikon* document, which the worthy Emperor Zeno of blessed memory uttered.

Then again, we also punish with the same anathema those who from another side have been moved by error against the true faith: and I mean Valentinus, Basilides, Marcion, Mani, Apollinaris, the senseless Eutyches who stumbled many times into the same snares and became a leper with a leprosy enduring and incurable; and those who after him were sick with this feebleness aggravated the disease as they took pains to defile the true and redemptive sufferings of Emmanuel as it were with abscesses, with an impassible and immortal body; and in their several ways they were dismayed, as the prophetic utterance declares (cf. Ez 36: 32), since they were unaware of the straight road of truth which proclaims that our Lord and our God and our Saviour

Jesus Christ is one and alone, who suffered in flesh which was capable of suffering until it destroyed (p. 32) death and utterly trampled it down by means of the resurrection; and he the same is impassible in divinity, as it has been affirmed. [There follows an encomium of Theodosius based on citations from the Old Testament.}

(p. 33) Pray, then, O my brother beloved above all, for My Lowliness also, that it may be adequate to resist the temptations with which it is continually beaten, and which at all times and with reverence keeps in mind the word of our Lord which declares: '*He who endures to the end, he shall live*' (Matt 10: 22); and may this thing come to pass for me, I beg you, through your holy prayers. For while I breathe this air, I shall not separate myself from spiritual union and brotherly fellowship with you in the divine struggles on behalf of the orthodox faith.

Greet the brotherly fellowship which is with you: that fellowship which is with us greets you in our Lord. And those who have brought your beloved and sacred letter I have received gladly according to my resources available to me: Eusebius, Uranius, Thomas, Timothy, and John, the reverend bishops; and the God-beloved presbyters Ammonius, Alphaeus, Theopemptus; and the chaste deacons John, Epimachus, Epiphanius. And I know that they who minister to your commands so fitting for the priestly office are worthy.

Here ends the Synodical Letter of our God-inspired Father Severus
to the reverend and holy Mar Theodosius.

7

HYMNS

Three of the hymns translated below were composed for feasts in the liturgical cycle: Hymn 8 (Text 29) probably for the Epiphany, Hymn 71 (Text 30) for the feast of the holy Cross and Hymn 109 (Text 31) for Pentecost. Hymn 147 (Text 32) on St Simeon Stylites the Elder belongs to a group in which various saints' days are commemorated, while 253 (Text 33) and 269 (Text 34) form part of a miscellaneous section of the hymn collection. Hymn 253, directed against proponents of the Council of Chalcedon who attributed a drought to the non-Chalcedonians, shows that the christological controversy was never far from Severus's mind. Hymn 269 contains strong warnings against attending games and the theatre which are to be found also in Severus's homilies.

Translated from *PO* 6/1: 51 (Hymn 8); *PO* 6/1: 115–16 (Hymn 71); *PO* 6/1: 147–9 (Hymn 109); *PO* 7/5: 604–5 (Hymn 147); *PO* 7/5: 701–2 (Hymn 253); *PO* 7/5: 716–17 (Hymn 269).

Text 29 Hymn 8

The kings of Tarshish and of the Islands shall bring him gifts
(Ps 72: 10)

The bodily birth of Emmanuel from the virgin Maryam
was not preceded by marital intercourse
but only by the descent of the holy Spirit,
and the imprinted seal of virginity, preserved also after giving birth,
confirms this wonder that is fitting for God.
But before one might behold and see the womb of the mother
and call him a child who is carried and in motherly arms,

the Magi approached entreating and urging one to behold the star,
and to contemplate in one's heart God the Word
who descended and drew near from heaven,
and to acknowledge him, one and the same, to be both terrestrial and celestial.
Let us bless, worship, and praise him as God the Saviour of the universe
and friend of humanity.

Text 30 Hymn 71

On the Holy Cross
Everybody who swears by him shall be praised (Ps 63: 12)

By your life-giving Cross, O Christ, the depth of the riches of wisdom and power can be seen.
For when you who are the power of God were nailed upon it, upon the wood of infirmity, that is, the Cross,
You changed it into a wood of power, such as befits God.
And since you are the wisdom of God and the Father,
through him you have made those who preached the good news of the Gospel fully wise.
Therefore fishermen and uneducated people
defeated and made useless the wisdom and the wise of the world.
And those from among the gentiles who believed and bore witness destroyed
and put to shame by their valour the might of the tyrants.
By one piece of wood all the wood and stone that had been carved and made into gods fled and perished,
And every lust of the body then vanished,
being killed by the nails of the Cross.
For *blessed is the wood through which comes righteousness* (Wis 14: 6–7 LXX), as it is written.
Praise be to you!

Text 31 Hymn 109

{On Pentecost}
In Judah God is known (Ps 76: 2)

God of all and Father, you became known already in the Law
and Prophets. You have explained and shown through them
your only Son and Word, and the holy Spirit, but not plainly,
because the (people) were not yet able to comprehend the
revelation of one Godhead of the Trinity.

As the Word and God appeared in the flesh and became a man
for our sake without change, he showed himself equal to you,
Father, by the astonishing deeds which he performed.

And today,[1] after he has ascended to heaven, he shows clearly
to those who have become perfect the Godhead of the Spirit
Paraclete, who in the form of the flames of fire descended
and settled upon (the heads of) the holy Apostles (cf. Acts 2:
1–11). (He did this) in order to burn away and bring about
the disappearance of the thorns which our father Adam's
transgression of the command once planted (there).

They also taught us to praise one God in three holy hypostases,
to whom, bowing, we say, 'Praise be to you'.

Text 32 Hymn 147

On the holy Simeon the Stylite
'Come and listen, let me tell you' (cf. Ps 66: 16)

The exalted and immense height of the upright and just
Simeon's way of life brings into the heart of the believers the
words of the Lord, which he spoke: *'A city on the top of a hill
cannot be concealed'* (Matt 5: 14).

As he ascended to the exalted height of virtues, he showed this
plainly, and by his appearance on the column, he made it clear
that he was the *pillar and foundation of the truth* (1 Tim 3: 14), as
it is written.

He drew both unbelievers and barbarians to the fear of God,
and those who were dwelling in the darkness of error (cf. Is 9:
1–2) (he drew) to the light of (true) knowledge – like a star,
which sends out rays on its appearance.

By his prayers, O Saviour of all, have pity and mercy upon us!

Text 33 Hymn 253

Another (hymn) concerning those who spread (the opinion) that the lack of rain was because the impure Synod of Chalcedon was anathematized.[2]

'You destroy all who are unfaithful to you for ever' (cf. Ps 73: 27).

We know, O Lord, that (it is) because of our transgressions and evil deeds which we have committed that you have prepared and drawn the bow of your wrath which is threatening us.

But the followers of the error of two natures said with their lips, scoffing and mocking, and shook their heads at us and said: 'Behold, they had trusted and relied on the Lord that he would rescue them. May he deliver and save them since he delights in them' (cf. Ps 22: 8).

But let us say weeping in pain: 'There is a God in heaven whom we serve, who has the power to save and rescue us from this suffering (cf. Dan 3: 16–18). And even if (he does) not – know that we will never agree to say in a Jewish way "two natures" about this one Christ, but as we have learned, so we declare, that there is (only) one nature in the incarnate Word.'

We confess One out of the Trinity who suffered for us in the flesh, him, who also through rain and dew, which are from him (cf. Ps 65: 11), blesses the crown of the year by his graciousness according to the abundance of his mercy.

Text 34 Hymn 269

Another (hymn) of warning concerning the spectacles of games and concerning dance
Hear this, all you peoples (Ps 49: 1)

If a single turning around and a mere gazing at the city of Sodom
made the wife of Lot the just a dead woman, and turned her into a statue of salt (cf. Gen 19: 15–26),
terror will overcome those who watch shows
and great fear those who listen to the shameful noise.
What will those then do who watch licentious swayings and mad dancing with many gyrations
while in the thought of their hearts they are as it were wandering in profound darkness?

It happens often to them that they are suddenly snatched away
from this life while terrible angels arrive and stand over them.
They however are inwardly filled with images of immorality and
debauched wantonness.
How then will they endure standing before the fearful
judgement-seat and the trial?
But as for us, Christ God, save us from every error, deliver our
souls and turn them to the worship of yourself,
according to the abundance of your bounteous mercy.

GLOSSARY

Anti-Chalcedonians or non-Chalcedonians These were the Christians who refused to accept the Definition of Faith of the Council of Chalcedon in 451.

Apollinaris/Apollinarian forgeries Born in Laodicea in *c*. 315, Apollinaris espoused a christological position in which the most striking expression was 'one incarnate nature of the Word' (*mia physis tou Logou sesarkomene*). He excluded from Christ's being the reason (*nous*) or higher soul. His writings were adopted by Cyril of Alexandria, because many of them were transmitted under the name of Athanasius of Alexandria, and subsequently they were also adopted by adherents of the one-nature christology.

Dioscorus The successor of Cyril as patriarch of Alexandria, Dioscorus supported Eutyches at the Council of Ephesus in 449, and was consequently anathematized at Chalcedon.

Docetism This term (from Greek *dokein* 'to seem') covers various attempts to explain Christ's incarnation and passion in a dualistic and spiritualistic way; that is, by excluding from it everything that seems unworthy of the Son of God. In this sense Christ only 'seems' to be human.

Dyophysites These are adherents of the christological position which affirms two natures in Christ.

Eutyches A monk, priest and archimandrite, Eutyches was a friend of Cyril of Alexandria, but was condemned at the Council of Chalcedon for his christological views. He asserted that Christ is not consubstantial (*homoousios*) with us and that from two natures before the union there resulted a single nature after it. He is considered the father of real, as opposed to verbal, monophysitism.

Henotikon This 'instrument of union' was an eirenic document promulgated by Emperor Zeno on 28 July 482, acknowledging the faith of Nicaea and Constantinople (381), without explicitly condemning the *Tome* of Leo or Chalcedon itself. Chalcedon was reduced to the status of a disciplinary council which had condemned Nestorius and Eutyches.

Monophysites   These are adherents of the so-called one-nature christology. They are also known as miaphysites or anti/non-Chalcedonians.

Peter the Iberian   A Georgian prince who died in 491, Peter consolidated the anti-Chalcedonian presence in Palestine. Despite his strong rejection of Chalcedon, he was not a radical monophysite, and held great attraction for the intellectual circles from which Severus came.

Synousiast   This name was given to the followers of Apollinaris because they maintained that in Christ human substance (*ousia*) and divine substance were united (hence *syn*), and that a single substance resulted from them.

Theopaschite   This term refers to the position of those who attribute suffering and death to God the Word.

Timothy Aelurus (the Cat)   Timothy II of Alexandria was present at the Council of Ephesus in 449, and subsequently organized anti-Chalcedonian opposition in Egypt. Like Peter the Iberian, although he took a strong stand against Chalcedon and Leo's *Tome*, he was a moderate monophysite, and served as a model for Severus of Antioch.

Tome of Leo   The *Tomus ad Flavianum* of Pope Leo I of Rome, written in June 449, affirmed two natures in Christ in one *persona*. It was recognized at Chalcedon as being in agreement with Cyril's doctrine, but regarded by anti-Chalcedonians as Nestorian.

Twelve Chapters or Twelve Anathemas   Composed by Cyril of Alexandria, these christological propositions were directed against Nestorius and Antiochene christology generally. After their acceptance by the Council of Chalcedon, they became a touchstone of orthodoxy in the debate about the Council.

NOTES

PART I SEVERUS'S LIFE AND WORKS

1 SEVERUS'S LIFE

1 See Hom. XXVII; *PO* 36/4: 563.
2 See Hom. IX; *PO* 38/2; 2 and Hom. XXXIV; *PO* 36/3: 477, with Darling 1982: 17, 99–100.
3 *Vie* 95–6; JBA 229.
4 According to George, bishop of the Arabs, Severus's family built the monastery for him (287–8).
5 See Honigmann 1951: 132–3 on Epiphanius and the staunch anti-Chalcedonianism in Pamphilia.
6 Michael, *Chron.* IX.8; 2: 259–60.
7 De Halleux 1963: 76 points out that not only was Philoxenus a generation older than Severus, but he was a Syriac-speaking Persian who had not enjoyed the privileges of a classical education in Alexandria and Beirut but a theological training in provincial Edessa.
8 *SL* I.1; p. 3. See de Halleux 1963: 68–9.
9 See e.g. Severus, Hom. CXXV; *PO* 29/1: 24.
10 Evagrius, *HE* III.44 mistakenly places the riots in the patriarchate of Macedonius: see Whitby 2000: 195 n. 175.
11 Zach. Rh. *HE* VII.10; de Halleux 1963: 70–73.
12 *Apologia Philalethis*; *CSCO* 319: 114. 26.
13 See further Chapters 2 and 3, below.
14 See further Chapters 2 and 3, below.
15 Ps.Dionysius of Tel-Mahre, *Chron.*: 13–14, trans. Witakowski; line division by P. Allen. The source is no doubt JBA 241.
16 On the date see Brière 1960: 11–13; see Honigmann 1951: 15 on the names of the participants.
17 Brière 1960: 11 notes that 18 November was in fact the day that Severus considered the anniversary of his ordination, because he preached anniversary homilies on this date in 513, 515 and 516.
18 Kugener 1902: 267–71; *pace* Downey 1961: 512, who sees this as the third delivery of the homily. See de Halleux 1963: 78–9 with n. 24.
19 *Life of Sabas* 158–9; in Cyril of Scythopolis, *Lives of the Monks of Palestine*, trans. Price.

20 For a different view on the stance of Apamea see Frend 1972: 228.

21 *SL* I.24: 84; cf. Frend 1972: 226.

22 On the city see Downey 1961, Liebeschuetz 1972, Darling 1982, Kondoleon 2000.

23 On the financial situation of Antioch see Downey 1961: 501–2; Frend 1972: 225; Darling 1982: 168–79.

24 Hom. XXVIII; *PO* 36/4; XXXIII; *PO* 36/3; XLVIII; *PO* 35/3; CV; *PO* 25/4.

25 Hom. XXXVIII; *PO* 36/3; CXIII; *PO* 26/3; CXV; *PO* 25/4; LXII; *PO* 8/2.

26 Hom. LXXXIX; *PO* 23/1; CII; *PO* 22/2; CXXII; *PO* 29/1.

27 An impression shared by Roux 2002: 139, with n. 19.

28 Jeffreys 1990: 7.

29 Theophanes, *Chron.* AM 5943; cf. Malalas, *Chron.* XV.6; Evagrius, *HE* III.10.

30 *CPG* 7070 (8); *Documenta* 1–5 (Theodosius) and 6–22 (Severus = Text 28 below).

31 JBA 243; trans. Darling 1980: 159. Cf. Kelly 1995: 118–9 on similar reforms executed by John Chrysostom, who, however, needed warm baths for his pitiful health (Kelly 1995: 113).

32 Philoxenus, *Letter to Abbot Simeon of Teleda*, fr. 4: 192, 1–4.

33 See e.g. Lebon 1909: 61–2; followed by most other scholars.

34 Preserved partially and only in Evagrius, *HE* III.31, 33 and II.5 (paraphrase). See Whitby 2000: 168 n. 97.

35 For the details see Whitby 2000: 194 n. 169.

36 *SL* VII.5: 379–80; trans. Brooks.

37 Letter XL; *PO* 12/2: 305, 309, 313.

38 *SL* I.3, 4, 12, 13, 19, 22, 38; II.2.

39 See *SL* I.43, the case of the monk Nonnus; and *SL* VII.4, the case of the monk Pelagius, where the *comes Orientis* was present with the patriarch and the accused in the bishop's palace.

40 De Halleux 1963: 86; Frend 1972: 226; Torrance 1988: 9–10, 13–14.

41 *SL* V.1: 280; trans. Brooks.

42 *SL* I.11, 43; IV.5; VII.1; VII.3.

43 *SL* I.29; V.3; X.6.

44 Allen 1999: 397–9; in general see Escolan 1999: *passim.*

45 See Torrance 1988: 7, who, however, follows Lebon in speaking of the synod of Tyre in 514. See above.

46 Hom. I, XXIII, XXX, LXII, CV, and CXII.

47 On the churches of Antioch see Downey 1961: 656–9.

48 See Honigmann 1951: 142 n. 3 for the sources.

49 Trans. Frend 1972: 234; line division by P. Allen.

50 On Timothy see Grillmeier 1996: 42–5.

51 These accusations came to light at the synod of 536 (on which see further below); *PO* 2/3: 342.

52 See further Honigmann 1951: 23 with n. 4; de Halleux 1963: 89.

53 On the details of his rapprochement with the West see Frend 1972: 234–7.

54 *SL* V.15: 358–9; trans. Brooks.

55 *SL* I.49, 50, 52; II.2; V.11, 12 (cf. V.15: 395); Letters XXII, XXVI (fr.), XXVII.

56 I.49: 148; trans. Brooks.

57 It is not known whether John hailed from Caesarea in Cappadocia or in Palestine. See Grillmeier 1995: 52 n. 91.

58 On the works of both John and Severus see Grillmeier 1995: 24–5, 52–79, and Chapters 2 and 3 below.

59 Hom. XXXIV; *PO* 12/2: 272; trans. Brooks.

60 John Eph., *Life of John of Tella*; *PO* 18/4: 515–16; Elias, *Life of John of Tella*, *CSCO* 8: 39.

61 On the date see Frend 1972: 269 n. 3.

62 *PO* 2: 303 and John Eph., *Lives of Five Patriarchs*; *PO* 18/4: 687; trans. Brooks.

63 On Gaianas and his party see Grillmeier 1996: 45–52.

64 Observation made by Youhanna Nessim Youssef.

65 Three of the published hymns are by John (*PO* 2/3: 327–30) and one by an anonymous Alexandrian monk (*PO* 2/3: 330–31). Other anonymous compositions remain unpublished (*PO* 2/3: 326).

2 SEVERUS'S THOUGHT

1 On Eustathius see *CCSG* 19: 391–476; Grillmeier 1995: 262–70.

2 The homily registered as *CPG* 7038 is in fact a fragment of Hom. XIV.

3 However, as shown by Roux 2002, when it comes to exegesis, Severus is as influenced by John Chrysostom as he is by Cyril.

4 *Ep. 3 ad Sergium*; Torrance 1988: 218. See further Lebon 1951: 454.

5 *Contra impium Grammaticum*, cited by Eustathius the monk, 417: 111–3. The extract does not survive in Syriac.

6 *Ep. 2 ad Sergium*; trans. Torrance 1988: 176.

7 Letter XV; trans. Brooks, *PO* 12/2: 210.

8 Letter X; *PO* 12/2: 203.

9 'Theandric' for Severus and ps.Dionysius meant, however, different things, for in the latter the soteriological role of the humanity of Christ is virtually absent. On this point see Torrance 1988: 110 n. 125 with literature.

10 Other renderings of the Greek include 'intellectually', 'formal' and 'abstractly considered'.

11 *Ad Nephalium*, *Or*. 1; *CSCO* 120: 6.27–7.5 (trans. Grillmeier 1995: 52).

12 Letter I (to Oecumenius); *PO* 12/2: 183 (trans. Brooks).

3 SEVERUS'S WORKS

1 On what follows see in detail Grillmeier 1995: 28–46.

2 Severus, Letter 1 to Sergius; Torrance 1988: 158.

3 Severus, Letter 1 to Sergius; Torrance 1988: 153.

4 Severus, Letter 2 to Sergius; Torrance 1988: 183–4.

5 Sergius, Letter 2 to Severus; Torrance 1988: 167–8.

6 See the beginning of Text 11 below.

7 *Contra impium Grammaticum*, *Or*. III.3; *CSCO* 93:19. 14–15.

8 *Contra impium Grammaticum*, *Or*. III.11; *CSCO* 93: 150. 10–12.

9 *Contra impium Grammaticum* III. 33; *CSCO* 102: 136.7–20.

10 See Michael Syr., *Chron*. IX. 27; Chabot 2: 225.

11 The Syriac fragments are edited with a Greek retroversion in Draguet 1924: 45*-78*; on the Greek fragments see *CSCO* 295: III.

12 See Severus's reply to this in *Apologia Philalethis*; *CSCO* 319: 112.28–113.25.

13 For a reconstruction of Julian's doctrine see Grillmeier 1995: 79–111.

14 *Apologia Philalethis*; *CSCO* 319: 113.20–114.12.

15 See e.g. *Apologia Philalethes*; *CSCO* 319: 247. 6–18.

16 On what follows see Allen 2001: 358.

17 See *CPG* 7032, adding the Syriac fragments in Peter of Callinicum: *CCSG* 32 and 35.

18 In Peter of Callinicum: *CCSG* 35: 310. 32–8.

19 In Peter of Callinicum: *CCSG* 32: 184. 56–65 = 35: 488. 322–9.

20 In Peter of Callinicum: *CCSG* 32: 258. 273.

21 For an overview of literature on the homilies see Allen 1998: 169–70 n. 4.

22 For inventory of all 125 homilies see Brière 1960: 50–62. On the catechetical homilies see Graffin 1960: 47–54.

23 Homilies I, XXIII, XXX, LXII, CV and CXII.

24 Homily LXXIV; *PO* 12/1: 110. 5–6; Homily LIII; *PO* 4/1: 40. 14–15; Homily XLI; *PO* 36/1: 16. 2. Cf. Olivar 1980: 434.

25 Homily LIX is the basis for Homily LXIV. On Severus's repeated homilies see Olivar 1980: 434, and cf. Allen 1998: 172–3.

26 On the developed angelology and mariology in Severus's homilies see Allen 1996: 165–77; on demonology see Allen 2002: 718–20.

27 For literature on the letters see Allen 1999: 388–90.

28 See Brightman 1896/2002: 144, 162–3, 181–2.

PART II TEXTS

4 DOGMATIC AND POLEMICAL WORKS

1 Sc. Fathers at the Council of Nicaea.

2 *ACO* II/1, 2: 125.16–22.

3 I.e. the second of Cyril's Twelve Chapters against Nestorius.

4 Cyril, *Apologia xii anathematismorum contra Theodoretum* (*CPG* 5222); *PG* 76: 400BC; *ACO* I/1, 6: 114.18–115.3.

5 Ibid.; *PG* 76: 437A; *ACO* I/1, 6: 137.1–5.

6 Ibid.; *PG* 76: 445B; *ACO* I/1, 6: 141.28–142.5.

7 Sc. Nestorius's.

8 *Apologia contra Theodoretum*; *PG* 76: 444AB; *ACO* I/1, 6: 140.15–17.

9 Ibid.; *PG* 76: 437B; *ACO* I/1, 6: 137.9–11.

10 Ibid.; *PG* 76: 436C; *ACO* I/1, 6: 136.22.

11 Ibid.; *PG* 76: 436D; *ACO* I/1, 6: 136.23.

12 Ibid.; *PG* 76: 437B; *ACO* I/1, 6: 137.10.

13 *PL* 54: 775: *ACO* II/2, 1: 31.9–10.

14 *PL* 54: 769; *ACO* II/2, 1: 29.10–11.

15 Nestorius, *Sermo x* (*CPG* 5699); Loofs 1905: 275.9–11.

16 Ibid.; 273.18–274.4.

17 *ACO* II/1, 2: 129.30–1.

18 *Adversus Nestorium lib. ii* (*CPG* 5217); *PG* 76: 92C; *ACO* I/1, 6: 45.33.

19 Ibid.; *PG* 76: 60D; *ACO* I/1, 6: 33.6–7.

20 *Ep. XVII* (*ad Nestorium*) (*CPG* 5317); *PG* 77: 120C; *ACO* I/1, 1: 40.28–30.

21 Sc. Andrew, bishop of Samosata, a supporter of Nestorius.

22 Cf. *Apologia xii capitulorum contra Orientales* (*CPG* 5221); *PG* 76: 329B; *ACO* I/1, 7: 39.28–32.

23 *Ep. I (ad monachos Aegypti) (CPG* 5301); *PG* 77: 25AD; *ACO* I/1, 1: 16.32–17 (paraphrase).

24 *PG* 76: 325C; *ACO* I/1, 7: 37.27–29.

25 *Ep. XVII (ad Nestorium*); *PG* 77: 116C; *ACO* I/1, 1: 38.21–2.

26 *Ep. IV (ad Nestorium*), *(CPG* 5304); *PG* 77: 45C; *ACO* I/1, 1: 27.1–2.

27 *PG* 77: 45C; *ACO* I/1, 1: 27.

28 *PG* 77: 45C; *ACO* I/1, 1: 27.2–3 (paraphrase).

29 *PG* 76: 92C; *ACO* I/1, 6: 45.33.

30 *PG* 76: 60D; *ACO* I/1, 6: 33.6–7.

31 *ACO* II/1, 2: 129.31.

32 *Ep. I (ad Succensum*), *(CPG* 5345); *PG* 77: 232C; *ACO* I/1, 6: 153.17.

33 Ibid.; *PG* 77: 233B; *ACO* I/1, 6: 154.2.

34 Ibid.; *PG* 77; 232D-233A; *ACO* I/1, 6; 153.20.

35 Cyril, *Apologia contra Orientales*; *PG* 76: 361CD; *ACO* 1/1, 7: 54.16.

36 Ibid.; *PG* 76: 361D-364A; *ACO* I/1, 7: 54.21.

37 This extract is in fact taken from Cyril's *Apologia contra Orientales*; *PG* 76: 329D; *ACO* I/1, 7: 40.7.

38 *Ep. XXXIX (ad Iohannem Antiochenum*), *(CPG* 5339); *PG* 77: 176D–177B; *ACO* I/1, 4: 17.9.

39 These events led to the Formula of Union (433), whereby Cyril was reconciled with the Antiochenes. See Evagrius, *HE* I.5.

40 The same words are attributed to Cyril, *Ep XXXIX (ad Iohannem Ant.)*: *PG* 77: 177AB; *ACO* I/1, 4: 17.9.

41 Possibly a reference to *Ep. XL (ad Acacium*), *(CPG* 5340); *PG* 72: 197ff.; *ACO* I/1, 4: 28ff.

42 *CPG* 2859; *PG* 31: 468C.

43 *Ep. XLIV (ad Eulogium presbyterum)*, *(CPG* 5344); *PG* 77: 225BC; *ACO* I/1, 4: 35.18.

44 Ibid.; *PG* 77: 224D-225A; *ACO* I/1, 4: 35.4.

45 In fact from ibid.; *PG* 77: 225D; *ACO* I/1, 4: 36.11–14.

46 This quotation cannot be located.

47 This quotation cannot be located.

48 This quotation cannot be located.

49 This quotation cannot be located.

50 An allusion to Cyril's *Ep. XXXIX (ad Iohannem Antiochenum*); *PG* 77: 173–81; *ACO* I/1, 4: 15–20.

51 This quotation cannot be located.

52 Lit.: 'substitutes'.

53 This quotation cannot be located.

54 Letter of John of Antioch to Cyril *(CPG* 5338); *PG* 77: 172D; *ACO* I/1, 4: 9.2.

55 *Ep. XXXIX (ad Iohannem Antiochenum*); *PG* 77: 180B; *ACO* I/1, 4: 18.26–19.1.

56 *Ep. XLIV (ad Eulogium presbyterum*), *PG* 77: 225C; *ACO* I/1, 4: 36.6–7.

57 Cited in ch. 10; *CSCO* 94: 140.3–6. The citation is from *Scholia de incarnatione unigeniti (CPG* 5225); *PG* 75: 1397CD.

58 *Ep. CI ad Cledonium (CPG* 3032); *PG* 37: 180A; *SC* 208.44, par 20.

59 This quotation cannot be located.

60 *Ep. XXXIX (ad Iohannem Antiochenum*); *PG* 77: 180B; *ACO* I/1, 4: 18.26–19.1.

61 *Ep. XLIV (ad Eulogium presbyterum*); *PG* 77: 225D; *ACO* I/1, 4: 36.10–12.

62 This quotation cannot be located.
63 This quotation cannot be located.
64 This quotation cannot be located.
65 This quotation cannot be located.
66 This work is attested only by fragments or excerpts in *catenae*: see *CPG* 7071 (38) and *Supplementum* 7070.
67 Sc. humanity.
68 This quotation cannot be located.
69 *Or.* 28 (*CPG* 3010); *PG* 36: 40A; *SC* 250: 120. 21–2.
70 Sc. the Trinity.
71 *Or.* 6 (*CPG* 3010); *PG* 35: 737B; *SC* 405: 152. 16–20.
72 *Or.* 34 (*CPG* 3010); *PG* 36: 248D; *SC* 318: 212. 1–4.
73 *Or.* 28 (*CPG* 3010); *PG* 36: 44A; *SC* 250: 128.22–4.
74 Sc. of the two elements in the composition of the incarnate Christ.
75 Sc. of the term as meaning.
76 Sc. the Chalcedonians.
77 *Adversus Nestorium lib. ii*; *PG* 76: 92C; *ACO* I/1, 6: 45.33.
78 *Ep. XL* (*ad Acacium*); *PG* 76: 192D–193A; *ACO* I/1, 6: 26. 7–9.
79 Ibid.; *ACO* I/1, 6: 26. 7–9.
80 Ibid.; *PG* 76: 193C; *ACO* I/1, 6: 27. 1–4.
81 Sc. into humanity and divinity.
82 Sc. of the two natures.
83 Cf. *Adversus Theopaschitas* (*CPG* 5752); Loofs 1905: 208–11.
84 Cf. *Sermo xxi. De fide seu oppositio fidei* (*CPG* 5710); Loofs 1905: 329.11–28.
85 *ACO* I/1, 6: 128.21–3.
86 Cf. *Adversus Theopaschitas*: Loofs 1905: 209.10–210.1.
87 Cf. ibid.; Loofs 1905: 209.5–9.
88 *CPG* 5217; *PG* 76: 229AB; *ACO* I/1, 6: 99.20–8; Loofs 1905: 229.
89 Sc. natures.
90 This quotation cannot be located.
91 This quotation cannot be located.
92 Sc. key words from formulae.
93 From an unidentified work of Nestorius; cf. Loofs 1905: 354. 7–11.
94 *Ep. XVII* (*ad Nestorium*); *PG* 77: 116; *ACO* I/1, 1: 38.4–8.
95 *Adversus Nestorium lib. ii*: *PG* 76: 84A; *ACO* I/1, 6: 42. 24–6.
96 *Or.* 38 (*CPG* 3010); *PG* 36: 328C; *SC* 358 138. 1–2.
97 Ibid.; *PG* 36: 325B; *SC* 358: 132.25–134.1. This whole passage must belong to lost parts of the *Philalethes*.
98 *Or.* 40 ; *PG* 36: 368AB; *SC* 358: 212.1–5.
99 *De prophetiarum obscuritate hom. ii* (*CPG* 4420); *PG* 56: 182.
100 Ibid.; 185.
101 This quotation cannot be located; however, see Loofs 1905: 330 e.
102 *CPG* 5217; *PG* 76: 36A; *ACO* I/1, 6; 22.35–6.
103 Loofs 1905: 328.
104 *CPG* 5217; *PG* 76: 84B; *ACO* I/1, 6: 42.5–6 (not exact).
105 Cf. *Sermo xii. In Matth. 22: 2ff.* (*CPG* 5701); Loofs 1905: 281.
106 From *De prophetiarum obscuritate hom. ii*; *PG* 56: 182. Cf. n. 99 above.
107 From *Adversus Nestorium lib. ii*, already quoted; see n. 95 above.
108 Gelasius (d. 395), bishop of Caesarea in Palestine and an ecclesiastical historian,

was the nephew of Cyril of Jerusalem. This fragment, which should be attributed to Eustathius of Antioch, also survives in Greek; see *CPG* 3520.

109 *Ep. XVII* (ad *Nestorium*); *PG* 77: 120D; *ACO* I/1, 1: 41.5–7.
110 *Or.* 40 (3010); *PG* 36: 328AB; *SC* 358: 212.1–5.
111 This is from Theodoret, *Eranistes* (*CPG* 6217), who is ostensibly quoting Gregory Nazianzen; *PG* 83: 192A; ed. Ettlinger 1975: 168.2–4.
112 *Oratio iii contra Arianos* (*CPG* 2093); *PG* 26: 385A.
113 *Or.* 38 (*CPG* 3010); *PG* 36: 328C; *SC* 358: 1–2.
114 *Or.* 38 (*CPG* 3010); *PG* 36: 325BC; *SC* 358: 132.25–134.29.
115 *Apologia contra Theodoretum*; *CPG* 76: 413D–416A; *ACO* I/1, 6: 124. 1–3.
116 Draguet 1924: 38*, 11–17 (Syriac); 73*. 22–8 (Greek).
117 Draguet 1924: 38*. 18–22 (Syriac); 74*. 1–5 (Greek).
118 A citation from Julian's *Tome*; Draguet 1924: 9*. 6–8 (Syriac); 49*. 7–9 (Greek); *CSCO* 244: 50. 21–51 (text); 245: 37. 18–20 (trans.).
119 Draguet 1924: 20*.2–6 (Syriac); 57.27–58.1 (Greek).
120 Draguet 1924: 21*.16–18 (Syriac); 59.1–3 (Greek).
121 Draguet 1924: 21*.19–20 (Syriac); 59.4–5 (Greek).
122 Athanasius, *Oratio contra Arianos iii*; *PG* 26: 392B.
123 Ibid.; *PG* 26: 392B.
124 Ibid.; *PG* 26: 437C-440A.
125 Cf. *Apologia contra Orientales*; *PG* 76: 376B.
126 Draguet 1924: 41*. 15–23 (Syriac); 76*. 13–20 (Greek).
127 *Ep. XLVI* (*ad Succensum*), (*CPG* 5346); *PG* 77: 241B; *ACO* I/1, 6: 159.18–160.2.
128 This citation cannot be identified.

5 HOMILIES

1   English translation in Leemans *et al.* 2003: 68–77.
2   *PO* 12/1:90; translated by Iain Torrance.
3   Both these martyrs are shadowy: Procopius seems to have been martyred at Caesarea (Palestine) in the reign of Diocletian, and Phocas was apparently a gardener martyred at Sinope.
4   There were at least three churches of this name in the vicinity of Antioch, one in the city itself and two in Daphne. See Downey 1961: 658.
5   Although the law which abolished the *chrysargyron* or *collatio lustralis* as recorded in *Codex Justinianus* X.1 bears no date, it seems that this oppressive tax ceased in May 498 (Mango-Scott 1997: 221 n. 5). It is unclear what prompted Severus to deliver Homily XIII between 23/25 January and 3 February 513 (Brière 1960: 52).
6   One folio recto and verso is missing at this point. Consequently the numbering of the paragraphs jumps accordingly.
7   I.e. the rhetorical device whereby to a proper name is attributed a descriptive phrase, or conversely a proper name is substituted for a quality which is associated with it.
8   Lit.: 'things made by hands'.
9   So reads the margin; the text reads 'more and more'.
10 Sc. on the Feast of the Hypapante, or Purification.
11 Lit.: 'crowns'.
12 This citation cannot be located.

13 In *PO* 37/1: 6–71, the missing first page in Jacob of Edessa's version of this homily is supplemented with the legible portions from that of Paul of Callinicum, but a lacuna remains.

14 Canon 51 of the synod of Laodicea in 364 forbids the celebration of martyrs' feasts if they fall on weekdays during Lent, but permits their transfer to the following Saturday and Sunday. See *PG* 137: 1409BCD; Percival 1899/1974: 156.

15 There is a lacuna at this point.

16 Cf. Hymn 156; *PO* 7/5: 615: 'the Forty Martyrs, equal in number to the perfect and holy days of the fast'.

17 Severus adheres closely to Basil's theoretical account of death by freezing (*PG* 31: 516AB) at this point.

18 One manuscript reads in the margin: 'In the Greek language, days are feminine. That is why, as mothers who conceive and give birth, these forty holy days of fast have been aptly personified by the teacher (sc. Severus), and not as "fathers" as I have rendered them in the Syriac language'.

19 For this image cf. Ephrem 559–60 (Assemani 351F) of the young boy.

20 Cf. Ephrem 691–706 (Assemani 354C) for the same image used of the speech of the mother.

21 Expansion of Basil, *PG* 31: 520B.

22 Severus was extremely distrustful of horse-racing: see especially Hom. XXVI.

23 Cf. Ephrem 616 (Assemani 325F) of the young boy.

24 For the image, cf. Ephrem 469–530 (Assemani 350B–351B), esp. 527–9, but the whole speech in Severus is similar to its lengthy equivalent in Ephrem.

25 Cf. Ex 14: 21–2; Josh 4: 16.

26 This phrase may indicate that a reading of Basil's homily was to follow.

27 Greg. Naz., *Or.* 38. 17; *PG* 36: 17 AB; *SC* 358: 144. 17–20.

6 LETTERS

1 On the formula and its influence see Grillmeier 2002: 338–56.

2 Laodicea was the third autocephalous metropolitan see in the eastern patriarchate of Antioch, and Nicias was one of the principal supporters of Severus. A fragment of this letter also survives in Greek. See Honigmann 1951: 35–6. On Severus's stance in this letter see also Escolan 1999: 273 n. 3. *SL* V.2 appears to be a follow-up letter to this.

3 The locations of these villages in Laodicea are unknown. Minidus is mentioned again in *SL* V.2.

4 Escolan 1999: 281 makes the point that during his patriarchate Severus had to cope with the lack of clergy committed to the anti-Chalcedonian cause. Yet the patriarch stood firm on clergy who had not been canonically ordained by anti-Chalcedonian bishops.

5 I.e. general principle.

6 The Greek word for 'expenditure' has been taken over into the Syriac text.

7 Lit.: God-loving.

8 See Escolan 1999: 340–44 on episcopal authority over monks in Syria.

9 Sc. than rightly it should be.

10 I.e. Syria Secunda.

11 *CPG* 2863; *PG* 31: 508–25.

12 This homily has not survived.

13 These two homilies, *CPG* 3184 and 3185, are by Gregory of Nyssa.

14 *Apokatastasis* is the belief that at the end of time all creation, including the devil, would be saved and restored to its original state. The theory was often ascribed to Origen.

15 What follows is in fact the 267th question from Basil's *Regulae Brevius Tractatae* (*CPG* 2875); *PG* 31: 1264–5, and is a reasonably close rendering of the Greek text.

16 In reality canons 32 and 33 respectively of the synod of Laodicea; *PG* 137: 1379B; Percival 1899/1974; 149–50.

17 Sc. The Fourth Book of Kings.

18 Variant reading: 'fineness'.

19 Lit.: 'daughter of the voice'.

20 Cf. Greg. Naz., *Or.* 40.26; *SC* 358: 258.26–33.

21 On Anastasia, who is perhaps identical with Anastasia the deaconess, to whom Severus wrote Letters 69–72 from exile, see *PLRE* 2: 76 under Anastasia 2. Georgia subsequently married, acquired the rank of 'patricia', and had a daughter (Letter 76, written between 532 and 538). See also Allen 1999: 392–4. This letter contains several lacunae, and the last paragraph may in fact not belong to it.

22 Lit.: 'mouth'.

23 Lit.: 'pass over'. Ps.Zachariah, the continuator of Zachariah Scholasticus, is speaking here.

24 This citation is unidentified.

25 I.e. until 534/5.

26 26 July 535.

27 Lit.: 'nuts'.

28 Sc. Christ.

29 By associating Julian with the docetic christololgies of these condemned heretics and with Apollinaris, Severus establishes Julian's pedigree as a heretic.

30 Or: 'in oral assault on the Scriptures'.

31 The monarchian christologies of Paul, Artemon and Photinus, whereby Christ was seen as a mere man, are aligned with the great representatives of the school of Antioch, Diodore of Tarsus, Theodore of Mopsuestia and Nestorius himself.

32 Like the other men mentioned in this catalogue, Irenaeus was a supporter of Nestorius. He was also twice married before becoming bishop of Tyre.

7 HYMNS

1 I.e. during the feast of Pentecost.

2 Sc. by the anti-Chalcedonians, and Severus himself.

BIBLIOGRAPHY

TEXTS OF SEVERUS

Dogmatic and polemical works

Severi Antiocheni orationes ad Nephalium, eiusdem ac Sergii Grammatici epistulae mutuae, ed. and trans. J. Lebon, *CSCO* 119 (text) and 120 (trans.), Louvain: Secrétariat du CorpusSCO, 1949.

Sévère d'Antioche, Le Philalèthe, ed. and trans. R. Hespel, *CSCO* 133 (text) and 134 (trans.), Louvain: Secrétariat du CorpusSCO, 1952.

Severi Antiocheni liber contra impium Grammaticum, ed. and trans. J. Lebon, *CSCO* 93 (text) and 94 (trans.) (textus orationis tertiae partis prioris), Louvain: Secrétariat du CorpusSCO, 1929.

Severi Antiocheni liber contra impium Grammaticum, ed. and trans. J. Lebon, *CSCO* 101 (text) and 102 (trans.) (textus orationis tertiae partis posterioris), Louvain: Secrétariat du CorpusSCO, 1933.

Severi Antiocheni liber contra impium Grammaticum, ed. and trans. J. Lebon, *CSCO* 111 (text) and 112 (trans.) (textus orationis primae et orationis secundae quae supersunt), Louvain: Secrétariat du CorpusSCO, 1938.

Sévère d'Antioche, La polémique antijulianiste I, ed. and trans. R. Hespel, *CSCO* 244 (text) and 245 (trans.), Louvain: Secrétariat du CorpusSCO, 1964.

Sévère d'Antioche, La polémique antijulianiste IIA, ed. and trans. R. Hespel, *CSCO* 295 (text) and 296 (trans.), Louvain: Secrétariat du CorpusSCO, 1968.

Sévère d'Antioche, La polémique antijulianiste IIB, ed. and trans. R. Hespel, *CSCO* 301 (text) and 302 (trans.), Louvain: Secrétariat du CorpusSCO, 1969.

Sévère d'Antioche, La polémique antijulianiste III, ed. and trans. R. Hespel, *CSCO* 318 (text) and 319 (trans.), Louvain: Secrétariat du CorpusSCO, 1971.

Homilies

The homilies of Severus are published in various volumes of *PO*. See *CPG* 7035.

Letters

The Sixth Book of the Select Letters of Severus Patriarch of Antioch in the Syriac Version of Athanasius of Nisibis, ed. and trans. E.W. Brooks, vol. 1, London: Williams & Norgate, 1902; reprint Farnborough, Hants.: Gregg International Publishers Limited, 1969 (text); vol. 2, London: Williams & Norgate, 1903; reprint Farnborough, Hants.: Gregg International Publishers Limited, 1969 (trans.).

A Collection of Letters of Severus of Antioch, ed. and trans. E.W. Brooks, *PO* 12/2, Paris: Firmin-Didot 1915; ²1973, Turnhout: Brepols; and *PO* 14/1, Paris: Firmin-Didot, 1920; ²1973, Turnhout: Brepols.

'Severos' Letter to John the soldier', ed. S. Brock, in G. Wiessner (ed.), *Erkenntnisse und Meinung*, vol. 2 (Göttinger Orientforschungen 1. Reihe: Syriaca, Bd. 17), Wiesbaden: Otto Harrassowitz, 1978, 60–4.

'Letter of Severus to Anastasia the deaconess', ed. and trans. Y.N. Youssef, *Bulletin de la Société d'Archéologie Copte* 40 (2001b) 126–36.

Hymns

The Hymns of Severus and Others in the Syriac Version of Paul of Edessa as revised by James of Edessa, ed. and trans. E.W. Brooks, *PO* 6/1: 1–179, Paris: Firmin-Didot, 1909; ²1981, Turnhout: Brepols.

The Hymns of Severus and Others in the Syriac Version of Paul of Edessa as revised by James of Edessa, ed. and trans. E.W. Brooks, *PO* 7/5: 593–802, Paris: Firmin-Didot 1911; ²1981, Turnhout: Brepols.

Other works

Defensio ad imperatorem, in *Historia Ecclesiastica Zachariae rhetori vulgo adscripta* 2, ed. and trans. E.W. Brooks, *CSCO* 87: 123–31 (text) and 88: 85–90 (trans.), Paris: e Typographeo Reipublicae, 1919; ²1952, Louvain: Secrétariat du CorpusSCO.

Epistula synodica ad Theodosium episcopum Alexandriae, ed. and trans. J.-B. Chabot, *Documenta ad origines monophysitarum illustrandas*, CSCO 17, Louvain: e Typographeo Marcelli Istas, 1908, ²1952, pp. 12–34 (text); 103, Louvain: e Typographeo Marcelli Istas, 1933, ²1952, pp. 6–22 (trans.).

Fragments

Dorival, G. 'Nouveaux fragments grecs de Sévère d'Antioche', in *ANTIΔΩRON. Hulde aan Dr. Maurits Geerard bij de voltooiing van de* Clavis Patrum Graecorum/*Hommage à Maurits Geerard pour célébrer l'achèvement de la* Clavis Patrum Graecorum, vol. 1, Wetteren: Cultura, 101–21, 1984.

Petit, F. *La chaîne sur l'Exode I. Fragments de Sévère d'Antioche*. Glossaire syriaque par L. Van Rompay (Traditio Exegetica Graeca 9), Leuven: Peeters, 1999.

'Letter to John the hegumenos', in F. Diekamp (ed.), *Doctrina Patrum de Incarnatione Verbi*, Münster i. W.: Aschendorff, 1907; 2nd ed. R. Phanourgakis and E. Chrysos, Münster: Aschendorff, 1981: 309, nr. XXIV: 15–25.

Contra Felicissimum: various fragments survive in scattered collections. See *CPG* 7032, and *CPG* Supplement 7032.

OTHER PRIMARY WORKS, INCLUDING TRANSLATIONS

Athanasius Scriptor, *Life of Severus: The Conflict of Severus, Patriarch of Antioch*, ed. and trans. E.J. Goodspeed and W.E. Crum, *PO* 4/6, Paris: Firmin-Didot 1907; [2]1981, Turnhout: Brepols.

——*The Arabic Life of Severus of Antioch attributed to Athanasius*, ed. and trans. Y.N. Youssef, forthcoming in *PO*.

Basil of Caesarea, *Homily on the Forty Martyrs of Sebaste*, *PG* 31: 508–26.

The Sixth Book of the Select Letters of Severus Patriarch of Antioch in the Syriac Version of Athanasius of Nisibis, ed. and trans. E.W. Brooks, vol. 1, London: Williams & Norgate, 1902; reprint Farnborough, Hants.: Gregg International Publishers Limited, 1969 (text); vol. 2, London: Williams & Norgate, 1903; reprint Farnborough, Hants.: Gregg International Publishers Limited, 1969 (trans.).

Codex Justinianus, ed. P. Krueger, in *Corpus Iuris Civilis* 2, Berlin: Weidmann, 1895.

Cyril of Scythopolis, *Lives of the Monks of Palestine*, trans. R.M. Price with an introduction and notes by J. Binns, Kalamazoo, MI: Cistercian Publications, 1990.

Documenta ad origenes monophysitarum illustrandas, ed. and trans. J.-B. Chabot, *CSCO* 17, Louvain: e Typographeo Marcelli Istas, 1908, [2]1952, pp. 12–34 (text); 103, Louvain: e Typographeo Marcelli Istas, 1933, [2]1952, pp. 6–22 (trans.).

Elias, *Life of Bishop John of Tella*, in *Vitae virorum apud monophysitas celeberrimorum*, ed. and trans. E.W. Brooks, *CSCO* 7: 29–95 (text); 8: 21–60 (trans.), reprint Louvain: Imprimerie Orientaliste, 1955.

Ephrem the Syrian, *Encomium on the Forty Holy Martyrs*, ed. J.S. Assemani, *S.P.N. Ephraem syri opera omnia*, vol. 2, Rome: Ex Typographia Pontificia Vaticana, 1743, 340–56.

Eustathius Monachus, *Epistula de duabus naturis*, ed. P. Allen, in *Diversorum Postchalcedonensium Auctorum Collectanea* 1, 390–476 (*CCSG* 19), Turnhout-Leuven: Brepols-Leuven University Press, 1989.

Evagrius Scholasticus, *Church History: The Ecclesiastical History of Evagrius Scholasticus*, trans. with introduction and notes by M. Whitby (*Translated Texts for Historians* 33), Liverpool: Liverpool University Press, 2000.

George, bishop of the Arabs: *A Homily on Blessed Mar Severus, Patriarch of Antioch*, ed. and trans. K.E. McVey, *CSCO* 530 (text) and 531 (trans.), Leuven: E. Peeters, 1993.

John of Beith Aphthonia, *Life of Severus: Vie de Sévère*, ed. and trans. M.-A. Kugener, *PO* 2/3, Paris: Firmin-Didot, 1907.

John, bishop of Assiut (?), 'A Homily on Severus of Antioch', ed. and trans. Y.N. Youssef, forthcoming in *PO*.

John of Ephesus, *Life of John of Tella* and *Lives of Five Patriarchs*, 513–26 and 684–90 respectively in *Lives of the Eastern Saints*, ed. and trans. E.W. Brooks, *PO* 18/4, Turnhout: Brepols, 1974.

John the Grammarian: *Iohannis Caesariensis presbyteri et grammatici opera quae supersunt*, ed. M. Richard (*CCSG* 1), Turnhout-Leuven: Brepols-Leuven University Press, 1977.

John Malalas, *Chronicle*: *The Chronicle of John Malalas. A Translation*, by E. Jeffreys, M. Jeffreys and R. Scott (Byzantina Australiensia 4), Melbourne: Australian Association for Byzantine Studies, 1986.

John Rufus, *Plerophories*, ed. F. Nau, *PO* 8/1, Paris: Firmin-Didot, 1912.

Josua the Stylite, *Chronicle*: *The Chronicle of Pseudo-Josua the Stylite*, trans. with notes and introduction by F.R. Trombley and J.W. Watt (*Translated Texts for Historians* 32), Liverpool: Liverpool University Press, 2000.

Julian of Halicarnassus, ed. R. Draguet, *Julien d'Halicarnasse et sa controverse avec Sévère d'Antioche sur l'incorruptibilité du corps du Christ*, Louvain: Imprimerie P. Smeesters, 1924.

Liberatus, *Breviarium*, ed. E. Schwartz, *ACO* 2/5: 98–141.

Michael the Syrian, *Chronique*, 4 vols, ed. and trans. J.-B. Chabot, Paris: Culture et Civilisation, 1899–1910.

Nestorius: *Nestoriana. Die Fragmente des Nestorius*, ed. F. Loofs, Halle: M. Niemeyer, 1905.

Peter of Callinicum: *Petri Callinicensis Patriarchae Antiocheni Tractatus Contra Damianum*, ed. and trans. R.Y. Ebied, A. Van Roey and L.R. Wickham; vol. 2, *Libri tertii capita I-XIX*, and vol. 3, *Libri tertii capita XX-XXXIV* (Corpus Christianorum Series Graeca 32 and 35), Turnhout-Leuven: Brepols-Leuven University Press, 1996 and 1998.

Philoxenus, *Letter to Abbot Simeon of Teleda* (frgs), ed. and trans. J. Lebon, 'Textes inédits de Philoxène de Mabboug', *Le Muséon* 43 (1930): 17–84, 149–220.

Ps.Dionysius of Tel-Mahre, *Chronicle*: *Pseudo-Dionysius of Tel-Mahre, Chronicle, Part III (known also as the Chronicle of Zuqnin)*, trans. with notes and introduction by W. Witakowski (*Translated Texts for Historians* 22), Liverpool: Liverpool University Press 1996.

Theodore Lector, *Church History*: *Theodoros Anagnostes, Kirchengeschichte*, ed. G.C. Hansen, Griechische Christliche Schriftsteller N.F. 3, 2nd ed., Berlin: Akademie-Verlag, 1995.

Theodoret, *Eranistes*, ed. G.H. Ettlinger, Oxford: Clarendon Press, 1975.

Theophanes, *Chronicle*: *The Chronicle of Theophanes Confessor. Byzantine and Near Eastern History ad 284–813*, trans. with introduction and commentary by C. Mango and R. Scott with the assistance of G. Greatrex, Oxford: Clarendon Press, 1997.

Zachariah Scholasticus, *Church History*: *The Syriac Chronicle Known as that of Zacharias Rhetor*, trans. F.J. Hamilton and E.W. Brooks, London: Methuen, 1899.

——*Life of Severus*: *Vie de Sévère*, ed. and trans. M.-A. Kugener, *PO* 2/1, Paris: Firmin-Didot, 1907.

SECONDARY WORKS

Allen, P. *Evagrius Scholasticus the Church Historian* (Spicilegium Sacrum Lovaniense 41), Leuven: Spicilegium Sacrum Lovaniense, 1981.

Allen, P. 'Severus of Antioch and the homily: the end of the beginning?', in P. Allen and E.M. Jeffreys (eds), *The Sixth Century – End or Beginning?* (Byzantina Australiensia 10), Brisbane: Australian Association for Byzantine Studies, 1996, 165–77.

Allen, P. 'A bishop's spirituality: the case of Severus of Antioch', in P. Allen, R. Canning, L. Cross (eds) with B.J. Caiger, *Prayer and Spirituality in the Early Church*, vol. 1, Brisbane: Centre for Early Christian Studies, 1998, 169–80.

Allen, P. 'Severus of Antioch and pastoral care', in P. Allen, W. Mayer, L. Cross (eds), *Prayer and Spirituality in the Early Church*, vol. 2, Brisbane: Centre for Early Christian Studies, 1999, 387–400.

Allen, P. 'Severus of Antioch as pastoral carer', *Studia Patristica* 2001; 35: 353–68.

Allen, P. 'Severus of Antioch as a source for lay piety in late antiquity', in M. Maritano (ed.), *Historiam Perscrutari. Miscellanea di studi offerti al prof. Ottorino Pasquato*, Rome: LAS, 2002, pp. 711–21.

Allen, P. and W. Mayer. 'Through a bishop's eyes: towards a definition of pastoral care in late antiquity', *Augustinianum* 2000; 40: 245–97.

Bacht, H. 'Die Rolle des orientalischen Mönchtums in den kirchenpolitischen Auseinandersetzungen um Chalkedon (431–519)', in A. Grillmeier and H. Bacht (eds), *Das Konzil von Chalkedon. Geschichte und Gegenwart*, Würzburg: Echter Verlag, vol. 2, 1951, 193–314.

Baumstark, A. 'Das Kirchenjahr in Antiocheia zwischen 512 und 518', *Römische Quartalschrift* 1897; 11: 31–66.

Blázquez, J.M. 'La vida estudiantil en Beyruth y Alejandría a final del siglo V según la Vida de Severo de Zacarías Escolástico. Paganas y Cristianos (I)', *Gerión* 1998; 16: 415–36.

Brière, M. 'Les homélies cathédrales de Sévère d'Antioche. Introduction générale à toutes les homélies', *PO* 29/1: 50–62, 1960.

Brightman, F.E. *Liturgies Eastern and Western*, Oxford: The Clarendon Press, 1896; facsimile reprint entitled *Eastern Liturgies*, Piscataway, NJ: Gorgias Press, 2002.

Brock, S.P. 'Some new letters of the Patriarch Severus', *Studia Patristica* 12 (Texte und Untersuchungen 115), Berlin: Akademie-Verlag, 1975, 17–24.

Brock, S.P., 1978: see under Severus's works (Letters).

Brooks, E.W. (ed. and trans.) *The Sixth Book of the Select Letters of Severus Patriarch of Antioch in the Syriac Version of Athanasius of Nisibis*, vol. 1, London: Williams & Norgate, 1902; reprint Farnborough, Hants: Gregg International Publishers Limited, 1969 (text); vol. 2, London: Williams & Norgate, 1903; reprint Farnborough, Hants: Gregg International Publishers Limited, 1969 (trans.) (see also under Other primary works).

Brooks, E.W. (ed. and trans.) *The Hymns of Severus and Others in the Syriac Version of Paul of Edessa as revised by James of Edessa*, PO 7/5: 593–802. Turnhout: Brepols, ²1981 (first edition Paris, 1911); see also under Severus's works (hymns).

Chesnut, R.C. *Three Monophysite Christologies. Severus of Antioch, Philoxenus of Mabbug and Jacob of Sarug*, Oxford: Oxford University Press, 1976.

Cumming, G.J. 'The liturgy of Antioch in the time of Severus (513–518)', in J.N. Alexander (ed.), *Time and Community. In Honor of Thomas Julian Talley*, Washington DC: The Pastoral Press, 1990, 83–103.

Darling, R. *The Patriarchate of Severus of Antioch, 512–518*, unpublished PhD diss., Chicago, 1982.

Downey, G. *A History of Antioch in Syria from Seleucus to the Arab Conquest*, Princeton, NJ: Princeton University Press, 1961.

Draguet, R. (ed. and trans.) *Julien d'Halicarnasse et sa controverse avec Sévère d'Antioche sur l'incorruptibilité du corps du Christ*, Louvain: Imprimerie P. Smeesters, 1924 (see also under Other primary works).

Duchesne, L. *L'Église au VIème siècle*, Paris: Ancienne Librarie Fontemoing & Cie. E. de Boccard, Successeur, 1925.

Escolan, P. *Monachisme et Église. Le monachisme syrien du IVe au VIIe siècle* (Théologie historique 109), Paris: Beauchesne, 1999.

Frend, W.H.C. *The Rise of the Monophysite Movement. Chapters in the History of the Church in the Fifth and Sixth Centuries*, Cambridge: Cambridge University Press, 1972.

Frend, W.H.C. 'Severus of Antioch and the origins of the monophysite hierarchy', in D. Neiman and M. Schatkin (eds), *The Heritage of the Early Church. Essays in Honor of G.V. Florovsky* (Orientalia Christiana Analecta 195), Rome: Pont. Institutum Studiorum Orientalium, 1973.

Garitte, G. 'Textes hagiographiques orientaux relatifs à Saint Léonce de Tripoli II. L'homélie de Sévère d'Antioche', *Le Muséon* 1966; 79: 335–86.

Graffin, F. 'La catéchèse de Sévère d'Antioche', *L'Orient Syrien* 1960; 5: 47–54.

Graffin, F. 'Jacques d'Édesse réviseur des homélies de Sévère d'Antioche d'après le ms. Syriaque Br. M. Add. 12159', in Orientalia Christiana Analecta 205 (Symposium Syriacum 1976), Rome: Pont. Institutum Studiorum Orientalium, 1978a.

Graffin, F. 'La vie à Antioche d'après les homélies de Sévère. Invectives contre les courses de chevaux, le théâtre et les jeux olympiques', in G. Wiessner (ed.), *Erkenntisse und Meinung*, vol. 2 (Göttinger Orientforschungen, 1. Reihe: Syriaca, Bd. 17), Wiesbaden: Otto Harrassowitz, 1978b, 115–30.

Grillmeier, A. *Christ in Christian Tradition*, vol. 2, *From the Council of Chalcedon (451) to Gregory the Great (590–604)*. Part Two, *The Church of Constantinople in the Sixth Century*, London-Louisville, KY: Mowbray-Westminster John Knox Press (with T. Hainthaler), 1995.

Grillmeier, A. *Christ in Christian Tradition*, vol. 2, *From the Council of Chalcedon (451) to Gregory the Great (590–604)*. Part Four, *The Church of Alexandria with Nubia and Ethiopia after 451*, London-Louisville, KY: Mowbray-Westminster John Knox Press (with T. Hainthaler), 1996.

Grillmeier, A. *Jesus der Christus im Glauben der Kirche*, Bd. 2/3, *Die Kirchen von Jerusalem und Antiochien nach 451 bis 600*, mit Beiträgen von Alois Grillmeier, Theresia Hainthaler, Tanios Bou Mansour, Luise Abramowski, Freiburg-Basel-Vienna: Herder, 2002.

de Halleux, A. *Philoxène de Mabbog. Sa vie, ses écrits, sa théologie*, Louvain: Imprimerie Orientaliste, 1963.

Honigmann, E. *Évêques et évêchés monophysites d'Asie antérieure au VIe siècle*, Louvain: Secrétariat du CorpusSCO, 1951.

Jeffreys, E. *Studies in John Malalas*, ed. E. Jeffreys with B. Croke and R. Scott (Byzantina Australiensia 6), Sydney: Australian Association for Byzantine Studies, 1990.

Kelly, J.N.D. *Golden Mouth: The Story of John Chrysostom–Ascetic, Preacher, Bishop*, London: Gerald Duckworth, 1995.

Kondoleon, C. *Antioch: The Lost City*, Princeton, NJ: Princeton University Press, 2000.

Lebon, J. *Le monophysisme sévèrien*, Louvain: J. Van Linthout, 1909.

Lebon, J. 'La christologie du monophysisme syrien', in A.Grillmeier and H. Bacht (eds), *Das Konzil von Chalkedon. Geschichte und Gegenwart*, vol. 2, Würzburg: Echter Verlag, 1951, 425–580.

Leemans, J., Mayer, W., Allen, P. and Dehandschutter, B. *'Let us Die That We May Live'. Greek homilies on Christian martyrs from Asia Minor, Palestine and Syria c. AD 350–AD 450*, London and New York: Routledge, 2003.

Liebeschuetz, J.H.W.G. *Antioch. City and Imperial Administration in the Later Roman Empire*, Oxford: Clarendon Press, 1972.

Loofs, F., 1905: see under Other Primary Works. Nestorius.

Maspero, J. *Histoire des patriarches d'Alexandrie depuis la mort de l'empereur Anastase jusqu'à la réconciliation des Églises jacobites* (Bibliothèque de l'École des Hautes Études 237), Paris: Librairie ancienne Édouard Champion, 1923.

Mayer, W. 'Monasticism at Antioch and Constantinople in the late fourth century: a case of exclusivity or diversity?', in P. Allen, R. Canning, L. Cross (eds) with B.J. Caiger, *Prayer and Spirituality in the Early Church*, vol. 1, Brisbane: Centre for Early Christian Studies, 1998, 275–88.

Moeller, C. 'Un représentant de la christologie néochalcédonienne au début du sixième siècle en Orient: Néphalius d'Alexandrie', *Revue d'Histoire Ecclésiastique* 1944–5; 40: 73–140.

Moeller, C. 'Le Chalcédonisme et le néo-Chalcédonisme en Orient de 451 à la fin du VIe siècle', in A. Grillmeier and H. Bacht (eds), *Das Konzil von Chalkedon. Geschichte und Gegenwart*, Würzburg: Echter Verlag, vol. 1, 1951, 637–720.

Olivar, A. 'Sever d'Antioquia en la història de la predicació', *Rivista Catalana di Teologia* 1980; 5: 403–42.

Olivar, A. *La predicación cristiana antigua*, Barcelona: Biblioteca Herder (Sección de teología y filosofía, 189), 1991.

Percival, H.R. *The Seven Ecumenical Councils of the Undivided Church. Their Canons and Dogmatic Decrees* (A Select Library of Nicene and Post-Nicene Fathers of the Christian Church, 2nd ser., vol. 14), Grand Rapids MI: Wm. B. Eerdmans, 1899; reprinted 1974.

Poggi, V. 'Severo di Antiochia alla Scuola di Beirut', in *L'eredità classica nelle lingue orientali* a c. di M. Pavan e U. Cozzoli, Rome: Enciclopedia Italiana, 1986, 57–71.

Richard, M. *Iohannis Caesariensis presbyteri et grammatici opera quae supersunt* (CCSG 1), Turnhout-Leuven: Brepols-Leuven University Press, 1977.

Roux, R. *L'exégèse biblique dans les Homélies cathédrales de Sévère d'Antioche* (Studia Ephemeridis Augustinianum 84), Rome: Institutum Patristicum Augustinianum, 2002.

Steppa, J.-E. *John Rufus and the World Vision of Anti-Chalcedonian Culture* (Gorgias Dissertations; Ancient Christian Studies 1), Piscataway, NY: Gorgias Press, 2002.

Torrance, I.R. *Christology After Chalcedon. Severus of Antioch and Sergius the Monophysite*, Norwich: The Canterbury Press, 1988.

Torrance, I.R. 'Severus von Antiochien', *Theologische Realenzyklopädie*, Berlin-New York: Walter de Gruyter, 2000; 31: 184–6.

Vööbus, A. 'Discovery of the biography of Severus of Antioch by Qyriaqos of Tagrit', *Rivista di studi bizantini e neoellenici* n.s. 12–13, 1975–6, 117–24.

Wallace-Hadrill, D.S *Christian Antioch. A Study of Early Christian Thought in the East*, Cambridge: Cambridge University Press, 1982.

Whitby, M. (ed. and trans.) *Church History: The Ecclesiastical History of Evagrius Scholasticus* (Translated Texts for Historians 33), Liverpool: Liverpool University Press, 2000 (see also under Other primary works).

Youssef, Y.N. 'Arabic manuscripts of the *Philalethes* of Severus of Antioch', *Proche-Orient Chrétien*, 2001a; 51: 261–6.

Youssef, Y.N., 2001b: see under Works of Severus. Letters.

Youssef, Y.N. 'The cult of Severus of Antioch in Egypt', *Ephemerides Liturgicae* 2001c; 115: 101–7.

Youssef, Y.N. 'Severus of Antioch in the Coptic Theotokia', in B. Neil, G.D. Dunn, L. Cross (eds), *Prayer and Spirituality in the Early Church*, vol. 3, Sydney: St Paul's Publications, 2003, 93–108.

GENERAL INDEX

INDEX OF MODERN AUTHORS